Archaeology and the Bible

In recent years archaeological discoveries in the Near East, particularly in Palestine, have been related in one way or another to the Bible, often in an effort to prove its historical veracity. But newer field methodologies, regional surveys and creative syntheses have called into question this traditional approach. *Archaeology and the Bible* examines these new developments and discusses what they imply for biblical studies. The book:

- traces the history of the development of Near Eastern archaeology, including the rise and fall of the so-called "biblical archaeology" movement
- describes how field archaeology is actually done so that the reader can visualize how archaeological discoveries are made, recorded and studied
- recounts the broader prehistorical/archaeological horizon out of which the Bible was born
- elucidates how recent archaeological discoveries and theorizing pose serious challenges to the traditional interpretations of such biblical stories as the "Exodus" and the "Conquest"
- explores the implications of new developments in the field for understanding Israelite religion.

Archaeology and the Bible presents a concise yet comprehensive and accessible introduction to biblical archaeology which will be invaluable to students.

John C. H. Laughlin is Professor of Religion and Chairman of the Department of Religion at Averett College. He has excavated at Tel Dan and served as Field Supervisor at the Capernaum excavations. Since 1989, he has been a Field Supervisor at Banias. He has published and lectured widely on the subjects of Near Eastern archaeology and the Bible.

Approaching the Ancient World
Series editor: Richard Stoneman

The sources for the study of the Greek and Roman world are diffuse, diverse, and often complex, and special training is needed in order to use them to the best advantage in constructing a historical picture.

The books in this series provide an introduction to the problems and methods involved in the study of ancient history. The topics covered will range from the use of literary sources for Greek history and for Roman history, through numismatics, epigraphy, and dirt archaeology, to the use of legal evidence and of art and artefacts in chronology. There will also be books on statistical and comparative method and on feminist approaches.

The Uses of Greek Mythology
Ken Dowden

Art, Artefacts, and Chronology in Classical Archaeology
William R. Biers

Reading Papyri, Writing Ancient History
Roger S. Bagnall

Ancient History from Coins
Christopher Howgego

The Sources of Roman Law
O. F. Robinson

Cuneiform Texts and the Writing of History
Marc van de Mieroop

Literary Texts and the Greek Historian
Christopher Pelling

Literary Texts and the Roman Historian
David Potter

Archaeology and the Bible

John C. H. Laughlin

London and New York

First published 2000
by Routledge
11 New Fetter Lane, London EC4P 4EE

Simultaneously published in the USA and Canada
by Routledge
29 West 35th Street, New York, NY 10001

Routledge is an imprint of the Taylor & Francis Group

© 2000 John C. H. Laughlin

The right of John C. H. Laughlin to be identified as the Author of this
Work has been asserted by him in accordance with the Copyright,
Designs and Patents Act 1988

Typeset in Baskerville by Keystroke, Jacaranda Lodge, Wolverhampton
Printed and bound in Great Britain by St Edmundsbury Press,
Bury St Edmunds, Suffolk

British Library Cataloguing in Publication Data
A catalogue record for this book is available from the British Library

Library of Congress Cataloging in Publication Data
Laughlin, John C. H. (John Charles Hugh), 1942–
    Archaeology and the Bible / John C. H. Laughlin.
        p.   cm. – (Approaching the ancient world)
    Includes bibliographical references and index.
    1. Bible. O. T.–Antiquities. 2. Middle East–Antiquities.
    I. Title. II. Series.
    BS621.L38 1999
    220.9'3 – dc21   99–19503
                                          CIP

ISBN 0–415–15993–8 (hbk)
ISBN 0–415–15994–6 (pbk)

Contents

Illustrations

Abbreviations

<table>
<tr><td>AAI</td><td>The Archaeology of Ancient Israel, A. Ben-Tor (ed.) (New Haven, CT: Yale University Press), 1992</td></tr>
<tr><td>AAIPP</td><td>The Architecture of Ancient Israel from the Prehistoric to the Persian Periods, A. Kempinski and R. Reich (eds) (Jerusalem: Israel Exploration Society), 1992</td></tr>
<tr><td>ABD</td><td>The Anchor Bible Dictionary, 6 vols, David Noel Freedman (editor-in-chief) (New York: Doubleday), 1992</td></tr>
<tr><td>ABI</td><td>Archaeology and Biblical Interpretation, L. G. Perdue, L. E. Tombs and G. Johnson (eds) (Atlanta, GA: Scholars Press), 1987</td></tr>
<tr><td>AJR</td><td>Ancient Jerusalem Revealed, H. Geve (ed.) (Jerusalem: Israel Exploration Society), 1994</td></tr>
<tr><td>ANET</td><td>Ancient Near Eastern Texts Relating to the Old Testament, 3rd edn, James Pritchard (ed.) (Princeton, NJ: Princeton University Press), 1969</td></tr>
<tr><td>ASHL</td><td>The Archaeology of Society in the Holy Land, T. E. Levy (ed.) (New York: Facts on File), 1995</td></tr>
<tr><td>BA</td><td>Biblical Archaeologist</td></tr>
<tr><td>BAR</td><td>Biblical Archaeology Review</td></tr>
<tr><td>BAReader</td><td>Biblical Archaeologist Reader</td></tr>
<tr><td>BASOR</td><td>Bulletin of the American Schools of Oriental Research</td></tr>
<tr><td>BAT</td><td>Biblical Archaeology Today, Proceedings of the International Congress on Biblical Archaeology, Jerusalem, April 1984, Janet Amitai (ed.) (Jerusalem: Israel Exploration Society), 1985</td></tr>
<tr><td>BAT 90</td><td>Biblical Archaeology Today, 1990, Proceedings of the Second International Congress on Biblical Archaeology, Jerusalem, June–July, 1990, A. Biran and J. Aviram (eds) (Jerusalem: Israel Exploration Society), 1993</td></tr>
<tr><td>BTC</td><td>Benchmarks in Time and Culture, J. F. Drinkard, Jr, G. L. Mattingly and J. M. Miller (eds) (Atlanta, GA: Scholars Press), 1988</td></tr>
</table>

CAH	*The Cambridge Ancient History*, 3rd edn, I. Edwards *et al.* (eds) (New York: Cambridge University Press), 1971, 1973, 1975
EA	El Armarna letters
EAEHL	*The Encyclopedia of Archaeological Excavations in the Holy Land*, 4 vols, M. Avi-Yonah and E. Stern (eds) (Jerusalem: Israel Exploration Society and Massada Press), 1977
FNM	*From Nomadism to Monarchy: Archaeological and Historical Aspects of Early Israel*, I. Finkelstein and N. Na'aman (eds) (Jerusalem: Israel Exploration Society), 1994
HBD	*Harper's Bible Dictionary*, P. J. Achtemeier (ed.) (San Francisco: Harper and Row), 1985
HNHAP	*The Hyksos: New Historical and Archaeological Perspectives*, E. D. Oren (ed.) (Philadelphia: University of Pennsylvania Museum), 1997
IEJ	*Israel Exploration Journal*
JBL	*Journal of Biblical Literature*
NDT	*The Nile Delta in Transition 4th–3rd Millennium BC*, E. C. M. van den Brink (ed.) (Tel Aviv: Edwin C. M. van den Brink), 1992
NEA	*Near Eastern Archaeology* (formerly *Biblical Archaeologist*; first issue, vol. 61, no. 1, March 1998)
NEAEHL	*The New Encyclopedia of Archaeological Excavations in the Holy Land*, 4 vols, Ephraim Stern (ed.) (Jerusalem: Simon & Schuster), 1993
OEANE	*The Oxford Encyclopedia of Archaeology in the Near East*, 5 vols, Eric M. Meyers (editor-in-chief) (New York: Oxford University Press), 1997
PBIA	*Palestine in the Bronze and Iron Ages: Papers in Honour of Olga Tufnell*, J. A. Tubb (ed.) (London: Institute of Archaeology), 1985
PEQ	*Palestine Exploration Quarterly*
REI	*Recent Excavations in Israel: Studies in Iron Age Archaeology*, S. Gitin and W. G. Dever (eds) (Winona Lake, IN: Eisenbrauns), 1994
WLS	*The Word of the Lord Shall Go Forth: Essays in Honor of David Noel Freedman in Celebration of his Sixtieth Birthday*, C. L. Meyers and M. O'Connor (eds.) (Winona Lake, IN: Eisenbrauns), 1983
ZAW	*Zeitschrift für die alttestamentliche Wissenschaft*

Chapter 1

Introduction: archaeology and the Bible

This book is concerned with field archaeology as it is practiced in the Near East, particularly in the modern state of Israel, and its implications for reading and understanding the Bible. It is not intended for archaeologists and/or biblical specialists. It is written for those who are only beginning a serious study of this complex subject. Consequently, I have tried to keep notes to a minimum while at the same time providing enough resources in the bibliography to enable further and more technical study for any interested reader. By its very format and intention, this small volume is but a general introduction to a very large field about which thousands of articles and books have been written, many of them quite technical and intended for specialists.

So I must begin with a caveat. It was Alexander Pope who observed that "fools rush in where angels fear to tread" (*An Essay on Criticism*, 1. 625). With all due respect, where this book is concerned, I would hasten to paraphrase him to read: "fools write books on subjects that angels would not dare." I say this because the issues, specialized studies, questions, controversies, methods, conclusions, as well as publications on the subject of archaeology and the Bible are so numerous and complex that no one person today can hope to be in control of them all. Thus the title, "Archaeology and the Bible," is as audacious as it is intimidating; as hopeful as it will be incomplete.

Yet of all archaeological work going on in the world today, none attracts any more attention than that thought to be associated with the Bible in some way. It is quite common to see headlines in newspapers about recent discoveries in Israel (or a neighboring country) believed to be related to the Bible (Davidson 1996). The cover of the December 18, 1995, issue of *Time* magazine reads: "Is the Bible Fact or Fiction? Archaeologists in the Holy Land are shedding new light on what did – and didn't – occur in the greatest story ever told" (cf. the cover story

– "God's City – Jerusalem's 3000 years: where David ruled, Jesus taught and Muhammad ascended to heaven" – of the same date in *US News & World Report*).

Thus it will be the purpose of this book to provide for the interested and serious student a brief overview of the history, methods and implications of archaeological discoveries and research that have gone on in the Near East during the past 150 years or so. But it needs to be understood that archaeological research does not sit idle,[1] and any current assessment of the situation is dated before a manuscript even reaches publication. However, there is value, one hopes, in stopping long enough to find one's bearings before journeying on. This volume, in my mind at least, is such a stop. The best I can hope is that the information here, while incomplete in most respects, will at least be accurate and clear; a pointer in the right direction for anyone seriously interested in the subject. My main concern will be with the question of how best to interrelate the data now known through archaeological discovery with the world and text of the Hebrew Bible, commonly called the Old Testament.

Chapter 2

A brief history

Palestine: "Where more sins have probably been committed in the name of archaeology than on any commensurate portion of the earth's surface."

(Sir Mortimer Wheeler, 1956)

As is always the case in trying to write the history of a complex subject, it is difficult to know where to begin. While it could be argued, and with good reason, that modern archaeology in Israel began with Sir Flinders Petrie at Tell el-Hesi in 1890 (Callaway 1980a), the public's interest in the Ancient Near East was piqued much earlier. This interest was due in no small part to three explorers and adventurers.

Hormuzd Rassam (1826–1910)

On the night of December 20, 1853, H. Rassam, a Chaldean Christian associated with the Englishman Layard, began to dig secretly on part of the mound of ancient Nineveh (in modern-day Iraq) that had been assigned to the French by Sir Henry Rawlinson, a British officer who was one of the first to decipher cuneiform. Two nights later Rassam broke into what turned out to be the library in the palace of Ashurbanipal (668–626 BC), an Assyrian king. Rassam was assailed both by the French and the British, but in the end thousands of clay tablets were taken to the British Museum (Rassam 1897: 23ff.; Lloyd 1955: 166ff.). As Rassam so brazenly put it: "because it was an established rule that whenever one discovered a new palace, no one else could meddle with it, and thus, in my position as the agent of the British Museum, I had secured it for England" (1897: 26).

Some nineteen years later, in 1872, George Smith, a precocious young man who had a keen interest in what was being discovered in the Near East, secured a position as a cataloguer at the British Museum. Smith acquired the ability to read the cuneiform text of the tablets and was assigned the task of sorting out and joining together the broken fragments. What happened next is the stuff of every scholar's dream.[1] He discovered a non-biblical flood story about a ship coming to rest on the mountains of Nizir and the sending forth of a dove which returned when it could find no resting place. When Smith reported his discovery in a paper read at the Society of Biblical Archaeology on December 3, 1872, "it created a very considerable sensation" (Lloyd 1955: 179).

As knowledge of his discovery became known, biblical students, in particular, were made aware that the Bible belonged to a much wider historical context than had hitherto been suspected. Thus an awareness of what archaeological discoveries might do for biblical studies began to emerge, and as one archaeologist put it, "Biblical scholarship . . . said to archaeology as Moses said to Hobab, ' . . . come thou with us and we will do thee good. . . . ' (Num. 10:29)" (Callaway 1961: 156).

This discovery by Rassam, and its subsequent publication by Smith, along with many other discoveries from Mesopotamia, especially inscriptions, alerted the world to the fact that the forgotten cultures of both the pre-biblical as well as the biblical worlds lay buried in ruins (called *tells*, which are artificial mounds) throughout the Middle East. Soon there would be a rash of excavations and discoveries and "Biblical Archaeology" would be born.[2]

Henry Layard (1817–94)

One of the most famous of these earlier "archaeologists," who represents the best and the worst of these early years, was Henry Layard. He was determined, well educated, resourceful, and very adept at dealing with the local inhabitants of the Middle East, especially the Arabs. But at his worst, he was little more than a treasure hunter with no understanding or appreciation of the complexity of an antiquity site.

> Layard dug as inclination directed wholly ignorant of the complex structures of ancient mounds, always seeking stone monuments and only recovering the most obvious and spectacular of small finds. Where stone sculptures lined mudbrick walls he was able to plan structures. When only mudbrick and mudbrick debris survived he was baffled.

(Moorey 1991: 8–9)

Layard was particularly interested in digging at Nineveh. He obtained his financial backing to excavate this site in 1846, and was assisted by Rassam. Thus the stage was set for the latter's nocturnal escapade in 1853.

Edward Robinson (1794–1863)

While treasure hunting continued unabated in Assyria, motivated by what W. K. Loftus described as a "nervous desire to find important large museum pieces at the least possible outlay of time and money" (quoted in Lloyd 1955: 161), the knowledge of the topography of Palestine was revolutionized by E. Robinson. A highly educated man, trained in both mathematics and biblical studies, Robinson made two extended trips to Palestine, first in 1838 and again in 1852.[3] Robinson was accompanied on his travels by one of his former students, Eli Smith, who had gone to Beirut as a missionary and was fluent in Arabic. This latter distinction of Smith's proved invaluable, since at that time most of the population of Palestine was Arab, and the key to the geographical identification of ancient biblical sites would prove to be the modern Arabic place names.

Robinson was not an archaeologist, but without his accomplishments later archaeologists would have had a far more difficult time in identifying ancient sites. During his two visits, and always traveling on horseback, he identified correctly more than 100 sites. So thorough was his work that a contemporary Swiss topographer said of him: "The works of Robinson and Smith alone surpass the total of all previous contributions to Palestinian geography from the time of Eusebius and Jerome to the early nineteenth century."[4]

Sir Flinders Petrie (1853–1942)

The honor, however, of being considered the "father of Palestinian archaeology" goes to Sir Flinders Petrie (Callaway 1980a). Having no formal education, Petrie was one of those remarkable individuals who because of personality, intelligence, opportunity and determination left an indelible mark on the emerging discipline of archaeology. Called a "genius" by W.F. Albright (1949: 29), Petrie introduced into archaeological field techniques two of its most important concepts: pottery typology and stratification. Up until his time most dating, to the extent that it was done at all, was through inscriptions. Consequently, little or no attention was paid to small, nondescript remains, and this was especially true of the thousands of pieces of unpainted pottery sherds found on a typical site in Israel and elsewhere in the Middle East.

Petrie came to Tell el-Hesi (which he mistakenly identified with the biblical site of Lachish) in 1890, after having established himself as an Egyptologist. He recognized that all small objects found in the debris of a site could be associated with a period of its occupation. The key to doing this was dating the pottery sherds: "once settle the pottery of a country and the key is in our hands for all future explorations" (Petrie 1891: 40).

Petrie also recognized, but little understood, that a tell was composed of different layers or strata of occupation. He seems to have envisioned these strata much like a well-made layered cake – each layer being uniform in size and shape and clearly distinct from all the others. Thus he created a system he called "sequence dating" (Figure 2.1), which really was not a method that allowed him to give absolute dates at all to the objects he found. Rather, it allowed him to arrange his materials into what he believed were natural groupings, separating what belonged to one family (based on shape, decoration, form, and so on) from another group. Each sequence could then be related to a stratum on the site (Callaway 1980a: 64).

While Petrie earned the praise he has received over the years, there are many weaknesses in his archaeological field techniques, not the least of which was his simplistic understanding of the formation of strata (cf. Davies 1988: 49; Dever 1980a: 42; Wheeler 1956: 29). Nevertheless, due to his pioneering efforts, the transformation of Middle Eastern

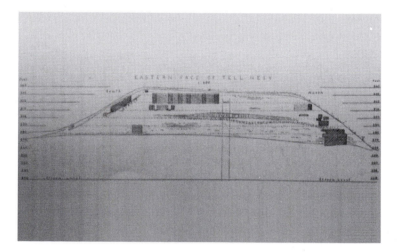

Figure 2.1 Petrie's "sequence dating" of Tell el-Hesi. From Petrie, *Tell el Hesy, Lachish*, 1891

archaeology from treasure hunting to scientific enterprise took a giant leap forward.

From Petrie to the present

It is customary to divide the archaeological history of the last 100 years or so since Petrie's work at Hesi into four or five periods.[5] Here only the briefest of summaries can be given.

Petrie to World War I

Petrie's work at Hesi was responsible for what W. G. Dever (1980a: 42) has described as a "Golden Age" of excavation in Palestine, that continued up until the outbreak of World War I. For the first time some of the major tells in Israel were excavated. These include the work of R. A. S. Macalister at Gezer (1902–9), and the German excavations at Jericho (1907–9) and at Megiddo (beginning in 1903). The Americans excavated at Samaria under D. G. Lyon and G. A. Reisner (1908–10).[6] In addition, an American, F. W. Bliss, continued the work Petrie had begun at Hesi, although Petrie's insight concerning the stratigraphy of a tell seems to have been lost on Bliss.

It should also be noted that several national societies of archaeology had already been established prior to Petrie's appearance on Palestinian soil: the Palestine Exploration Fund (British, 1865); the American Palestine Society (1870); the German Palestine Society (1878); and the French School of Bible and Archaeology (École Biblique, 1890).

Despite all of this flurry of archaeological activity, many mistakes were made regarding both method (lack of proper stratigraphical techniques led Macalister to identify only eight out of twenty-six strata at Gezer), and dating (Macalister was off at Gezer by as much as 800 years). Their lack of better methods and understanding of tell formation is clearly reflected in the publications of this period which have been described as "vast treasure houses of intriguing, but often useless information" (Dever 1980a: 42). Nevertheless, given the hardships these early pioneers had to overcome or learn to live with, their achievements were remarkable.

1918–40

The description "the Golden Age of Archaeology" has been reserved for this period by Moorey (1991: 54; cf. Dever 1980a: 43–4). Call it what one will, many developments and influential people in the field of archaeology emerged during this time that have left an indelible stamp upon archaeology in the Middle East, and in Israel in particular. Politically, the British took control of Palestine and established a Department of Antiquities (known today as the Israel Antiquities Authority), thus providing some stability and control over the excavations in the region. Major excavations were carried out by several of the national schools: Beth Shan (1921–23) and Megiddo (1929–39) by the Americans; Jericho (1929–36) and Samaria (1931–35) by the British. The excavation at Samaria is singularly important because it introduced Dame Kathleen Kenyon to archaeology in Israel. Her meticulous application of stratigraphic analysis would almost single-handedly lead to what Dever called his third "revolution" (1980a: 44).

This period also witnessed for the first time the appearance of Israeli archaeologists such as A. Biran, who has had the longest-running excavation ever conducted in Israel, Tel Dan, which was begun in 1968 and at this writing (1998) is still in progress. B. Mazar excavated the important Philistine site of Qasile, and there are others. The Israeli school of archaeology, for obvious reasons, is now the leading factor in Palestinian archaeology.

But the genius of this period was W. F. Albright (1891–1971).[7] His excavation at Tell Beit Mirsim (TBM) between 1926 and 1932 led to his mastery of pottery analysis and typology. This mastery, coupled with his stratigraphical understanding of the site (which he identified with biblical Debir, an identification disputed by most archaeologists today), was so great that he revolutionized the chronological framework for the Bronze and Iron ages (ca. 3300–540 BC; on chronology, see below). His influence has also been widely felt among many students, either trained by him or exposed to his methods. One of his outstanding students was Nelson Glueck, a rabbi, (1901–71); see Mattingly (1983) for a helpful critique of Glueck. Glueck established his reputation exploring the regions of the Transjordan (Glueck 1940; see Moorey 1991: 75–7). G. E. Wright (1909–74), then, was Albright's most influential student (Wright 1957; see King 1987). It was Wright, above all others, who popularized Albright's views and who trained a new generation of archaeologists at Shechem. It was also Wright who founded the periodical *The Biblical Archaeologist* in 1938.

1948–70

By 1948 World War II was over, and Israel was an independent state, the British Mandate in Palestine having also come to its end. Archaeological excavations were once more begun with renewed vigor as well as controversy. The controversy was created primarily over the question of field methodology. K. Kenyon (1906–78) introduced an elaborate stratigraphic technique, first at Jericho (1952–58), then at Jerusalem (1961–67). Her method meant less exposure of a site as well as working at a much slower pace (Moorey 1991: 94–9).

Many Israeli archaeologists, who started digs at some of the largest tells in Israel, such as Yadin at Hazor and Biran at Dan, were reluctant to adopt Kenyon's method exclusively. Their primary concern was with the exposure of the architectural remains of the sites (Dever 1980a: 45). However, it is only fair to point out that, while there may still be no agreement among all Israeli archaeologists on field methodology, they all draw stratigraphic sections today (for brief, but informative summaries of Israeli archaeology, see Ussishkin 1982; A. Mazar 1988).

1970 to the present

Since about 1970 (according to Dever) there has been a different kind of revolution in "Biblical Archaeology." The impact of the so-called "New Archaeology," first practiced in America, began to be felt in Israel. While over-simplification always runs the risk of distortion, the main thrust of this movement seems to have been with providing *explanations* for cultural changes recorded in the material remains, rather than *descriptions* of those changes, as heretofore had been the norm. Thus a natural outgrowth of this shift in paradigms was the emphasis on multidisciplinary staff. No longer could a single "genius" like Petrie or Albright single-handedly run a dig and expect to answer all the questions now being raised. Scientists from many disciplines, such as geology, botany and zoology, were now beginning to make invaluable contributions to the overall knowledge attained from excavations (Dever 1980a, 1985b, 1988, 1989, 1992a; Moorey 1991: 114–75).

Regional surveys made in the last several years also have had a major impact on archaeology in Israel and in Jordan. Such surveys are essential if a holistic picture of the culture that flourished at any particular time and place is to be appreciated. Such surveys, as will be seen, can have a profound impact on particular areas of interpretation, such as the "Conquest of Canaan" by Israel (see below, Chapter 7).

Another change that occurred, at least in some cases during this period, is in the planning and operation of digs. Excavations are now carried out for shorter periods of time, perhaps with the goal of trying to answer a specific question. Many salvage digs are conducted each year by archaeologists from the Antiquities Authority. Unfortunately, many of these digs are necessitated by the rapid development now taking place in Israel, which is destroying antiquity sites at an alarming rate. Student volunteers, many from American colleges and universities, now do much of the manual labor.

The Wheeler-Kenyon field method of stratigraphical analysis, however modified, is here to stay. There is more cooperation between American and Israeli archaeologists, though the Israelis are doing more and more excavations (A. Mazar 1988: 112–14). And, of course, every dig now has its computer technician, often right in the field, daily recording the activities of the dig. At the moment, however, there is no systematic unity among archaeologists with regard to computer programming. This has limited the use of the data created by computers. It is to be hoped that it will soon be possible for computer information from all digs (past and present) to be readily accessed so that research and study can be conducted in the most comprehensive way possible. With the technology currently available and still more, no doubt, on the way, the kinds of questions posed by archaeologists and the kinds of data available to answer those questions are limited only by the creativity practiced in field operations and the computer recording techniques themselves.

Archaeology and the Bible

The title of this volume presupposes that archaeological discoveries in the Middle East, particularly in Palestine, can have a bearing upon the interpretation and appreciation of the Bible. However, the issues and questions involved are many and complex. In fact, even what to call what archaeologists do in this part of the world is controversial. For years archaeological research in Palestine (and in adjacent countries) was called "Biblical Archaeology." Some scholars, particularly Dever of the University of Arizona, have called for the abandonment of this term and have suggested such replacements as "Near Eastern Archaeology" or more often "Syro-Palestinian Archaeology."[8] Dever has claimed that the term "Biblical Archaeology" is an American phenomenon linked primarily to Protestant professors of religion. It was in an effort to establish archaeology in the Levant as an independent, secular and professional discipline that he has argued for the name change.

Reaction to his argument has varied. H. D. Lance, an American biblical scholar and archaeologist, has argued that biblical archaeology "is a *biblical* discipline which exists for the benefit and interest of biblical studies. So long as people read the Bible and ask questions about the history and culture of the ancient world which produced it, those questions will have to be answered; and the sum total of those answers will comprise biblical archaeology" (1981: 95).

V. Fritz, a German archaeologist, has also resisted the name change. In his book, significantly entitled *An Introduction to Biblical Archaeology*, he concludes: "From a scholarly point of view there is no reason to abandon the term 'Biblical archaeology' since a relationship between the two disciplines is justified. At any rate the term, when used, can refer only to the archaeology of the whole region throughout all periods and not to a study of antiquities that is exclusively related to biblical texts" (1994: 12).

Amnon Ben-Tor, of the Hebrew University, and editor of a volume on the archaeology of Israel written exclusively by Israeli scholars, has also opposed the suggestion to abandon the term "biblical archaeology": "The two fields are naturally related and mutually enriching. It is as unreasonable as to demand that classical archaeology be separated from Homer and other writings of antiquity. Eliminate the Bible from the archaeology of the Land of Israel in the second and first millennia BCE, and you have deprived it of its soul" (*AAI*: 9).

In all fairness, it should be noted that Dever has never, to my knowledge, suggested that the Bible ought to be eliminated from the archaeology that goes on in Israel. Rather, what he has called for is an honest dialogue between those who do archaeology on the one hand, and those who do biblical studies on the other. As he sees it: "The crucial issue for biblical archaeology, properly conceived as a dialogue, has always been (and is even more so now) its understanding and use of archaeology on the one hand, its understanding of the issues in biblical studies that are fitting subjects for archaeological illumination on the other – and the proper relationship *between* [emphasis in the original] the two" (1985a: 61; see Moorey 1991: 133–45).

Dever's concern is a reminder that the meaning of neither archaeological data nor of biblical texts is self-evident. To be competent in either of the disciplines requires highly specialized training, which the increasing complexity of both fields makes nearly impossible for a single individual to achieve. It is thus tempting for someone who has been trained in both archaeological and biblical studies to be defensive. However, Dever has made a valuable contribution if for no other reasons than having raised the question and forced a discussion of the issues. I would like to believe that there is still a place for those in positions where they must teach both disciplines if the contributions of biblical scholars *and* archaeologists are to reach a wider audience. It is very unlikely in this economic period of "down-sizing" and other restraints that small, private schools can afford the luxury of a full-time "Syro-Palestinian" archaeologist. If students, especially those planning seminary careers, as well as interested lay-persons, are to be informed about what is bunk and what is not bunk when it comes to archaeology and the Bible, there is still, I believe, a place for those trained in both disciplines. Training in archaeology ought especially to be required for those students who plan to enter the professional ministries of the church, if for no other reason than that it is archaeologists who in recent years have been at the forefront of a new evaluation of the history and culture out of which the Bible came.[9]

During the first half of this century and even up through the 1960s, many archaeologists were optimistic that archaeological discoveries had validated many of the historical claims of the Bible, if not the theological interpretations given to that history by the biblical authors. For example, Albright triumphantly declared in the mid-1930s: "Discovery after discovery has established the accuracy of innumerable details, and has brought increased recognition of the Bible as a source of history" (1974: 128). Albright's most famous student, G. E. Wright, also believed that archaeology and the Bible were very closely aligned when he concluded that biblical archaeology's "chief concern is not with strata or pots or methodology. Its central and absorbing interest is the understanding and exposition of the scriptures" (quoted in Dever 1985a: 55).

Many Israeli archaeologists still seem to operate from this perspective. Shortly before his death, Y. Yadin (whom Dever once called a "secular fundamentalist"!) wrote concerning the conquest story in the Bible: "The fact is that excavation results from the last 50 years or so support in a most amazing way, except in some cases, the basic historicity of the Biblical account" (1982: 18).

Such sentiments as the above are examples of what Lemche has recently referred to as: "the pervasive mania within certain archaeological circles for correlating text with excavation before either the text or the excavation has had an opportunity to speak for itself" (1985: 388). This highly optimistic view of what archaeology can do for biblical studies – historically speaking, at least – is now all but absent except among the most conservative of archaeologists and biblical historians. The contemporary view of most archaeologists is that the purpose of archaeology, however defined, is not to prove the Bible true in any sense, historically or otherwise (Dever 1990a: 26).

Given the revolution that has taken place in the discipline of "Biblical Archaeology" since the 1970s, the problem, as stated recently by one archaeologist, "is that it is not actually clear what archaeology can do for biblical studies" (Strange 1992: 23). This leads to the basic question of the purpose of archaeology in the first place. What is it that archaeologists ought really to be trying to do if they are doing what the logic of the discipline dictates?

Perhaps we can begin by stating what archaeologists do not do. Archaeologists do not dig up history, whether of the Bible or of anything else. Neither do we excavate ancient economic, political or social systems. We certainly do not recover ancient religions. The only thing the archaeologist discovers from the past are *artifacts* – the material remains left by human and/or natural activities (the latter are sometimes called "ecofacts"). Properly interpreted and understood, these artifacts may indeed inform us about all of the above issues (cf. Dever's "material correlate," 1992c: 550). However, archaeologists can only *excavate* the material reality of the past, in whatever form that reality takes. Any *interpretation* of this recovered material data is an *addition* to the material remains themselves. The problem, of course, is that artifacts, even if they include inscriptions or texts, do not interpret themselves and are usually open to more than one meaning. Although there is always one best explanation or inference with respect to any given artifactual data, we can never be absolutely certain, as P. de Vaux pointed out years ago, that we have it. It should come as no surprise, then, that archaeologists can study the *same* data but come to *different*, if not totally opposite, conclusions. All such interpretations are highly subjective, which is why different archaeologists can "see" the same things but disagree violently on what these things mean. These disagreements will become obvious as we explore issues below (see the comments by Knoppers 1997: 44).[10]

Since the 1970s the amount and kinds of artifactual data now being recovered from antiquity sites have greatly increased due to the use of multidisciplinary staff discussed above. This has resulted in the recovery of a wider assortment of material concerning the total setting of ancient sites including their natural environment. But despite the increase in sophisticated recovery techniques as well as in the overall complexity of contemporary digs, the most important challenge facing the archaeologist is still "the development of reliable means for inference justification" (Binford 1989: 3). Just how difficult "inference justification" can be will be seen when we raise the question of archaeological data and the rise of early Israel (see below, Chapter 7).

For the student interested in "Biblical Archaeology" there are two sets of data: the archaeological and the biblical. The Bible can no longer be accepted uncritically as a "historical" account of ancient Israel, if by historical we mean all the modern connotations of that term. Rather the Bible interprets through theological, and even mythological, lenses what archaeologists must interpret through scientific/historical ones. The case of the story of the destruction of Jericho in the Book of Joshua is a classic example. The temptation was, and still is in some quarters, to interpret the archaeological data to "fit" a preconceived interpretation of the Bible. Garstang, in the 1930s, interpreted his findings at Jericho to support his literal interpretation of the biblical story. Indeed, there are those today who have sought to rewrite the entire chronological framework of the Near East in order to make the biblical stories fit their preconceptions. As my former teacher, Joseph Callaway, was fond of cautioning us, we need to be careful lest we make up in imagination what we lack in knowledge.

The more it is appreciated that whatever history there is in the Bible, particularly of the earlier periods, has been edited after Israel's catastrophes, especially that of 587 BC (the "Exile"), the more obvious it seems that the Bible does not contain a contemporary witness to many of the events it describes.[11] The conclusion reached by Joseph Blenkinsopp seems to reflect the consensus of most biblical scholars: "We assume that the Hebrew Bible is a product of the Second Temple period and that it inevitably reflects the concerns of that time and the ideology of the religious and intellectual elite responsible for its final redaction" (1995: 119). However, this does not mean that no parts of the Bible were in a written form prior to the exilic or post-exilic periods (see below, Chapter 8).

Given this literary nature of the Bible and the fact that there is much archaeological data the interpretation of which denies the Bible much of its historical value, what can archaeology do for biblical studies? The rest of this book will be concerned with trying to answer this question. But it must be admitted here that archaeology simply has not done for the Bible what earlier practitioners had hoped it would. For a non-believer this development is not particularly troublesome. But for those who claim the Jewish or Christian faith as their own, the consensus now developing in archaeology as well as in critical literary studies raises many acute questions concerning the use of the Bible as a source of religious truth. The believer seems to be caught, as one observer recently noted, "between the rock of the biblical claim and the hard place of the archaeological contradiction" (Willis, in Charlesworth and Weaver 1992: 77).

The issue is complicated even more when one considers the fact that the archaeological picture in Palestine is woefully incomplete. In most cases excavators discover only bits and pieces left from the past. All of these fragments are important, to be sure, but the best we can do is draw only tentative conclusions in most cases. Thus any assessment of archaeology and the Bible must always be open to modification, if not outright rejection, when new evidence so warrants. Still, despite such limitations, archaeology has made many valuable contributions to our understanding of the Bible. The following are only a few suggestions which will be developed further as we proceed:

1   Archaeological data in many cases provide the only contemporary witnesses we have for many "events" described in the Bible. This is especially true for the paradigm stories of the "conquest" of Canaan and the rise of early Israel.
2   Archaeological data allow us to create a different point of view (see Lance 1981) from which we can begin to evaluate the biblical point of view, especially with regard to the way the biblical writers understood Israel's history and culture, and particularly their religion (see below, Chapter 8). Often these two very different points of view will clash. When they do, critical judgments have to be made. These judgments may sometimes be difficult, tentative and even ambiguous, but this is the fault neither of the Bible nor of the methods of the archaeologist. It is simply a reflection of the complex world in which we all live.

Archaeological discoveries have helped to make crystal clear that the Bible is not a book of inerrant history and certainly not of inerrant science. Rather, they have reinforced the conclusions reached by literary studies that the Bible is a book reflecting theological sensitivities of generations of thinkers who struggled with some of life's most troublesome and difficult, but at the same time, exciting and ultimate questions. Sometimes archaeological discoveries have forced the honest student to question and/or reject the "historical" reconstruction found there and certainly to reject much that passes for contemporary biblical interpretation by fundamentalists who insist on confusing truth with literalism and faith with fact. Even if archaeological data could substantiate the historicity of the biblical stories, this substantiation could say nothing concerning the theological usage made of such "historical events" by the biblical writers. The claims the Bible makes with regard to ultimate truths can only be affirmed or denied, not proven or disproven by archaeological or any other scientific data. Archaeological discoveries and interpretations may bring one to the threshold of faith, but they cannot carry one across.

It will be my concern in the chapters that follow to suggest just what this "archaeological point of view" can contribute to our understanding of the Bible. To set the tone for our quest it will suffice here to quote from P. King, who has spent a good part of his professional life struggling with the same issue:

> Archaeology prevents the Bible from being mythological by keeping it in the realm of history. Archaeology provides the geographical and chronological context of biblical people and events. Archaeology recovers the empirical evidence necessary for clarifying the biblical text. Archaeology illuminates the daily life of biblical people by recovering their pottery, utensils, weapons, seals, ostraca, and architecture. As Palestinian archaeology lengthens its geographical horizon to the Arabian peninsula and expands its chronological perspective to the prehistoric period, it is possible to understand the Bible in a much larger context.
>
> (1983b: 3–4)

Chapter 3

How it's done: an introduction to field work

Excavators, as a rule, record only those things which appear to them important at the time, but fresh problems in Archaeology and Anthropology are constantly arising. . . . Every detail should, therefore, be recorded in the manner most conducive to facility of reference, and it ought at all times to be the chief object of an excavator to reduce his own personal equation to a minimum.

(Lieutenant-General Pitt-Rivers, 1887)

Today archaeological excavations are very complex and multifaceted undertakings. They require any number of specialists in various disciplines, including computer technicians. Overall, excavations consist of three major interrelated activities: site selection, field work and publication.

Site selection

Obviously, the first task that must be accomplished before an excavation can take place is the selection of a site. In the beginning of archaeological excavations in Israel, most of the sites selected were large tells (ruins that are mound shaped – see Figure 3.1) that were identified (correctly or not) with major biblical cities. While the early pioneers, such as Petrie, Macalister, Sellin and Watzinger, deserve the admiration and gratitude of today's excavators, their field techniques often left much to be desired. Consequently, through the years many of these same sites have been re-excavated in order to check, and more often than not, correct or modify the conclusions reached by the earlier excavators (Megiddo, for example). Thus, it is not unusual for students to discover in their research into the history of excavations that some sites have been repeatedly

Figure 3.1 Tel Beth Shan. Photo: J. Laughlin

excavated. In fact, archaeologists today hope, and expect, that their site will be re-excavated in the future when better recovery techniques will be available. Consequently, it is common practice now deliberately to leave areas of a site undisturbed so future archaeologists will have the opportunity to reach independent conclusions against which to check those established by earlier excavators. This is a timely warning that all interpretations presented in archaeological publications, regardless of how impressive they may be, are tentative and open to correction and modification.

Many excavations in Israel today are salvage digs usually conducted by archaeologists from the Israel Antiquities Authority. In these cases the site is "selected" for the archaeologist, who is usually given a specific and normally quite short time to excavate before the site is partially or totally buried or destroyed.

Other sites are chosen for their accessibility or because they are thought to contain remains from time periods in which the excavator is particularly interested. Any combination of the above, as well as other factors, might influence the choice of a site. At Banias (Caesarea Philippi), where I am currently involved, contemporary political realities as well as the occupational history of the site affected the choice. Before 1967 this site was in Syria and inaccessible to archaeologists working in Israel. When it became available after the Six Day War in 1967, it was 1988 before an archaeologist interested in the historical periods reflected in the material remains (primarily Early Roman to Ottoman) could organize an excavation. Of course, before any legal excavation can proceed in Israel, a license must be obtained from the Antiquities Authority.

Field work

Archaeology has often been described as the systematic destruction of an antiquity site (I once heard it called "controlled vandalism"). If such destruction is to be justified at all, the way in which the site is "destroyed" must be recorded so that the knowledge obtained about the site is as accurate and as complete as possible. To help achieve this goal, field excavation techniques have been developed and improved through the years. It is only when the excavator uses consciously developed and accepted methods that positive, useful results can be expected.[1] Even though archaeology has sometimes been described more as an "art" than a "science," many scientifically developed procedures, from satellite imaging to microscopic paleo-botanical analysis, are used. Digs now have as many specialists working as money and interests allow. However, in this chapter the major concern will be with the more normal, day-to-day field activities that a student volunteer is likely to encounter on a typical dig.

Once a site has been selected, much preparation has to be done before the excavation can begin (Dessel 1997). Surveyors must prepare a topographic map that shows the elevation contours of the site (Blakely 1997; see Figure 3.2). This type of survey can be very helpful in planning the overall strategy of the excavation. To a trained eye, such surveys and plans may suggest the location of buried defensive walls or the possible location of water sources. As architectural remains are uncovered and drawn to scale on the map, the overall layout or plan of some period in the site's occupational history may be suggested. The plan also allows future archaeologists to locate previously excavated areas which may have eroded or been removed.

Once this task has been completed, the site is usually divided into fields or areas designated by numbers or letters. At Banias, we used letters: Areas A, B, C and so on. Also, it should be noted that in some systems, "area" designations refer to individual "squares." Each area or field is drawn on a "top plan," usually on a 1:50 scale. This plan is oriented on a north–south axis and divided into a grid composed of squares. These squares are normally represented as measuring 5 meters in length on each side. However, this is a purely arbitrary number, and each excavator may choose to modify the size of the grid to meet his or her own objectives. Regardless of the modifications to the grid system, it

Figure 3.2 Topographic plan of Tel Dan showing areas of excavation as of 1992. From *Dan I*. Courtesy of A. Biran, Tel Dan Excavations, Hebrew Union College, Jerusalem, 1996

is now used by all archaeologists working in the Near East.[2] However, as the excavation proceeds, this grid pattern may be changed dramatically as conditions warrant. It cannot be emphasized too much that the aim of all archaeological work is, or should be, to recover the physical data left by both human and natural activity on a site and to explain the interrelations of these data in order to understand human cultures of the past. Excavation recovery techniques are the means to this end, not the end in itself, and there is nothing sacred about them.

Nevertheless, the grid system has proved its usefulness due to the way antiquity sites were formed in the Near East. Many of the sites were occupied over long periods of time by different peoples. At Megiddo, for example, some twenty-five periods, or strata, of occupation have been identified dating from the fourth millennium BC, down to the fourth century AD. Not until recently has there been much of an effort to understand how tells were formed, and many mistakes in the excavating strategy of past excavations have occurred accordingly (see Chapter 2).[3]

Stratigraphy

It was Sir Mortimer Wheeler who observed many years ago that "There is no right way of digging, but there are many wrong ways" (1956: 15). One wrong way would be to give pickaxes to a group of workers and let them dig wherever they pleased (see plate 4a in Wheeler). This method, if it can be so called, will not work for obvious reasons. Not only is it impossible to control and record accurately what is happening, it also makes impossible a viable interpretation of the data. Another wrong way, under normal circumstances, would be to dig using large (or even small!) mechanical earth-moving equipment, such as bulldozers. However, under abnormal or unusual circumstances, such equipment cannot only be useful but actually required by common sense. For example, some sites are covered with thousands of cubic yards of modern debris or fill material containing little or no diagnostic remains. Once this has been established by careful probing, the use of modern earth-moving equipment can save countless and boring hours of having to remove this material by hand. But this is only an exception that proves the rule. Most excavating must be done by hand. Subtle changes in soil composition, superimposed floor levels, foundation trenches for walls, countless small objects and many other data would be completely destroyed and lost using only mechanical equipment. The common sense of the excavator and the particularities and research objectives of each unique excavation should play a decisive role here.

In order to assign properly the archaeological data (walls, floors, streets, pits, cisterns, tombs, graves, sherds, fills and so forth) to their proper time period, the various, and often complex, layers of a tell must be removed in a way that is controlled as much as possible. The time period to which recovered material data are assigned is usually called a "stratum" (see note 3). This controlled removal technique is provided by digging squares, leaving, normally, a 1 meter wall between each square (Figure 3.3). On a grid where the side of each square is 5 meters in length (a 5 meter square is a popular but arbitrary size, and circumstances may dictate squares of different dimensions, even on the same site), an effective digging square of 4 meters on a side is created. The artificial walls created between each square are called "balks." No one that I know believes that ancient people lived in 5 meter (or 10, or 20 meter!) squares oriented on a north–south axis. But it is the vertical face of the balk, called a "section"(Figure 3.4) that provides the excavator with his or her best chance to distinguish correctly between the superimposed layers that exist on that part of the site. Only when this has been accomplished, and all finds have been assigned correctly to each layer or stratum, can the excavator begin to form a stratigraphical profile of the site.

Understanding the stratigraphy of a site is one of the most difficult challenges facing the excavator. This is especially so on sites which have

Figure 3.3 Archaeological site using the "grid" method.
Photo: J. Laughlin

Figure 3.4 Excavated section showing tagged layers. Note the Roman stone earth fill-in top half. Photo: J. Laughlin

been occupied many times over thousands of years. There are any number of reasons why this is so. Only now are we beginning to understand something of the complex processes that formed ancient tells (see note 3). They are the repositories of material remains left by many and various activities, lasting in some cases for millennia. No two tells are exactly alike in formation or remains. Everything from geographical location to climate affected their formation and history.

Starting from the top of a tell, one expects to uncover the latest stratum of occupation first. But even this is not always the case, as the latest period of occupation may have been located at the bottom of the tell. Sometimes it is helpful to dig what is called a "stepped trench" from the top of the tell to the bottom to gain an overall understanding of the tell's occupational history (Figure 3.5).

Figure 3.5 Archaeological site using the "stepped trench" method.
Photo: J. Laughlin

The strata of a tell are naturally associated with any architectural remains. However, buildings, streets, floors and other remains may have gone through several stages of use and re-use within the same period or stratum of occupation. Furthermore, once occupation on the tell has ended, for whatever reason, activity within the material remains of the site may continue indefinitely. Burrowing animals may cause materials from later occupations to appear in earlier periods and vice versa.[4] Storage pits, cisterns, tombs, foundation trenches for walls from other, later periods may all intrude upon earlier deposits. This type of disturbance frequently leads to what is sometimes called "upward migration," a process whereby earlier objects are brought up and mixed with later material (Schiffer 1987: 122–5). It is also quite common to find materials from earlier strata re-used later, sometimes centuries later, by other groups occupying the site. There is also the chance that erosion caused by both wind and water has redeposited artifacts and soils or destroyed them altogether. And we are just now beginning to try to understand how the environment helped to shape and was shaped by human activity on these tells. All of the above, and no doubt other activities as well, helped create the very complex stratigraphical history that is common on most Near Eastern tells. One of the main goals of the excavator is to recognize each layer or stratum and to identify correctly all of the material that belongs to each one.

Locus

Essential to the recording system on most digs is the concept of *locus* (Lance 1978; Nakhai 1997b; Van Beek 1988). Everything that is excavated must belong to a locus, which may be defined simply as any three-dimensional part of a site that needs to be distinguished from any other three-dimensional part. Thus a locus is anything that needs to be recorded as being discrete from everything else that is around it. This includes such things as soil layers, floors, fills (Boraas 1988), destruction debris, ash layers, pits, walls (in some recording systems walls are given separate designations), pavements, streets, water pipes, thresholds, water channels, tombs, graves and so on. Different excavators use different systems of recording loci, but however it is done, everything recovered from an archaeological site must be assigned a locus number.

At Banias, the site was divided into areas designated by letters of the alphabet (Areas A, B, C . . .). At the beginning of each season, that season's number was prefixed to the area being excavated. The first locus number assigned to each area was the number "001." Thus, "10B025" would refer to locus 25 from Area B of the tenth season. In practice it is better to have too many loci than too few. If on closer reflection and study it is discovered that materials originally assigned to separate loci belong together, the loci numbers can be collapsed into one. On the other hand, if data that belong to separate loci are excavated as one locus, it is normally impossible to separate them later. This is especially true of pottery baskets (see below).

Another important though sometimes difficult task of the area supervisor is to provide a detailed description of each locus in his or her area or field. This description must include an identification of the type of locus (such as floor, fill, doorway, pit), its horizontal boundaries and its top and bottom levels. Such description is essential if the larger stratigraphical profile of the area being excavated is to be understood.

Each individual locus must be related to adjacent loci both vertically and horizontally. One of the practical functions of balks is that they provide fixed reference points for loci description. Once one or more of the balks have been removed other reference points must be established. "Balk removal," by the way, is another locus designation.

The basket number

Every artifact that is found in a locus must be recorded. This is accomplished by tagging the collected materials with *basket numbers* (Blakely and Toombs 1980: 87–108; Van Beek 1988: 155ff.). Since the most commonly collected artifact on Near Eastern tells since the Pottery Neolithic period (6th–5th millennium BC) is the lowly potsherd (usually just called "sherd"), most basket numbers refer to the pottery collected in each locus. Thus the basket numbers form the basic framework of the supervisor's field diary (Lance 1978: 75–6). A single locus may produce many baskets, each one representing a three-dimensional part of the locus from which it came. The basket (in many cases today it is actually a bucket) tag contains vital information which follows the material from the field, through the cleaning, and where required, the restoration process, to the storage lab and finally to the interpretative and publication phases of an excavation.

A typical basket ticket will contain the following basic information: the name of the site being excavated; the license number for that season granted by the Antiquities Authority; the date the basket was excavated; the area or field and locus from which the basket came; the top and bottom levels of the basket; and a brief description of the type of locus from which it was excavated – for example, "surface material," "threshold in building B2036," "collapse" and so on. At Banias we used a system designed specifically for computer use. Thus a typical basket number might look like this: "14D0120p." The number "14" designates the fourteenth season of the excavation, in this case the summer of 1996; the letter "D" refers to the area from which the basket came; the number "0128" to the 128th basket excavated; and the letter "p" to the contents of the basket – in this case, the ceramic sherds. Had the number read "14D0128l," it would have indicated marble fragments (denoted by the letter "l" in our system) found in the same locus and material as the pottery basket described above.

The pottery basket is basic, because on a Near Eastern tell it is usually sherds that provide the most reliable date for the cultural horizon ("Middle Bronze Age," "Iron Age I" and so forth) from which the material is coming. Other artifacts, such as the marble fragments in the above case, would be dated according to the date of the pottery remains found in the same locus. This assumes that the locus is "clean" or sealed. Otherwise intrusions can, and often do, occur. If the locus happens to be a "fill" or "pit," the sherds could come from different periods and the marble fragments mentioned above conceivably could come from still another period. If this sounds rather confusing and complicated, it is (or can be). That is another reason why controlled recovery and recording techniques are essential if the excavation is to succeed.

All material excavated from a locus is tagged and prepared for further study in the lab. It may include such items as bones, coins, tesserae (from mosaics), oil lamps, flint, sea shells, plaster fragments, charcoal, metal fragments, scrapers and, if one is lucky, some type of inscription. And there is always that twisted corroded "thing," or odd-looking piece of ceramic material that nobody seems to be able to identify. All of these materials, as well as many others found on a typical dig, must be carefully cleaned, often researched, and studied after the dig is over. Many of these studies require specialists and can involve a long and expensive process.

On the other hand, the baskets of sherds collected each day are usually cleaned and "read" in the field. Different digs use different methods for doing this. One system that seems to work fairly well requires each day's pottery finds to be soaked overnight in water. They are washed and dried the next morning and "read" in the afternoon after the field work is finished. The disadvantage of this method is that the reading is one day behind the field work. But whatever system is used, it is essential that the pottery washing, drying and arrangement for reading, and the marking and storage of diagnostic pieces be well organized, otherwise chaos and confusion will be the usual results.

However it is done, pottery reading is essential, both for its immediate value in informing and guiding the excavator in the field, and in the final identification and dating of the strata of the site overall. Since the precise location from which the sherds came can be pinpointed on the grid, the date of the activity that left behind the debris being excavated hopefully can be estimated (again, assuming that the pottery is not "mixed"). By fitting together all such data collected over the course of the life of the dig, it is possible to reconstruct the overall occupational history of the site. However, every experienced archaeologist knows that something hidden just a few inches inside a balk or in a square not yet excavated can change dramatically one's understanding of (perhaps) the date of a phase of occupation, or the function of a building. Thus tentative conclusions open to modification in light of new evidence would seem to be the best policy for archaeologists to follow.

Computer recording and analysis

Since the introduction of computers into field archaeology in the 1970s, vast strides have been made utilizing the ever-increasing technical advancements in this field. It is now commonplace for excavations to have a computer specialist recording the daily activities of the dig. J. Strange[5] has identified three major uses of the computer which is now ubiquitous on archaeological excavations. First, the use of computers enables the contemporary excavator to establish a database of an ever-increasing number of artifacts. What would have required boxes of handwritten card files a few years ago can now easily and quickly be recorded in a computer. Second, computers enable the management of these databases, one of the most obvious results of which is the creation and publication of reports. The third major use is the analysis of the archaeological data. Here the possibilities are many. Depending upon the goals of the excavator, the kind of site being excavated and the computer programs being utilized, everything from descriptive analysis of all artifacts recorded to "analytical" or "inferential statistics" is possible (Longstaff 1997). It is also now possible to create plans and add photographs and video recordings directly into the computer.

Architects and surveyors

As already noted (above, p. 19), one of the most important tasks of the dig's architect and/or surveyor is the drawing of the topographic map, which is essential if a well-designed research strategy is to be conceived and put into operation.[6] Also, if an excavation can afford the luxury of having the services of a professional architect throughout the dig, it is the responsibility of that architect to provide professionally drawn plans of all structural remains, including hypothetical reconstructions of buildings, streets, cisterns, pits, walls and so on, as well as "section drawings" (Figure 3.6) and up-to-date top plans.[7] It should always be remembered that relatively few people actually dig a site. When the dig is completed, all that is left of the site are holes (hopefully in the shape of "squares") in the ground, and even these, unless considerable effort is put forth for preservation, will soon be completely unrecognizable from vegetational growth and erosion.

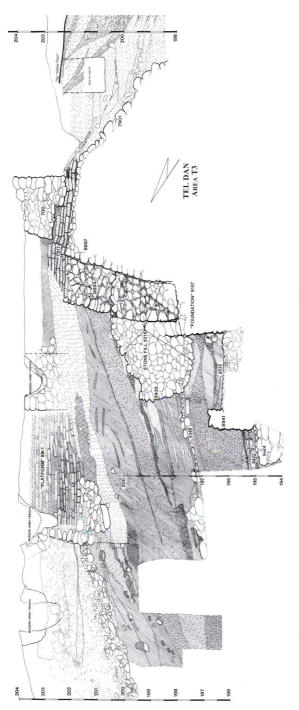
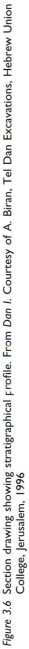

Figure 3.6 Section drawing showing stratigraphical profile. From *Dan I*. Courtesy of A. Biran, Tel Dan Excavations, Hebrew Union College, Jerusalem, 1996

Thus, until the accurate publication (see below) of all the excavation's activities and results are available, the dig is of little value. Essential to these publications are all architectural drawings. Since it is quite common for years to elapse between the first drawings and final publications, it is necessary that all architectural drawings be carefully filed so they will be available for future reference.

The actual tasks of the architect have been described in any number of field manuals and space limitations prohibit full discussion here (see note 3 and the discussion above). The importance of the architect's work is that it provides a kind of pictorial complement to the verbal description of an excavation. The need and contributions of a professional architect have been well summarized by De Vries:

> Architectural drawing relies on precise measurement and scale reproduction of the features and objects on a site. A primary goal is to provide a three-dimensional framework in which everything excavated can be located, including both the site's stratigraphic features and the artifacts found within the strata. In this sense, architectural drawing is akin to mapping, and the various drawings are integral components of a master site map. Vertically, all features and objects are locatable on sitewide sections related to their distance above sea level (asl). Such a three-dimensional framework gives an accurate location for everything on the site in question and makes it possible to determine their comparative dimensional relationship to features at other sites.
>
> (1997: 198)

Publications

Without publications, the best of archaeological field work is a failure. Field work itself has no intrinsic value except for the very few people who have participated in it.[8] Publishing the results of excavations not only provides permanent records that will survive the excavators, it also allows for archaeological research by other archaeologists, including those yet unborn. Also a well-published volume with plans, drawings, photographs and so on, enables others to reconstruct in their own minds exactly how the site was excavated. If a trained archaeologist cannot do this, then the publication is faulty and of limited, if any, use. A good publication also allows other archaeologists to interpret for themselves what the archaeological data mean. While there may be one best explanation for the material remains recovered in any excavation, archaeologists frequently and, sometimes, vigorously, disagree over what it is. The reason good publications are so important was well put by H. D. Lance several years ago: "the excavation of any particular piece of archaeological data can only occur once. There is no way to repeat the experience, as it were, even if it was done incompetently" (1981: 49).

Lance identified and discussed three major types of archaeological writings: primary reports, criticism and synthesis (1981: 53–8). He further divided primary reports into three types: informal reports, reports written primarily for specialists (which are again subdivided) and final reports. As Lance pointed out, it is imperative that any student of archaeology be able to use these sources critically.[9] Finally, he warned that:

> the researcher will have to trace carefully the course of publication, accepting the fact that every dig will follow a different pattern. Some go from current reports to final reports without producing preliminary reports. Some, because of the death or disinterest of the excavator, never go beyond preliminary or even current reports. Current reports certainly and sometimes even preliminary reports appear unpredictably in different publications. Final reports can be published years later by persons who were not even present during the digging.[10] In short, the system of publication is irregular, uncertain, and wasteful of excavated evidence.
>
> (1981: 56)

Appendix: a note on chronology

The dates of the various archaeological time periods have been debated from the very beginning. The problems and differences of opinion are so great that this field of research has become a specialized study in itself. One should not be discouraged when reading different dates in other publications. The important thing here is for the reader to become conversant with the terminology used to identify these time periods and their approximate, if not exact, dates.

For the most part, I have followed the suggestions in the *OEANE*, vol. 5, p. 411 and/or those in the *NEAEHL*, vol. 4, pp. 1529–31.

Prehistoric periods

Paleolithic	1,200,000–18,000 BC
Mesolithic	18,000–8500 (8000) BC
Neolithic	8500–4500 (4200) BC
Pre-pottery Neolithic (PPN)	8500 (8300)–6000 (5500) BC
Pottery Neolithic (PN)	6000 (5500)–4500 (4200) BC
Chalcolithic	4500 (4200)–3300 BC

Historic periods

Early Bronze Age	3300–2200 (2000) BC
EBA I	3300–3000 BC
EBA II	3000–2700 (2800) BC
EBA III	2700–2200 (2800–2400) BC
EBA IV (Middle Bronze I)	2200–2000 (2400–2000) BC
Middle Bronze Age	2000–1550 (1500) BC
MBA I (MBA IIA)	2000–1800 (1750) BC
MBA II (MBA IIB)	1800–1650 BC (others date MB IIB from c. 1750–1550)
MBA III (MBA IIC)	1650–1550 BC
Late Bronze Age	1550–1200 BC
LBA I	1550–1400 BC
LBA IIA	1400–1300 BC
LBA IIB	1300–1200 BC (others see LB II as one period – 1400–1200)
Iron Age	1200–587 (540) BC
Iron I	1200–1000 BC (others divide Iron I into two periods: IA: 1200–1150; and IB: 1150–1000)
Iron IIA	1000–923 BC (1000–900 in others)
Iron IIB	923–700 (900–700)
Iron IIC	700–540 BC (others date this period from 700 to 586)

Chapter 4

The rise of civilization: the Neolithic through the Early Bronze Age (*ca.* 8500–2000 BC)

The largest single step in the ascent of man is the change from nomad to village agriculture.

(Jacob Bronowski, 1973)

The Background

It is now known that human beings lived in Palestine over a million years ago in what is called the "Paleolithic" ("Old Stone") period. For hundreds of thousands of years these people remained hunters and foragers.[1] But sometime during the ninth millennium BC, Bronowski's "largest single step in the ascent of man" (1973: 64) was taken. Over the next six and a half thousand years the people of the Near East would learn how to build and maintain complex social, political, economic and religious structures that culminated in the great fortified cities of the Early Bronze Age (below). Between the end of the so-called "Middle Stone Age" (*ca.* 18,000–8500 BC) and the beginning of the Early Bronze Age stand two very important archaeological periods: the "Neolithic" ("New Stone," *ca.* 8500–4200 BC), and the "Chalcolithic" ("Copper-Stone," *ca.* 4200–3300 BC). Both of these stages in the development of man have received thorough treatments by specialists and deserve serious study. However, due to space limitations, I can mention them here only in passing and refer the interested reader to the bibliography.[2]

The Neolithic period

This period as a whole is divided into two major subperiods: the Pre-pottery Neolithic = PPN (8500–6000 BC) and the Pottery Neolithic = PN (6000–4200 BC). Several hundred Neolithic sites (Figure 4.1) have

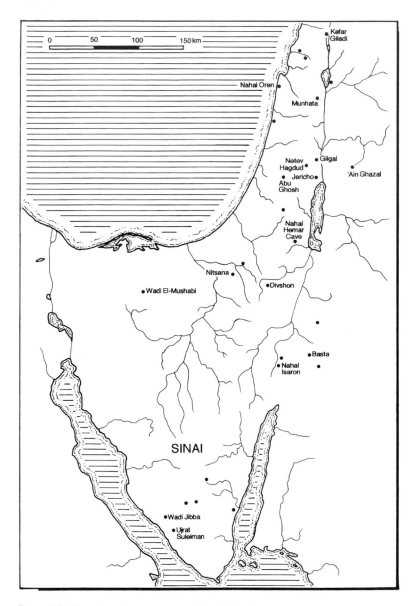

Figure 4.1 Map showing pre-pottery Neolithic sites

been identified in the Near East, stretching from the Middle Euphrates in Syria to the Sinai Desert in the southern Levant. One of the most famous Neolithic sites is Jericho, still called "the oldest city in the world" (see Kenyon 1979). One of the major accomplishments of this long prehistoric period was the "discovery" of pottery sometime during the sixth millennium BC. It has been suggested that the use of plastered fireplaces, known from the preceding PPNB era, may have led to this most important development (A. Mazar 1990: 49). From this time forward, the pottery remains found on Near Eastern sites are one of the major diagnostic tools at the disposal of the archaeologist, not only for establishing absolute chronologies but also for understanding many other aspects of ancient societies.

The Chalcolithic period

Sometime during the fifth millennium BC, the technology necessary to produce copper emerged in the Near East. This development did not replace the use of stone, thus the name "Chalcolithic" to describe this period. While many Chalcolithic sites are known, this period is still something of a mystery both in terms of its beginning and ending. More than 200 sites have been found in Palestine alone (Figure 4.2). They stretch from the Golan in the north to the Negev in the south; the coastal plain in the west, and the Transjordan in the east. Three of the most important permanent sites are Shiqmim (Levy 1995a) and Gilat in the Beersheba region and Teleilat Ghassul in the Transjordan. These sites have yielded most of what is known of this period.

One of the truly surprising achievements of this culture is in craft specialization. The high quality of the material remains suggest the existence of a professional class of skilled artisans. This development is reflected especially in the copper items produced, the most famous examples of which were found in the "Cave of the Treasure" in 1961 (Bar-Adon 1980; Moorey 1988; Figure 4.3). This hoard contains 416 copper items as well as ivory products carved from both hippopotamus and elephant tusks. Other products of this period include a basalt industry in the Golan (Epstein 1977), anthropomorphic ivory statuettes from Bir Safadi (Figure 4.4) and elsewhere (Levy 1986: 92), and enigmatic wall paintings from Teleilat Ghassul (Cameron 1981). In addition, the earliest gold products yet discovered in Palestine date to this time (Gopher and Tsuk 1991). Special mention should also be given to the many small violin-shaped objects found at many sites. These objects are usually made from stone (granite or chalk) and are 8 to 10 inches in

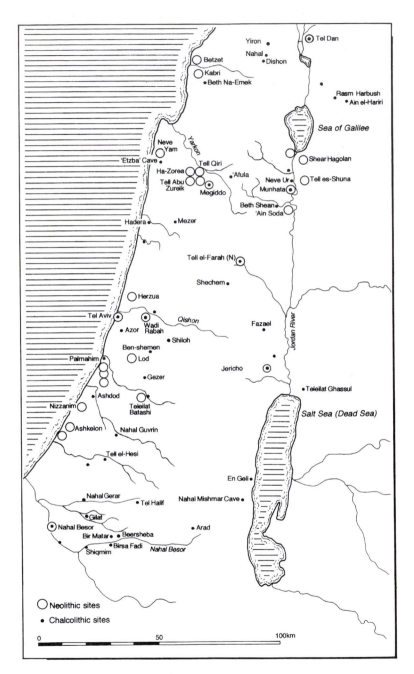

Figure 4.2 Map showing major Neolithic and Chalcolithic era pottery sites

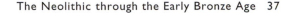

Figure 4.3 Chalcolithic copper hoard, Judean desert treasure, first half of the 4th mill. BC, Nahal Mishmar. Collection of the Israel Antiquities Authority. Photo Israel Museum, David Harris

length. A remarkable example of these objects, made from bone, was found at Shiqmim (Levy 1996). This figurine is only about 4 inches in height and is decorated with several rows of punctures. It also has a face emphasizing the eyes and nose. Levy has interpreted this object as representing syncretistic and mnemonic aspects of Chalcolithic culture heretofore unrecognized.

Another unique aspect of the Chalcolithic culture is the formal cemeteries located away from the inhabited areas. Some of these are man-made caves, many of which are located along the coastal plain. Secondary burials, often in *ossuaries* (ceramic bone boxes often resembling a house – Figure 4.5), became a popular practice for adults. Children, on the other hand, were often buried beneath house floors (Teleilat Ghassul) or in large pithoi.

After a thousand years of existence, the Chalcolithic people disappear. Most sites seem simply to have been abandoned and never resettled.

Figure 4.4 Chalcolithic ivory figurines, first half of the 4th mill. BC. Collection of the Israel Antiquities Authority. Photo Israel Museum/ Jerusalem

The reason for the sudden departure is not known. Everything from political and social changes to environmental catastrophe to economic disruption has been suggested. In fact, neither the exact cause of their disappearance nor where they disappeared to is known. Gonen, in his study, has summed it up well:

> The Chalcolithic period thus remains a mysterious period from beginning to end. If no significant breakthroughs in the appreciation

Figure 4.5 Chalcolithic ossuary. Photo: J. Laughlin

of its true essence are forthcoming, we will be left only to contemplate its creations, admire them, and wonder who their creators were, how they lived, in what manner they interpreted the world around them, and why they finally disappeared from the stage of human history.

(1992a: 80)

The Early Bronze Age (3300–2000 BC)

The understanding of the Early Bronze Age by archaeologists has seen something of a major revolution in the past fifteen to twenty years. The publications on this time period have mushroomed into a seemingly endless stream of books, general articles and technical specialized studies of all sorts.[3] Older syntheses rested primarily upon data extracted from the major tells of Palestine, such as Arad, et-Tell ('Ai), Beth Shan, Hazor, Jericho, Gezer, Megiddo, Tell el-Far'ah (N), Yarmuth, Lachish and others. Today these older data have been greatly expanded by recent surveys and excavations of many single-period sites. Furthermore, the older political/historical paradigm has been replaced with a more holistic approach that allows for newer ways of understanding the past through models drawn from anthropology and the social sciences. The end result has been a large increase of data relative to everything from settlement patterns to political, social and economic stratification; gender role identification; environmental relationships; trade patterns; land use; and other questions. While these newer approaches need to be used with proper caution, it can only be expected that the information base will continue to expand as more sites are discovered and/or excavated.

The chronology for the Early Bronze Age has also seen revisions over the past decade or so. The major disputed areas involve both the beginning and the ending dates. In the case of the latter, there has also been a lively discussion concerning terminology for the period, leading to confusion.[4] Based on carbon-14 dates and correlations with Egyptian periods, the following four-fold division (with some subdivisions) seems to be gaining a consensus among most archaeologists – at least among those who write about this period; see in particular Dever (1980b, 1995b), both with full bibliographies.

Palestine	Egypt
Early Bronze I: 3400–3100 BC	Gerzean: 3700–3100
Early Bronze II: 3100–2700	Early Dynastic: 3100–2700
Early Bronze III: 2700–2300	Old Kingdom: 2700–2200
Early Bronze IV: 2300–2000	First Intermediate: 2200–2000[5]

Furthermore, to call all the years between *ca.* 3400 and 2000 BC the Early *Bronze* Age is something of a misnomer. Bronze (an alloy composed of copper and, usually, tin) is not widespread until the so-called "Middle Bronze Age" (2000–1550 BC). In fact, until recently it was argued that it did not show up at all until this later period.[6] However, there is now evidence that bronze was known, at least during the EB IV period. This evidence is in the form of bronze daggers found in an EB IV tomb in the Huleh Valley near 'Enan. There is also literary evidence that bronze was known in Syria (Ebla) by the 24th century BC (Palumbo 1991: 107–8).

No one knows how many Early Bronze Age sites/settlements there are, or were (Figure 4.6). Many, especially single-period sites, may have been completely destroyed by nature or by human activity, and many

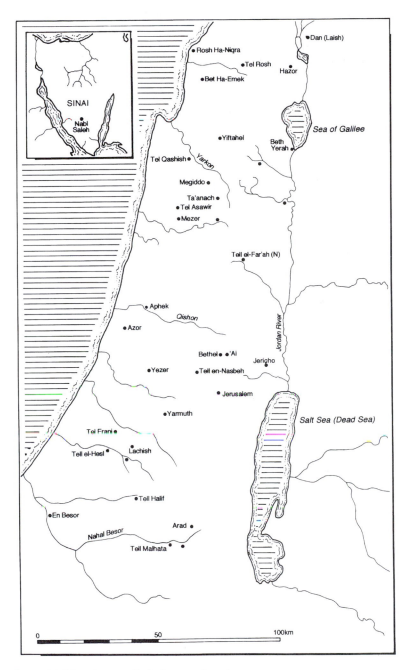

Figure 4.6 Map showing Early Bronze Age sites

others simply have not been found. But for the entire 1400-year period, thousands of sites (including both settlements where people actually lived, and burial grounds) have been discovered. However, barely 100 of the settled areas have been excavated to any extent.[7]

The excavations, surveys, specialized studies (such as pottery) and other issues that have become topics for publications in one form or another for this long, important period are far too many to be discussed in any detail in this brief summary. The reader is referred to the bibliography.

Early Bronze Age I (3300–3000 BC)

Because for a long time the EB I period was known primarily from finds in cemeteries (and still is to a certain extent), earlier archaeologists explained the appearance of the EB I populations as outsiders who either migrated to Palestine peacefully or conquered it by force.[8] While the question of the disappearance of the Chalcolithic populations and the origin(s) of the people who inhabited the EB I sites is still debated, there is a growing consensus to trace the EB I culture to the indigenous groups who developed from the preceding Chalcolithic period (Hanbury-Tenison 1986: fig. 14; Richard 1987; Schaub 1982). Amiran has argued that certain ceramic and basalt vessels of the EB I evolved directly from Chalcolithic forms and thus demonstrate continuity between the two periods (1985a; but see now Hanbury-Tenison 1986: 72–103). Amiran has also suggested that increased contact with Egypt and further development of an agropastoral economy during EB I, both of which developments were anticipated during the Chalcolithic period, point to an indigenous origin of the EB I culture.

Hanbury-Tenison's study (1986) is the most intensive yet in this regard. Comparing such things as settlement patterns, economic models, pottery and lithic traditions, craft specialization and architecture, she concluded that while there was a complete break between the two periods, there was a "gradual transition, rather than abrupt change, between the Late Chalcolithic and the Early Bronze I. There are no grounds for an invasion hypothesis or for seeking the roots of the Early Bronze I outside Palestine and Transjordan" (1986: 251; cf. Richard's conclusion, 1987: 24).

However, due to the difficulty that is always present when one tries to *interpret* the meaning of changes in the material culture, not all archaeologists agree that the transition from the Late Chalcolithic to the Early Bronze Age was a local, indigenous affair only. A. Mazar, in his recent survey of this period, concluded: "Thus it appears that the material culture of EB I Palestine was an intermingling of new features – originating in Syria, Anatolia, and Mesopotamia – with elements rooted in the local culture of the preceding period" (1990: 105; cf. Gophna 1995). Nevertheless, there is a growing body of data that indicate that indigenous elements played a much larger role than was believed just a few short years ago.

One of the most obvious changes during the EB I period was the choice of settlement areas. In contrast to the preceding Chalcolithic period where the settlement pattern often included arid regions, such as the northern Negev, it has been estimated that 90 percent of the EB I sites are in new settlement areas (Ben-Tor 1992:84). These areas include especially the Central Hill Country of Palestine, the Jordan Valley and the Shephelah (Hanbury-Tenison 1986).

Notable in this pattern is the large increase in settlements in the north and almost total abandonment of sites in the south. Finkelstein and Gophna have reported that in the Negev the number of sites shrank from seventy-five in the Chalcolithic period to eight in EB I. On the other hand, in the Central Hill country, the number of sites increased from twenty-eight during the Chalcolithic to more than sixty during EB I (Finkelstein and Gophna 1993). This occupational pattern of the Central Hill country during EB I would be repeated only twice more: once during the Middle Bronze Age (2000–1550 BC), and again during the Iron Age (1200–587/540 BC; Finkelstein and Gophna 1993: 6; cf. A. Mazar 1990: 95).

Finkelstein and Gophna also concluded that this increase in the number of sites occupied was not due to some "population explosion" as suggested by some, but to the economic advantages offered by the highlands environment. This environment is well suited to the growing of olives and grapes as well as to the raising of animals. The large-scale production of olives and wine during EB I opened up trade possibilities, particularly with Egypt (1993: 12–13).[9] The establishment of trade patterns implies a certain amount of central organization and political and social stability. This may help explain why, as in the preceding Chalcolithic periods, most EB I sites were unfortified. In any event, an economy based on pastoralism (primarily goat- and sheep-herding) and olive and wine production became the basis for economic life in Palestine (Ben-Tor 1992: 85; Richard 1987; Hanbury-Tenison 1986).

While most archaeologists divide the Early Bronze Age I into two major periods (EB I and EB II),[10] because of space considerations we will consider the period as a whole. Many major Bronze Age cities, such as

Hazor, 'Ai, Jericho, Lachish, Megiddo, Gezer and Arad, to name a few, had preceding EB I remains. However, many EB I settlements were quite small and of relatively short duration.[11] An example of such a site is Ein Shadud, an unwalled EB I village located a few miles northwest of Afula, excavated in 1979 (Braun and Gibson 1984; Braun *et al.* 1985). The economy of this village was based on agriculture and animal husbandry, as no doubt were most such villages of this era. Sometime towards the end of EB I, the site was abandoned and never resettled.

Another important EB I site is Hartuv, located close to Beth-Shemesh in the Shephelah (A. Mazar and P. de Miroschedji 1996). One of the major discoveries here is a structure identified as a sanctuary containing standing stones called *massebot*. Such pillars figure prominently throughout Canaanite and Israelite religion (see below). Here, they were interpreted by the excavators as "memorial" stones for dead patriarchs.[12] Hartuv was also abandoned at the end of EB I, indicating that the transition to the EB II period was peaceful. In this case, the excavators suggested that the inhabitants of Hartuv may have been absorbed by the emerging urban site of nearby Tel Yarmuth, which became a large fortified city during EB II.

The *massebot* and "sanctuary" from Hartuv, as well as material remains from other sites identified as "temples," raise the question of the nature of the religious cult(s) during this early period. The fact that these so-called "temples" are so far the only public buildings known from EB I may indicate that religious leaders (priests?) had considerable power during this prehistoric era (A. Mazar 1990: 98). In this context may also be mentioned a group of drawings found on a courtyard pavement associated with the "double" temple from Megiddo (Stratum XIX). The figures included images of animals, human-like images and other decorations. These drawings, along with scattered seal impressions on pottery vessels, represent most of the "art" work known from the EB I period.

Early Bronze Age I pottery

The importance of pottery remains found on Near Eastern sites cannot be overestimated. The cultural and/or ethnic (these two are not the same) identification of a people, their relationships with other groups, both foreign and local, the absolute chronology of their habitation, as well as other issues, are all reflected in the ceramic assemblages collected and studied by the archaeologist. The question of "ethnicity" is as important as it is complex. The debate concerning this issue has become full-blown, especially as it relates to the question of the origin and identity of "early Israel" (see below, Chapters 8 and 9, with references). There is a growing debate over whether or not pottery remains are a true ethnic marker (see particularly Dever 1993b, 1995c; Finkelstein 1996; and below). The arguments are complex and technical, and only specialists are qualified to deal with the issues in detail. Nevertheless, pottery assemblages are very important, especially in the absence of written texts, as is the case of those living in Palestine and the Transjordan during the Early Bronze Age. Most publications of field work, whether preliminary or final, include pages of technical descriptions of the pottery repertoire (Figure 4.7). To be able to "read" pottery takes years of field experience and study. Here only the briefest of summaries can be offered.[13]

Discussions of EB I pottery usually center on three major groups: "red-burnished," "gray-burnished" and "red-painted." However, some archaeologists have used different names for the same pottery, thus creating unnecessary confusion. Kenyon, for example, called red-burnished ware "Proto-urban A" or PUA; the red-painted, "Proto-urban B" or PUB; and the gray-burnished ware, "Proto-urban C", or PUC (1979). In addition, since the gray-burnished pottery was first found in the Esdraelon Valley, particularly at Megiddo, it is sometimes called "Esdraelon Ware."

Furthermore, there is still some debate among archaeologists regarding the chronology of the appearance of certain types, as well as the origin and distribution of these types. Some believe that the different pottery types point to regional variations during the EB I period. For example, most of the gray-burnished ware is found in northern sites and the Transjordan.[14] At issue here is the chronology of certain pottery types and what their presence on archaeological sites tells us about the transition from Chalcolithic to the Early Bronze Age I, as well as the transition from the pre-urban EB I to the urban EB II.[15]

In addition to these distinctive EB I pottery forms, there is also what is usually called "plain" ware that appears throughout the periods (Hanbury-Tenison 1986:119–21; 129–31, fig. 23). Part of the problem is that very few sites have been found with pottery sequences for all of EB I. Hanbury-Tenison identified two: Shunah North, and Umm Hammad, both on the east side of the Jordan. The pottery from Umm Hammad is singled out: "The sequence at Umm Hammad shows local development punctuated by distinctive forms well known elsewhere, grey-burnished, Jawa-type, and proto-urban D pottery, thus providing for the first time a sequential chronological slot for these wares" (1986: 120).

No.	Object	Reg. No./ IAA no.	locus	Description
1	Platter	232/2	18	Light red paste (10R 6/8): white and red grits. MW.
2	Platter	169/5	18	Reddish yellow paste 5YR 7/6); white and brown grits; burnished rim; MW.
3	Platter	169/3	18	Light red paste (10R 6/6); white and grey grits; red slip int. and ext.; pattern burnish int.; burnished rim; MW.
4	Platter	230/4	18	Light reddish brown paste 2.5YR 6/4); gray core; white and red grits, inclusions; red slip int. and rim; well fired (MW?).
5	Bowl	237/4	18	Reddish yellow paste (5YR 7/6); white, red and gray grits, inclusions; thin red slip int. and over rim; medium fired.
6	Basin	237/2	18	Light red paste (10R 6/8); light red core; white and red grits; pattern combing; MW.
7	Cooking pot	169/8	18	Red paste (2.5YR 5/6); white, red and gray grits; smoke-blackened ext.; medium-fired.
8	Cooking pot	169/4	18	Reddish brown paste (5YR 5/4); white, gray and calcite grits; smoke-blackened, medium-fired.
9	Jar	148/10	18	Pink paste (7.5YR 8/4); white and gray grits, inclusions; red decoration; medium fired.
10	Pithos	235/1	18	Light red paste (2.5YR 6/6); pinkish gray core; white and red grits; pattern combing; MW.
11	Bowl	23200/1	4663	Light red paste (2.5YR 6/8); surface light red (2.5YR 6/6); white, red and brown grits, inclusions; wheel-turned; well-fired.
12	Cooking pot	23223/5	4674	Light reddish brown paste (5YR 6/4); white, gray and calcite grits, inclusions; smoke-blackened ext. and rim; well-fired.
13	Ledge-handle	23200/7	4663	Light red paste (2 5YR 6/6); white and calcite grits; pattern combing; smoke-blackened ext; medium fired.
14	Knob-handle	23248/7	4674	Gray paste (10YR 5/1); quartz grits; multiple twig impressions; MW.

Figure 4.7 key

This is an important conclusion, because it is only by finding the pottery remains in clear stratigraphical contexts that justifiable chronological judgments can be made. Such contexts have not always been the case in tombs where most of the EB I pottery has been found.

Early Bronze Age I burial practices

Since a major portion of our knowledge of EB I has come from burials, it is no surprise that they have received special attention by archaeologists.[16] In the past, particular emphasis has been given to the cemeteries discovered at Jericho, Bab edh-Dhra' and elsewhere. Three types of burial seem to have been common during this period; disarticulated (the bones of skeletons have been removed); secondary (the bones are reburied after the flesh has decomposed); and articulated (the bones are not disturbed). Many of the tombs of this period are artificial caves dug into hillsides (Jericho), or natural caves (Tel el-Far'ah North). Others are chamber tombs (Bab edh-Dhra'), entered by way of a vertical shaft cut into the rock. The number of chambers varies between one and four. There is also some evidence for cremation at Gezer and in the charnel houses at Bab edh-Dhra' (Hanbury-Tenison 1986: 234, 238), as well as at other sites. However, cremation does not appear to have been as common as the other forms of burial. Why some bodies

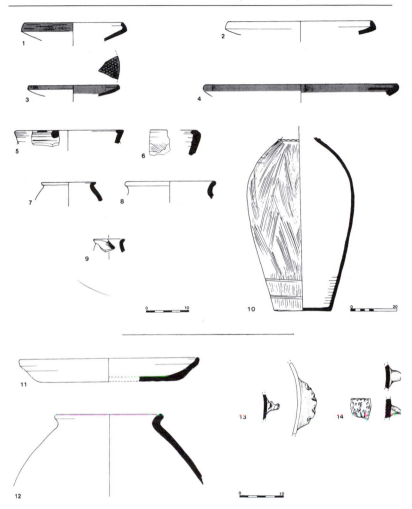

Figure 4.7 EB III pottery typology. From *Dan I*. Courtesy of A. Biran, Tel Dan Excavations, Hebrew Union College, Jerusalem, 1996

were cremated at all is still something of a mystery (Hanbury-Tenison 1986: 247).

Another form of burial is in *dolmens* (from Celtic *dol* = "table" and *men* = "stone"), most of which are found in the northern Levant. While there are differences in dolmen construction, many are made from large rock slabs which are used for the sides and top, and sometimes the ends. They are usually built on a mound of stones and may contain a carved window or door. This form of construction particularly applies to those that have been discovered in the Transjordan. There is no agreement on their dates, but Hanbury-Tenison points to the large dolmen field at Jebel Mutawwaq, in northern Transjordan, as providing evidence for placing them in EB I (1986: 244–5, and fig. 38). Zohar (1993), on the other hand, while dating them as early as the Chalcolithic period, dates their major use to the EB IV – MB I periods (*ca.* 2200–1800 BC).

Egyptian connections

There is considerable evidence for the presence of Egyptians in Palestine, particularly in the coastal region, during EB I. Much of this evidence comes from the site of Tel ʿErani, where more than 1000 Egyptian pottery vessels were found (Ben-Tor 1991; Brandl 1992, 1997). In the past, this evidence has been interpreted as a sign of Egyptian military oppression. But more recently there has been an emphasis on identifying these Egyptian enclaves as nothing more than "trade settlements."[17] In his study, Ward (1991) concluded that Egyptian colonists were present in the northern Sinai and Negev during EB I for "commercial," not military reasons.

The non-military interpretation of Egyptian presence has also been supported by finds from the site of En Besor. It has been argued that for nearly 200 years there was a local Egyptian population here of several hundred living alongside the indigenous inhabitants. Part of this argument is based on the presence of many sickle blades, but few arrowheads. This occurrence has been interpreted to imply that the population was civilian, not military (Ben-Tor 1991).

However, during the following EB II period, relations with Egypt declined dramatically. Whether this was a consequence of the social/political/economic changes that occurred during this period or one of the causes of the changes is not clear. What is clear is that a dramatic change did occur which resulted in the construction for the first time of huge fortifications.[18] Nevertheless, the commercial contacts with Egypt that were begun during EB I were only the beginning of what one archaeologist has described as "an intricate web of relations . . . that would last through three millennia" (Richard 1987: 27).

Early Bronze Age II–III (3000–2300/2200 BC)

The Early Bronze II–III periods are the heart of the Early Bronze Age in Palestine/Transjordan. This was the time of the "city-states," the first real "urban" era in the history of this region. However, the terms "city-state" and/or "urban" need to be understood clearly. In a survey that identified some 260 EB II–III sites in Palestine, over 60 percent (158) were 2.5 acres or less in size (Broshi and Gophna 1984). Thus the word "city," when applied to these early settlements, has none of its modern connotations in terms of size. Some of these "cities" existed throughout the long EB II-III periods, including Dan (Laish), 'Ai, 'Erani, Yarmuth, Jericho and Bab edh-Dhra'. Others were either abandoned or destroyed during EB II. Among the latter are Arad and Gezer. By the end of EB III, all of these settlements would be destroyed or abandoned, and many, such as Arad and 'Ai, would not be re-occupied for centuries.

While in the past emphasis has been placed on the large tells spanning the major portions of the EB period, recent surveys (Finkelstein and Gophna 1993; Palumbo 1991) have shown that during the EB II–III periods, rural communities and hamlets thrived. It seems logical that these small, rural sites would be related economically/politically to the much larger cities. In fact, in Broshi's and Gophna's study, twenty sites, encompassing nearly half of the total area of space occupied during these periods, were over 25 acres in size. Some of these sites, such as, Tel Dan (50 acres), Hazor (25 acres), 'Ai (27 acres) and Lachish (37 acres), will figure in the story of the biblical Israelites centuries later.

In the Sinai during EB II, Beit-Arieh (1981) found what he described as an "extensive expansion of settlement" with ties to Arad. He also concluded that the material remains point to a "single ethnic group" who was responsible for this growth (p. 50). While Beit-Arieh did not identify this "single ethnic group," others have argued that the walled settlements of EB II–III were not the result of new peoples coming into the area, but of internal processes (social/economic) set in motion by the long preceding EB I (Gophna 1995: 274; Hanbury-Tenison 1986). For an older, but very influential perspective, see Kenyon (1979: 84–118). Furthermore, Richard concluded that the similarity of the material culture points to an "integrated society" (1987: 29).

However, many questions remain. How were these villages and fortified settlements related? Why were such massive fortifications needed? Did the non-urban villages supply needed materials for the cities, such as food and other products? What sort of "administration" existed to oversee such critical issues as land and water use and the distribution of goods? All of these issues led Richard to suggest that during this time there was a three-tiered ranking society composed of "cities, towns, and villages with a fully integrated society among which there were complex interrelationships and interdependencies" (1987: 29).

While some EB II sites were abandoned or destroyed and not re-occupied during EB III (such as Arad, Tell el-Far'ah North), others were rebuilt (for example, Tel Dan, Megiddo, 'Ai, Beth Shan and Jericho). In the case of Jericho, Kenyon reported that in some places the EB walls were repaired a total of seventeen times (1979: 29)! To make matters even more complex, some sites were apparently founded during the EB III period, such as Bethel, Beth-Shemesh, Tell Beit Mirsim and Hazor. In the northern part of Palestine, some sites became more important during EB III. These include Tel Dan, Tel Abel Beit Ma'acah, Tel Qadesh, Hazor, Megiddo, Ta'anach, Beth-Yerah and Beth Shan. In the Judean hills, 'Ai became an important regional center, as apparently did Arad in the northern Negev.[19]

One of the major architectural characteristics of this period was the erection of massive fortifications. The wall at Megiddo, for example, was 25 feet thick, and major fortifications were erected at 'Ai and elsewhere. The defensive wall at Arad was over 3800 feet long! Nevertheless, despite such constructions, by 2300 BC, these great fortified tells had either been abandoned or destroyed. After surviving some 700 years, the fears that led to such massive fortifications were realized. What exactly happened to bring about the demise of this era is not clear. Perhaps there was conflict between the urban centers and the non-urban populations (pastoral nomads?); perhaps, as some inscriptions indicate, the Egyptians raided some of the cities. Perhaps there were environmental causes. Whatever the reason(s), the urbanized Early Bronze Age collapsed. It would be three centuries before such settlements would exist again.

Early Bronze Age IV (2300/2200–2000 BC)

Since the late 1970s there has been such an intensive study of the last three centuries or so of the third millennium BC that this period has become a field of specialized research all on its own.[20] Despite this interest by archaeologists and historians, many questions remain unanswered. Who or what brought to an end the long urban culture of EB II–III? What was the origin (or origins) of the peoples who inhabited the hamlets and villages, towns and caves of EB IV? What is the nature of the relationship between the culture of the EB IV era and the preceding EB II–III? What connections, if any, existed between this culture and the following Middle Bronze Age?

While final answers to these and other questions are still lacking, in some cases older theories and conclusions have been replaced, or seriously modified. In the 1960s and 1970s it was popular to argue for a complete break between the period called here "EB IV" and the preceding urban era. This break was usually attributed to an invasion by Amorites or some other group from the north (so Kenyon 1979: 119–47; cf. Lapp 1970; de Vaux 1971). Also, until recently, because most of the material culture of this era was known from tomb deposits, it was frequently referred to as a "Dark Age."

Because so little was known about this period, there was also disagreement (and there still is) over what to call it. Kenyon, based mainly on her interpretation of tomb remains from Jericho, called it the "Intermediate Early Bronze–Middle Bronze" (1979: 119). Others have called it "Middle Bronze I" (cf. the terminology in *NEAEHL* and the *OEANE*). There is still no unanimity on the nomenclature for this period, though "EB IV" seems to be gaining support among all but Israeli scholars and will be used here.

One of the major reasons the older "Amorite Hypothesis" has been discarded is that it rested on the assumption that most or all of the EB III cities met a violent end. In some cases, such as 'Ai, Jericho and Bab edh-Dhra', this seems to have been the case. But the majority of sites appear to have been abandoned, not destroyed. These latter include Hazor, probably Dan, Tell Beit Mirsim, Megiddo, Lachish, Ta'anach and others. Furthermore, the archaeological data now available indicate that no one theory or model fits all the evidence. In the last fifteen or twenty years surveys have identified thousands of EB IV sites (Palumbo 1991; Haiman 1996). Furthermore, in the Transjordan, fortified settlements, such as Khirbet Iskander (Richard and Boraas 1984, 1988; Schaub 1982) have provided clear evidence of cultural continuity with the preceding EB III culture. Thus the older view that the EB IV period (or whatever it was called) was characterized only by nomadic or semi-nomadic lifestyles is giving way to more inclusive views that take into account that during this period there was an extensive sedentary element that required permanent agricultural activities.

Dever suggested years ago that the model of "pastoral nomadism" was perhaps the best way to explain the material data as it was then known (Dever 1980b; and bibliography). This model was based in part on Dever's work at Beer Resisim in the Negev Highlands, which Dever interpreted to be a seasonal site. He has also emphasized the regional nature of this period, particularly as this regionalism is expressed in the pottery assemblages. In fact, he identified six regional groups that he believed could function as chronological indicators. This led him to propose three major sub-phases for the EB IV period: EB IV A–C. Others have questioned his chronological interpretations (Palumbo 1991; Goren 1996; Gophna 1992),[21] but his insistence on regional differences appears to be generally accepted.

In his latest summary of the EB IV period, Dever (1995b: 295) suggested the model of "Ruralism" for understanding this cultural horizon. He based this on the thousands of rural sites now known from surveys. What all of this means is that during the last 300 years or so of the third millennium BC, the society of Palestine and the Transjordan was far more complex than earlier generations of archaeologists had suspected. This complexity limits the usefulness of most models suggested for this period, such as "Nomadism," "Pastoral Nomadism," "Nomadic Interlude," "Amorite Invasion," or whatever. The more obvious it becomes that different subsistence strategies were used by different peoples in different locations, the more obvious is the inadequacy of the older models.[22]

Conclusions about this period must remain tentative and open to correction and/or modification as more sites are identified and excavated. Any assessment of the period must take into account its extreme diversity. Dever has clearly shown that for any model to be useful it must be able to explain the fact that during the EB IV period there was "a shift of economic strategies and social organization along a *continuum* [emphasis in the original] – an almost infinite variety of interrelated adaptive responses on a theoretical scale from 'urban' to 'nomadic'" (1995b: 295).

Site location

While some EB IV sites were built on top of previous EB III deposits (such as Jericho), most were constructed in previously uninhabited areas, or on sites which date before the Early Bronze Age began (Palumbo). More than 1000 EB IV sites have been identified in the Negev and Sinai (Haiman 1996), many of which are so well preserved they have been called "open-air museums" (Gophna 1992: 134). Most of them are very small (0.25–1.2 acres) and have been constructed in previously uninhabited areas. Larger sites have been found, two of which have been excavated: Beer Resisim (about 3.7 acres) and Har Yeruham (1.2 acres; see Gophna 1992: figs 5.4–6, for plans of both sites). At these sites, as well as others in the same area, the domestic structures were oval-shaped, measuring some 6.5–13.0 feet in diameter. Most of these sites are single- period occupations, perhaps not used for more than two or three generations. This latter characteristic led Gophna, in his study, to call them "transient settlements" (1992: 137).

In sharp contrast to the EB IV culture in the Negev and Sinai is the Transjordanian area where surveys and excavations have revealed a major EB IV region. Apparently, regional differences existed here just as they did in the Cisjordan, indicated by differences in pottery assemblages. But the presence of such sites as Khirbet Iskander, with monumental architecture, fortifications and residential quarters, suggests that in some cases, at least, cultural continuity with the EB II–III culture was not broken (see Richard and Boraas 1988 for details). It is obvious from this brief survey that the settlement pattern of the EB IV varied greatly between regions. Whether or not this has implications for the identity of the people(s) who inhabited these regions remains to be seen.

Of interest are the burial practices of this period, which included shaft tombs as well as tumuli. In the latter case, the body was placed in a shallow grave which was then covered with a mound of stones or earth. These tumuli are found scattered in different parts of the region. Dolmens were also used and thousands have been found in the Golan and Transjordan (Gophna 1992: map 5.2; Zohar 1993).

Finally, for whatever the reason, compared to the previous EB II–III periods, more copper objects have been recovered, mostly in the form of weapons such as daggers, spears, battle-axes and arrowheads (cf. Gophna 1992: 147–52). There are still many unanswered questions concerning these objects. Were they imported, and if so, from where? Who were the craftsmen who produced them? What was the source of the copper? Small personal ornaments including rings, bracelets and earrings have also been found.

Conclusions

The archaeological material remains from the EB IV period clearly reveal a wide range of adaptation and economic subsistence for this period. Grinding stone and flint tools, along with floral remains of barley, wheat and other crops, point to grain cultivation as a major source of the economy. On the other hand, bone remains of sheep, cattle, pigs and goats all point to animal husbandry. However, not all varieties of animal are found in the same regions. This is another indication that regional differences persisted throughout the period. The presence of gazelle and antelope bones also indicate that hunting played some role in the overall economic scheme. Pottery remains and special finds, such as the famous silver cup found in a tomb near 'Ayin Samiyu (Gophna 1992: figs 5.21, 5.22), point to trade relations with areas north of Palestine. Syria is the place most often suggested (Richard 1987: 38).

Perhaps the most far-reaching conclusion indicated by the evidence is that the last three centuries of the third millennium BC were as sedentary as they were nomadic. Thus the change may not have been nearly as abrupt as the older model of "nomadism" implied. In fact, Richard and Boraas identified fourteen characteristics of EB IV that link it with the preceding EB III (1988: 127). It should be obvious from such studies that older models are no longer sufficient to explain this complex and varied society. It is to be hoped that Dever's call for a "more focused, sophisticated, and disciplined fieldwork and research in the generation to come" (1995b: 295) will be heard and responded to.

Chapter 5

The Middle Bronze Age (2000–1550 BC)

> This is Canaan in its rise, its flourishing, and its decline as reflected
> in ancient Israelite tradition. It is the first really historical period in
> Eretz-Israel from which written documents have been preserved . . .
> that give flesh and blood to the sinews of the bare archaeological finds.
>
> (Y. Aharoni, 1978)

Sometime during the twentieth century BC, there began the rebirth of
towns and cities and the emergence of a high level of material culture
in Palestine that would last for nearly 800 years. Archaeologists have
divided this long period into two basic subperiods: the Middle Bronze
Age (MBA) and the Late Bronze Age (LBA). The Middle Bronze Age
occupied the first half of the second millennium BC. Based upon the
material remains from excavated MBA sites (Figure 5.1), several
distinguishing characteristics of this period can be identified (see Ilan
1995). These include the widespread use of bronze, especially in the
manufacturing of weapons; new settlement patterns, accompanied by
the construction of large, fortified cities; and the widespread use of
the potter's wheel. Written documents also appear, particularly from
Egypt and Mesopotamia, in which for the first time Palestinian cities
are named, some of which are mentioned in the Bible. There is also
monumental architecture that included, in addition to massive rampart
walls and tripartite city gates, palaces and so-called "patrician" houses.
New burial practices (intraburials) are found. There is also evidence of
international trade and political and social hierarchical rankings.

In recent years there have been several summaries of this period,
many with full bibliographies. They are highly recommended not only
to gain a good overall impression of the MBA, but also to see how the
understanding of this period has changed over the last twenty to thirty

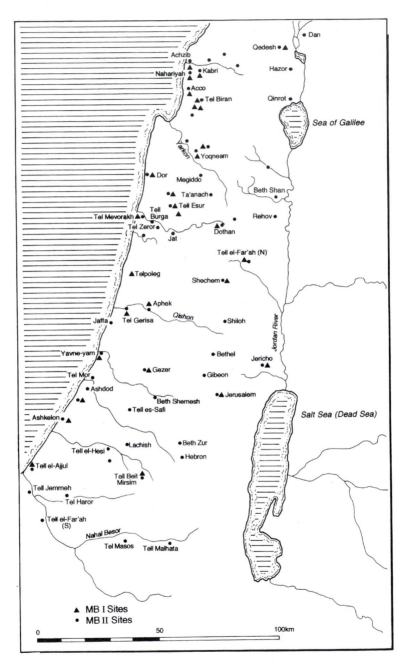

Figure 5.1 Map showing Middle Bronze Age sites

years: see B. Mazar (1968); Kenyon (1973a); Dever (1987a); A. Mazar (1990: 174–231); Kempinski (1992b); Ilan (1995). In addition to these summaries, there have been many specialized studies of various aspects of the MBA. The list is far too long to list here, but many of them will be referred to in this chapter.

MBA chronology

Very few periods in Near Eastern archaeology have as confusing and controversial a chronology and nomenclature as those of the MBA. While all authorities place the MBA (at least the major part of it) in the first half of the second millennium BC, there is still much disagreement on sub-phases, descriptive nomenclature and absolute dating.[1] Here, in order to be consistent, I will use the nomenclature and dates suggested for the MBA in the recent publication of *OEANE*, vol. 5: 411. I do this for two reasons: first, this major publication will no doubt become a standard reference work for Near Eastern archaeology for many years to come; and, secondly, except for some in the Israeli school, most other archaeologists seem to be adopting this scheme (see the discussion in Dever 1987a). In this publication the MBA is divided into the following phases and dates:

MB I: 2000–1800
MB II: 1800–1650
MB III: 1650–1500

What is essential is to realize that the same period(s) may be named and dated differently by other authorities (for example, MB I = MB II). It is to be hoped that one day all of this confusion will cease. However, it gets worse. Not only do archaeologists debate the issues of the nomenclature and relative dates for each subperiod listed above, they also vigorously debate the issue of absolute chronology for the MBA (*inter alia*, see Beck and Zevulun 1996; Bietak 1991; Dever 1991a, 1992b; Ward 1992; Ward and Dever 1994; Weinstein 1991, 1992, 1996). The discussions are often quite technical and tedious, and involve assumptions on the part of the archaeologists that include everything from methodology, stratigraphical profiles, pottery typology and dating, to the proper use of Egyptian chronology, as well as the value and use of cylinder seals and scarabs. The use of ancient Egyptian chronology, in particular, has come under attack recently from Ward, who has argued persuasively that Egyptian chronological evidence is "inconclusive" and conclusions based upon it reflect more "personal judgment" than any absolute dates established by the Egyptians (Ward 1992: 54).[2] Those who date the beginning of the MBA to the twentieth century BC are said to hold an "ultra high" chronology, while those who date the beginning to the eighteenth century (namely, Bietak) argue for an "ultra low" chronology.

Dever has defended a high chronology (1992b, and others), arguing that the MB I began at least as early as the nineteenth century BC. He cites archaeological evidence from tombs and from such sites as Shechem, Gezer and Avaris (Tell ed-Dab'a) to support his conclusions (see particularly, 1992b, fig. 1). Bietak, on the other hand (1991, and bibliography cited there), has argued for a very low chronology beginning for the MBA based on his interpretation of the same excavation results from Tell ed-Dab'a. Their disagreements on this issue should alert one to the fact that archaeology is not the dry, dusty, objective stuff that it is sometimes made out to be. Archaeologists disagree on the meaning of the same data precisely for the same reason that literary experts disagree on the meaning of the same text: training, life experiences, dispositions, presuppositions – all play a part in trying to make sense out of data that is subject to more than one interpretation or meaning. The best approach, perhaps, is to learn to live with tentative conclusions, and move on with caution. The last word is never spoken, because all those interested in the issues know that a single new discovery can force a total re-evaluation of a previously held position. In this regard, Dever's conclusion is very timely:

> While the ultimate goal of all archaeological and historical chronological studies is an absolute chronology, fixed with such scientific precision that it commends itself to all scholars, that goal is rarely attainable. Thus all chronological arguments for the ancient Near East begin with relative sequences, based on exceedingly complex chains of evidence that are largely circumstantial. With even one piece of new data, one link may break, and the chain will fall apart.
>
> (1992b: 1)

While most studies of the MBA divide the period into at least two subperiods – MB I and MB II – due to space considerations, I will discuss the period as a whole.

The origin of the Middle Bronze Age

Just as archaeologists continue to disagree over the dating of the MBA, so too do they argue over the origin of the population that began it. There are really only three common-sense options: either the population group(s) of the time came from the preceding EB IV, and thus were indigenous to the country, or they came from the outside. Or, as is most likely, the population of MB I was made up of a combination of the above. In the 1960s and 1970s it was popular to argue that the MBA culture was created by the arrival of a new group (or groups) from the north, particularly from Syria, who were identified as "Amorites" (see especially Kenyon 1973a; 1979: 148–79; Dever 1970, with bibliography). These Amorites, in turn, were responsible for establishing the so-called "Canaanite"[3] culture met in the Ugaritic texts and in the pages of the Bible. On the other hand, others (Gerstenblith 1980; Tubb 1983) have argued that the MBA period in Palestine was an "indigenous development of the population in response to a resumption of more favourable conditions, both climatic and economic, which allowed the return to urban settlement" (Tubb 1983: 59).

More recently, Ilan (1995) has concluded that the changes identified in the material remains of the MBA reflect a "complex combination of exogenous and endogenous factors" (p. 297). As he rightly points out, the real issue here is that of establishing a valid methodology that enables us to identify population movements based upon the archaeological record.[4] He has suggested four criteria to support his conclusion that immigration from Syria into Palestine did occur during the MBA, or at least the "transfer of information" (a rather ambiguous expression). His criteria are interesting and deserve consideration (1995: 300–1):

1   In several cases, such as at Tel Dan (Canaanite Laish), Acco and Ashkelon, MB mudbrick gates were built only to be quickly blocked up due to rapid deterioration caused by the wetter climate. Ilan's point is that the sun-dried mudbrick did not work as well in Palestine as it did in Syria.
2   The presence of new burial practices (intraburials) that supplemented, rather than replaced, local traditions (see esp. 1995: 318–19).
3   Bone analysis of skeletal remains that indicates that more than one population was present during this time.
4   Locally made pottery ("monochrome painted cream ware") whose style, form and so on point to a Syrian source.

Whether or not these new people were "Amorites" is a different question (Ilan 1995: 301). But Ilan's conclusion that at least part of the population of the MB I period did have connections with the north seems reasonable.

Historical texts

One of the most important achievements during the MBA is the development of writing, both in Egypt and in Syro-Mesopotamia. In fact, sometime during the first half of the second millennium BC, the Phoenicians gave the world one of its greatest gifts: the alphabet (see below, Chapter 7). Consequently, important discoveries of written documents dating to this period have been found and for the first time provide the archaeologist with texts contemporary with non-textual material remains.

Two important discoveries from Egypt are called "execration" texts (inscriptions with a curse). The earliest group, purchased in Thebes, is written on bowls and are now in Berlin and have been dated to the twentieth century BC. The other group is inscribed on figurines that are now in museums in Cairo and Brussels. They are dated to the mid-nineteenth century. Both groups of vessels contain the names of towns and cities the Egyptians considered to be their enemies. The vessels were smashed, apparently in some type of ritual, to ensure their defeat. These vessels contain names of some of the major cities mentioned in the Bible such as Beth Shan, Jerusalem, Laish (Dan), Shechem, Hazor and Beth-Shemesh (*ANET*: 238–9; see also Kempinski 1992b: 159–60).

Another written source that is believed to shed some light on the era is called "The Story of Sinuhe" (*ANET*:18–22). Whether fictitious or not, the story is dated to the twentieth century BC and is about a man, Sinuhe, who voluntarily moved from Egypt to northern Canaan. There he became very successful only to long for his homeland. Before returning to Egypt at the request of the Egyptian ruler, San-Usert I (*ca.* 1971–28 BC), he encountered nomads in Palestine. Finally, from the first half of the eighteenth century BC, come the so-called "Mari Texts" (Malamat 1970), which contain trade records. According to these records, tin was traded at such Palestinian sites as Hazor and Laish (Dan). Tin, of course, was desired in order to make bronze.

Settlement patterns

Recent studies (for example, Broshi and Gophna 1986; Gophna and Portugali 1988) have emphasized regional patterns in the spread and growth of MBA sites. Broshi and Gophna divided Palestine into 10 regions and catalogued some 400 sites. Furthermore, based on a formula of 250 persons for every 2.5 acres of occupational area, they estimated the MB I (their MB IIa) population to be about 106,000. For the MB II period, they estimated a population of about 140,000.[5] They also estimated that over 75 percent of the settlement sites were quite small, ranging in size from 0.25 to 2.5 acres.

The area of greatest concentration was the coastal region (Gophna and Portugali 1988: figs 7–9). During MB I there were some forty-nine sites occupying over 450 acres. During MB II, the number of sites increased to sixty-five with an occupational area of over 500 acres. That a good part of this coastal population came from elsewhere (whether inside or outside Palestine) is indicated by the fact that 80 percent of the identified sites were found to contain no earlier EBA remains (Broshi and Gophna 1986: fig. 2).

Other areas also saw an increase in the number of settlements during MB II. Lower Galilee, for example, went from four sites with about 5.5 acres of occupied area to fifty-seven sites with over 85 acres. The Middle and Lower Jordan Valleys had sixteen sites on some 34.5 acres during MB I; thirty-four sites with some 39 acres during MB II. Some of the most dramatic changes took place in Samaria. With only four sites identified from MB I occupying about 27 acres, the area went to 105 sites with 205 occupied acres in MB II. All of these data clearly illustrate the spread of MBA sites during the latter part of this period (see Kempinski 1992b: 166).

While Broshi and Gophna identified some 410 sites, there may have been many more, especially small sites which have been lost beyond recovery. Gal (1991) reported from his survey of the Jezreel and Beth Shean Valleys that many rural farming villages have probably been buried under alluvial soil where they are extremely difficult to find. One such village was even found under a fish pond at Kibbutz Kfar Rupin, where it had gone unnoticed for thirty years (Gal 1991: 29)!

Whatever the actual number of MBA sites there turns out to be, very few of them have been excavated. In the north, Tel Dan and Hazor are the most important. In the Middle Jordan Valley, Beth Shan (about a 12-acre MBA site) is the most important site so far excavated. In the Jezreel Valley, Megiddo became a major city during MB II and is listed in the Poesner group of execration texts discussed above. The city featured a large city wall, palaces and a new city gate during this period. During this time it was some 40 acres in size.

While most MBA sites in Samaria date to MB II, Shechem is an exception. Dominating the Central Hill country throughout the Bronze Age, this city (*ca.* 12.5 acres[6] during MB I) may have been a center for rural settlements, especially during and after MB II (Kempinski 1992b: 172). In Judah, Bethel (Canaanite Luz), first built in MB II, was around 5 acres in size. On the other hand, Gezer existed throughout the MBA and attained a size of about 30 acres. Other important Judean sites from the MBA are Hebron, Lachish and Jerusalem. The latter city is estimated to have been around 10 acres in size during this period.

By far the greatest concentration of larger sites was on the coastal plain. In the north, eight sites occupied some 230 acres. All but one of these sites were occupied throughout the MBA. The largest site is Tel Kabri at nearly 100 acres. Six of these sites had rampart defensive systems (see below). South of Mt Carmel, several sites have been discovered that also existed throughout the MBA. The largest of these is Yavne Yam (160 acres). Other sites include Ashkelon (125 acres), Aphek (25 acres), Dor (25 acres), and Tell el-'Ajjul (30 acres). 'Ajjul has been identified with ancient Sharuhen of Hyksos fame (see below). Aphek was an important site in the Yarkon basin (Kempinski 1992b: 170). Here, remains of large buildings identified as palaces and a patrician's house have been discovered, dating from MB I–II. The patrician house had a thick lime floor which has been described as "most characteristic" of floors in palaces and such houses of this period (Kempinski 1992b: 170). Such houses have been discovered at other MB sites such as Megiddo (1992b: 172, fig. 6.7). The people of Aphek also practiced intraburials under their houses' floors as they did at Megiddo. By contrast to these sites, the MBA settlement of the northern Negev was very sparse. Only two small MB II sites have been found. On the other hand, several port cities along the coast have been discovered, such as Mevorakh, Tel Poleg, Jerishe and Nahariya. The existence of so many of these types of settlements has been interpreted to indicate coastal trade between Syria and Palestine during the MBA (Kempinski 1992b).

How the larger "cities" were related to the smaller towns and rural villages is still unknown for certain. Some of the more prominently located sites, such as Shechem and Jerusalem, have been interpreted as "control centers" by some, with each city ruled by a different "chief" (see Finkelstein and Gophna 1993). On the other hand, others (for example, Bienkowski 1989) have argued that there was a fragmented political system in which different city-states competed for resources, which ultimately led to the collapse of the MBA culture.

Ilan, in his study (1995: fig. 6), identified what he called "gateway cities" that existed through the MBA II–III periods (*ca.* 1800–1550 BC). Ilan has suggested three different kinds of "gateways," based on geographical location, size and economic indicators: "first order," such as Hazor and Tell el-Dab'a (Avaris, in the Nile Delta); "second order," including Ashkelon, Kabri and Pella; and "third order," such as Jericho and Dan (Laish). In addition, he ranked other settlements as "regional center(s)" (such as Megiddo, Beth Shan and Shechem); "subregional," including Tell el-Hayyat and Afula. The last two categories are "village," and "farmstead" or "hamlet" (Ilan 1995: 305).

The assumption seems to be that the larger sites, such as Hazor, controlled their surrounding countryside. The picture emerging from these recent social/anthropological studies is that of a complex society that supported an elite class located in major cities, many of which contained "palace-temple" institutions with a rural peasantry that existed on the social/political periphery (Ilan 1995: 306; Kempinski 1992b).

MBA architecture

Taken as a whole, the MBA architectural remains can be divided into four major categories: domestic; royal (palaces); cultic (especially temples); and defensive (gates, walls and ramparts).

Domestic remains (Kempinski 1992b: 194–6; Ben-Dor 1992: 99–102)

The most common domestic dwelling during this time was a courtyard house that began during MB I and continued throughout the Bronze Age. However, due to the penchant of archaeologists to concentrate on public monumental remains such as "palaces" and defensive systems, little domestic architecture has been recovered. A fairly typical layout of a domestic dwelling consisted of a courtyard usually surrounded by several rooms (Ben-Dor 1992: especially figs 1 and 2). In walled enclosures, houses normally shared common walls out of consideration for space. Good examples have been found at Megiddo and Tel Nagilah (Ben-Dor 1992: figs 3, 4). These courtyards vary in size measuring from around 7–10 feet by 13–14 feet. Furthermore, they seem to have been used for gatherings of both people and animals, especially in the small unwalled villages.

A special type of domestic building larger than the more common ones is called a "patrician" house. Albright first used this term to describe a structure he discovered at Tell Beit Mirsim (Kempinski 1992b: 195–6, fig. 6.25; Ben-Dor 1992: 101–2, fig. 7; Oren 1992: 115–17). This structure is almost 30 feet long and 16 feet wide. Other such houses have been identified at Megiddo (Kempinski 1992b: fig. 6.26), Ta'anach, and Tell el-'Ajjul. It is assumed by most authorities that these houses were for an elite ruling/wealthy class. However, in light of the fragmentary nature of much of the remains, and in the absence of contemporary written texts describing such buildings and their functions, their true use is still unknown for certain.[7]

Palaces (Oren 1992: 105–15; Kempinski 1992b: 196)

The same difficulty in identifying material remains as "patrician" houses is also true of "palaces," and for the same reason: what is left of such structures is either an accident of nature and/or what has been left by ancient and modern robbers. However, remains identified as MBA palaces have been found on such sites as Megiddo, Tell el-'Ajjul, Aphek and Shechem (Oren 1992: figs. 1, 6, 8, 9 respectively). Megiddo, Strata XII–X, has longed served as a model of a Palestinian Canaanite city. The remains of what have been identified as eight palaces have been uncovered in three areas: AA, BB and DD. The best-preserved remains are in AA and have been dated to the end of the MBA. According to Oren (1992: fig. 2) this palace continued in use into the Late Bronze Age with very little change.

All known structures identified as palaces consist of a courtyard surrounded by rooms on at least three sides. This is the same general description given to private houses above. However, one of the major differences between the two is in the size. Palaces are much larger, with many more rooms (though the function of most of the rooms is only a guess), ranging in size from 8000 square feet (Megiddo, Stratum X) to 12,000 square feet (Tell el-'Ajjul). However, compared with their counterparts from Syria and Mesopotamia, Palestinian palaces are much smaller and simpler. At Mari, in Mesopotamia, one of the palaces found measured over 250,000 square feet, with more than 300 rooms. Many archaeologists believe that palaces from these regions had considerable influence on the construction of palaces in Palestine.

If it is safe to describe such remains as palaces, then politically it is also safe to conclude that during the latter half of the MBA there existed in Palestine a hierarchical political system centering on city kings or rulers.

Dever, in his most recent summation of this period (1987a), concluded that the large urban sites (for Dever, sites more than 20 acres in size) dominated other settlements, creating a "three-tiered, hierarchically arranged settlement" (see especially pp. 152–3). Another archaeological indication of this domination are the massive remains of many fortifications.

Fortifications

Beginning as early as the MB I at such sites as Dan and Hazor in the Huleh Valley, Jericho in the Lower Jordan Valley, and at over a dozen or more sites on the coastal plain, large fortifications began to be built that included three-tiered entry-way gates and large earthen embankments called "ramparts." The spread of such massive structures by the MB II period has been called "the single most characteristic feature of the fully developed phases of this period" (Dever 1987a: 153). In their survey, Broshi and Gophna (1986) identified some twenty-five fortified sites dating to MB I (their MB IIa). Of these, some ten sites continued on into the later phases of the MBA. These sites range from a few acres in size to much larger settlements such as Hazor (200 acres) and Yavne Yam (160 acres).

Ramparts

One of the major physical characteristics of many MBA cities and settlements is the earthen rampart (Kempinski 1992b: 175, fig. 6.11). For many years it was believed that the main purpose of this edifice was protection from outside enemies (for example, Kenyon 1973a: 115). In particular it was thought that the ramparts protected the city from such tactics as battering rams, undermining and fires. Furthermore, it is usually assumed (see Kempinski 1992b: 175–6) that this type of construction originated in northern Syria and Mesopotamia. Recently, however, defensive explanations have given way to new theories. Bunimovitz (1992) has argued that the ramparts were constructed more as a status symbol for local leaders (city-state kings) than for military purposes. Constructing such massive structures provided a "symbolic expression of the capability and power of the ruler" (Bunimovitz 1992: 225). Finkelstein (1992) has also re-evaluated the traditional interpretation and concluded that they were built more for "propaganda" on the part of local rulers who wanted to show off their power and wealth.

These critiques by Finkelstein, Bunimovitz and others do not, however, rule out defensive motivations. Ramparts were massive earthen-stone projects that, even if not constructed solely for defensive purposes, or even primarily so, would still have given protection to the inhabitants within. Many of these structures measure over 100 feet in width at their bases and originally stood over 40 feet high (Ilan 1995: 316). At Tel Dan (Biran 1994: 58–73; illustrations 32, 34, 36, 38-41) the rampart was built sometime during the nineteenth–eighteenth centuries BC, spanning both MB I and II. Its core was discovered to be over 20 feet thick and it was preserved to a height of over 30 feet (Figure 5.2). The rampart was constructed on both sides of the core in order to keep the outside mass from pushing down the wall-core. Biran has estimated the width of the rampart at its base to be nearly 200 feet. It was also

Figure 5.2 Middle Bronze Age rampart wall at Tel Dan. Note stone core at top. Photo: J. Laughlin

discovered that the core of the wall differed depending upon its location. That is, the builders used whatever materials were available, adapting to the natural shape of the terrain. There was no one way to construct the rampart.[8] In addition to Tel Dan, ramparts are known from many other Palestinian sites, including Hazor, Jericho, Beth Shan, Lachish, Ashkelon and Gezer.

City gates (Kempinski 1992d: 134–6).

All fortified settlements must have a way of getting in and out for the inhabitants; thus the need for gates. While not all gates of the MBA were built the same, the most common style was a three-entry-way gate such as those found at Tel Yavne Yam, Shechem, Hazor, Tel Dan and Alalakh (Turkey) (Kempinski 1992d: figs 18–22). Of all gate remains

Figure 5.3 Middle Bronze Age gate, Tel Dan. Photo: J. Laughlin

Figure 5.4 Reconstructed model of Middle Bronze Age gate, Tel Dan.
Photo: J. Laughlin

discovered so far dating to the MBA, none is more spectacular than the one uncovered at Tel Dan (Figure 5.3). Discovered in 1979 (Biran 1994: 75–90) on the southeastern corner of the site, the mudbrick gate was composed of two towers, each one nearly 17 feet wide; a recessed triple-arched entryway; and four chambers, each one about 15 by 8 feet in size (Figure 5.4). Ceramic remains found on the floor of one of the chambers dated the gate to MB I–II (MB IIA–B, in Biran's nomenclature), or around the mid-eighteenth century BC. In all, the gate complex stands some 23 feet high, with seventeen courses of mudbrick preserved above the arches. The entry-way itself is over 10 feet high and almost 8 feet wide. Each arch contains three radial courses of brick. The entire gate structure is about 45 feet long and 50 feet wide. The distance through the recessed arches is nearly 35 feet. The approach to the gate from the outside was by stone steps, twenty of which were cleaned for a distance of some 36 feet to the east. Steps were also found leading down into the city on the inside. About 20 inches beneath the outside steps, another row of steps was found. This discovery, plus that of an earlier threshold, led the excavator to conclude that the gate went through at least two stages of use before it was blocked up and incorporated into the MB rampart.

Temples – cult sites (Dever 1987a: 165–71; A. Mazar 1992a)

It is always difficult to try to rethink the thoughts of ancient peoples, even when there are written texts contemporary with the time one is investigating. Nowhere is this more true than in the realm of religious beliefs and practices. Always present is the danger of reading one's own notions into the artifactual evidence or missing entirely the true meaning of what material data there are. Nevertheless, there does seem to be a good amount of what we may call "cultic" material evidence from the MBA. Among such material is what has been identified as the remains of temples. These remains have been uncovered at such sites as Hazor, Shechem and Megiddo. The remains from Shechem consist of such thick walls (over 16 feet) and overall size (86 by 69 feet), that it has been called a *migdal* or fortress temple (cf. G. E. Wright 1965: 80–102). A similar building has been found at Megiddo. Associated with the Shechem building were standing stones or *massebot*. In particular, the excavator, G. E. Wright, concluded that in the center of the entrance to this temple there once stood a stone column over 2.5 feet in diameter. Some commentators have associated this Shechem installation with the biblical stories in Joshua 24: 21–27 and Judges 9: 6 (Campbell 1983). This structure is sometimes called a "long building" (A. Mazar 1992a: 169), the architectural tradition of which has been traced back to Syria. Other "broad-room" temples are believed to have been indigenous to Canaan and south Syria (for a general discussion, see A. Mazar 1992a: 164–9).[9] Also dating to the MBA are two buildings interpreted as temples from Tell ed-Dab'a (Avaris) from the time of the Hyksos.

In addition to cultic buildings, open-air sites have also been discovered. Two especially merit mention. One is at Nahariya (A. Mazar 1992a: fig. 1), north of Acco on the Mediterranean coast. A large quantity of incense burners was found at this site along with a number of female figurines made of clay and bronze. Another well-known MB open-air site is the "High Place" at Gezer. This site consists of ten standing stones or pillars. Dated to the end of MB II by Dever, they are believed to represent, perhaps, ten towns or sites or even rulers that had formed some kind of league.

Other cultic objects from this period include female figurines, such as the two made of gold from Gezer. These spectacular finds have been interpreted by Dever as representing 'Asherah, the Canaanite fertility goddess (1987a: 168). Other finds have been identified as votive offerings in the form of miniature pottery vessels or zoomorphic figurines. All of these objects were probably associated with fertility rites with which the Canaanite deities were connected.

Arts and crafts

The artistic production of the MBA includes sculptures reflecting Syro-Mesopotamian styles (Kempinski 1992b: figs. 6.31–33). One of these is a basalt statue found at Hazor believed to be of a ruler. It has been described as the "only statue so far discovered in the Land of Israel that may clearly be ascribed to the Syrian school" (Kempinski 1992b: 200).

Wooden boxes with bone inlays were also popular during the MBA. Some of those found vary in size from 3 x 5 to 5 x 7 inches and have been found in tombs (Kempinski 1992b: figs 6.34, 35). The craftsmen who constructed these items were also familiar with faience (made by adding sand to clay before firing), and vessels made by this process began to appear by MB II (Kempinski 1992b: fig. 6.36). Many of these objects reflect Egyptian forms and are taken by some archaeologists as evidence of Egyptian influence on local burial practices.

Both imported and locally made alabaster were known. The difference between the two, according to Kempinski (1992b: 202), is that Egyptian alabaster is made of calcium carbonate and was shaped by drilling, while locally made vessels are formed from calcium sulphate and were shaped using a chisel. Other objects from this period include cylinder seals, both imported and locally made. The imported ones came mainly from Syria, whereas local counterparts reflect Egyptian influence (Kempinski 1992b: 202–3, fig. 6.37).

Metal figurines and jewelry have also been recovered. Those found at Nahariya were also interpreted as representing fertility goddesses. Unlike the gold figurines from Gezer, these were molded from silver. A magnificent discovery at Tell el-'Ajjul also shows that gold was used for personal jewelry (Kempinski 1992b: 204, figs 6.40, 41, 44; see also plate 31 in the same volume). According to Kempinski, the personal use of gold did not occur until late in the MBA. The reason was not a lack of goldsmiths, but a lack of means to pay for it (1992b: 204).

Weapons (Kempinski 1992b: figs. 6.47–52; 206)

Weapons of the MBA were cast in bronze and included axes, javelins and daggers. The shape of the weapons does show an evolutionary development. Thus the so-called "duckbill" ax of MB I gives way to the "notched" ax of MB II. While the war chariot was known in Syria by the nineteenth century BC (Kempinski 1992b: 208), there is very little evidence for its use in Palestine during the MBA. Except for a harness found at Tell el-'Ajjul, no other discoveries from the MBA can be related to the possibility of chariots existing here during this time.

Pottery

With the widespread use of the fast potter's wheel, the ceramic output of the MBA was unsurpassed during the long Bronze Age (for an older, but still useful description of MBA pottery, see Amiran 1970b: 90–123; see also Dever 1987a: 161–3). The ceramicists of this era produced a variety of forms that included bowls, kraters, mugs, goblets, cooking pots, jars, lamps, jugs and juglets (in addition to the above, see Kempinski 1992b: 161–6; Figs 6.3–4; 14–15). The sources for such pottery included Byblos on the Lebanese coast, Syria, and the local ware, usually made in villages (Kempinski 1992b: 165–6). The international flavor of this period is also seen in imported ceramic ware. By the end of the period, Cypriot pottery in several varieties was widespread. The presence of such ware, as well as the Tel el-Yehudiyeh ware from Egypt, clearly shows that Palestine during the MBA participated in international trade.

The Tell el-Yehudiyeh ware is a special import of the period. Named after the Egyptian site in the Delta where it was first found, the ware first appears at the end of MB I (Kempinski 1992b: 165, fig. 6.1 and plate 30). The uniqueness of the vessels is in the technique of rubbing a white substance (lime or pigment) into incisions on the surface, which is made of black clay. A rare find in this style is the fish-shaped vessel found at Tel Poleg. Dever has suggested that Palestinian exports also included grain, olive oil, wine, timber, cattle,[10] and perhaps copper and even slaves (1987a: 162).

The Hyksos Period (Dever 1985; Hayes 1973; Oren 1997; Redford 1970; Van Seters 1966; Weinstein 1997a)

One of the most discussed political events of the MBA is the arrival in the Egyptian Delta of a group of people the Egyptians called "Asiatics" or "Sand Dwellers" (Wilson, *ANET*: 416). Taking advantage of, and perhaps contributing to, the collapse of Egyptian rule (the so-called "Second Intermediate period"), these people set up a capital at Avaris, identified with Tell ed-Dab'a. The leaders of these "Asiatics" were called *kikau-khoswet*, from which it is believed came the word *hyksos*, which is now used to describe this people as a whole (see Hayes 1973: 54–5). The word *hyksos* is a Greek term universally taken to mean something like "rulers of foreign lands." The word comes from the writings of the third century BC Ptolemaic writer Manetho, by way of Josephus, the first-century AD Jewish historian (see *Against Apion*, book 1, chapter 1).

The Hyksos established the Fifteenth Dynasty and ruled over Egypt (at least the northern part) for more than 100 years, from the middle of the seventeenth to the middle of the sixteenth century BC. Exactly who these people were in terms of ethnic identity is still unclear, though the study of their names occurring on scarabs, as well as the material evidence from Tell ed-Dab'a, indicate they were basically Semitic. The older theory that they gained dominance over Egypt in a single assault has recently been challenged, especially in light of the recent excavations at Avaris (Tel ed-Dab'a). Their rise to power now appears to have been the result of the infiltration of several groups of Asiatics over a long period of time (Hayes 1973: 54–5; Dever 1987a: 173). In fact, Dever has argued that the takeover of Egypt in the seventeenth century was more the result than the cause of the internal collapse of Egyptian control during the Second Intermediate period.

However they managed it, by the end of the eighteenth century they seem to have been well established in the Nile Delta, having built their capital at Avaris. The location of this city is probably indicative of close ties they maintained with Palestine, from which they had come, as well as the fact that they were never in full control of Upper Egypt, which remained in the hands of Theban princes during this time. It is from within this latter group that the Egyptians' struggle to overthrow the Hyksos began with the efforts of Ka-mose, the last Upper Egyptian ruler of the Seventeenth Dynasty. However, credit for the ultimate expulsion of the Hyksos from Egypt goes to Ka-mose's brother, Ah-mose (*ca.* 1552–1527 BC), the founder of the Eighteenth Dynasty. By 1540 BC he had succeeded in driving the Hyksos back into Palestine as far as Sharuhen, now identified with Tell el-'Ajjul (Weinstein 1991; Kempinski 1992b: 189–92). Following a three-year siege of the city, Ah-mose successfully drove them out.

The full extent of Hyksos rule and influence is still unclear, but the evidence points to Egypt, Palestine and parts of Syria. Also, to what extent they should be credited with the introduction into the area of such developments as the rampart, war chariot and the composite bow is still not entirely clear, though the latter two are thought more likely than the first. Politically, they organized Palestine into a city-state system producing a feudal society with its concomitant uneven distribution of wealth. Nevertheless, Palestine experienced one of its most prosperous periods under Hyksos rule. Along with Horites and other groups, the Hyksos formed the population from which came the "pre-Israelites" (Dever's term) at the end of the LBA and the beginning of Iron Age I.

The End of the MBA[11]

While there is still some debate among archaeologists over the cause(s) of the end of MBA, there appears to be little doubt that the overriding cause was the reassertion of Egyptian power in the region at the end of the Seventeenth and beginning of the Eighteenth Dynasties (Weinstein 1981, 1991). Dever has concluded that the massive ramparts described above were built precisely to defend against Egyptian retaliation (1987a: 174) and not intercity rivalry. Almost all MB sites in Palestine that have been excavated show destruction levels dating to the end of the MBA. Some sites, such as Shechem, show more than one level of destruction during this time. By analyzing the stratigraphic archaeological evidence from some thirty sites in Palestine, Egyptian textual sources, and Hyksos names found on scarabs at Palestinian sites, Weinstein (1981) concluded that the MBA destruction was primarily limited to settlements under Hyksos control in the southern and inland regions of the country. Thus, for him, the Egyptian reprisals were out of hatred for the Hyksos, not imperialistic goals.

The Middle Bronze and the Bible

A few short decades ago many biblical historians and archaeologists would have agreed with Albright's conclusion that "the Middle Bronze Age corresponds to the Patriarchal Age of the Bible" (1949: 83). Many introductory textbooks, especially those written during the first six or seven decades of this century, place the biblical Patriarchs (Abraham, Isaac, Jacob) historically during this period. De Vaux, in his *magnum opus* (1978: 257–66), while a little more cautious than Albright and others, concluded that although it was impossible to give exact dates for the patriarchal period , the MBA was the "most suitable period for Israel's ancestors' first settlement in Canaan" (1978: 265).

What seemed to be a scholarly consensus a short time ago has recently been challenged by literary studies by such scholars as T. L. Thompson (1974) and J. Van Seters (1975). Although the conclusions reached in their studies have not received a wide endorsement among biblical scholars in general, Thompson, Van Seters, and others like them, have succeeded in opening a new, and often heated, debate on all issues raised by the patriarchal stories in the Bible. Particularly, they have radically re-dated the traditions to the post-exilic period and seriously questioned the historicity of the patriarchal stories.

While there are many questions involved, two of the most important and most often discussed are the date and historicity of the patriarchal narratives. With regard to the date of these traditions, part of the problem is that the Bible itself does not give the kind of chronological precision necessary to formulate clear, exact dates by modern historians. There is little in the biblical stories that can be related to known historical or political events of antiquity (McCarter 1988: 3ff.; de Vaux 1978: 257–66). Furthermore, as has often been noted, the chronology imposed by the biblical authors on the stories in Genesis is very problematic. Not the least of the problems is the unusually long life spans given to the patriarchal characters: Abraham, 175 years (Gen. 25: 7); Isaac, 180 years (Gen. 35: 22); Jacob, 147 years (Gen. 47: 28); and Joseph, 110 years (Gen. 50: 26). These long life spans, if taken literally, are very difficult, to say the least, to reconcile with archaeological data from thousands of ancient tombs and graves, many of them dating long before any possible date for the Patriarchs, which suggest that the life expectancy of people in antiquity was less than fifty years. Consequently, the biblical data concerning the life spans of these figures are of little use in trying to establish an absolute chronology for the period as a whole.

Even where the Bible does seem to give a useful chronological reference, problems exist. According to I Kings 6: 1, Solomon built the temple in Jerusalem 480 years after the Exodus. Dating Solomon to the tenth century BC (for the problem of Solomon, see below, Chapter 8), this would place the "Exodus" and "Conquest" sometime during the fifteenth century BC. Such a date cannot be reconciled with the archaeological data known from this time. On the other hand, the biblical writers seem clearly to place the time of the Patriarchs long before that of Moses and the Exodus. Furthermore, if these traditions are as late as Thompson, Van Seters and others have suggested, it is a major curious fact that not one personal name in Genesis is compounded with the name of the Israelite God, YHWH (usually translated as "Lord" in English Bibles). But there are several compounded with "El," the chief god of the Canaanites, such as "Ishmael," and even "Israel" (see Hendel 1995 for details).[12] It has also been argued that the social, political and economic world view reflected in Genesis is much closer to the world of the Middle Bronze Age known from archaeological discoveries than to any other period in Israel's history (see, for example, the comments by

A. Mazar 1990: 225). Nevertheless, the consensus, if that is what it was, established by Albright and others a generation ago has unraveled beyond recognition. Many questions have not been satisfactorily answered to all concerned. It should be no surprise, then, that authorities on the subject widely disagree on proposed solutions.[13]

What role archaeology can or should play in the current debate is also unclear. If the stories are indeed post-exilic and fictional in character, then archaeologists can add little to the discussions (see Dever and Clark's comments, 1977). On the other hand, if the biblical stories, or at least parts of them, can be placed in an earlier setting, as suggested above,[14] archaeologists can illuminate the culture of that period. This is a long way from "proving" the stories true. There are two totally separate issues here: the date(s) of the biblical traditions *about* the Patriarchs; and the question regarding the *historicity* of the Patriarchs themselves. Even if the last question could be positively answered, that in itself would not "prove" the historicity of what the biblical writers have them do and say. (Wyatt Earp existed historically as a real person. But it is very questionable that he "did" and "said" everything attributed to him.) That the Bible is supposed to be an "inspired" text hardly solves this problem except for the most conservative reader.

Before a serious, critical discussion of this question can take place, two sets of complicated, complex and wide-ranging data must be understood and appreciated: the archaeological data now known about the Near East in general, and Israel in particular (as well as the theories/methods used to interpret these data); and contemporary literary critical studies of the biblical traditions. If one, much less both, of these components is missing, the resulting picture will be skewed, to say the least. What is being called for is a balanced approach that seeks to deal fairly and even-handedly with both sets of data (see particularly Dever's comments, in Dever and Clark 1977: 71–9). The ever-present temptation to use what is known from archaeological discoveries to correlate with some biblical text must be avoided, unless the clear context of both sets of data is established independently. This means that the archaeological evidence cannot be used to date the biblical stories and then the biblical stories used to suggest dates for the archaeological record. Such circular reasoning is no stranger to these discussions. What does seem clear is that the old attempt to try to "prove" the historicity of the patriarchal period in the Bible is all but over except among the most conservative of scholars. Even those who believe that the Patriarchs were real people can only argue indirectly from the material data for their position, as the latest attempt by Kitchen (1995) illustrates. But even this approach does not provide conclusive results, as Hendel's critique has demonstrated (1995).

Where does all this leave us? First, it is impossible in light of current debates to know how old the biblical stories of the Patriarchs really are (whether or not they were historical figures seems more questionable than ever, except by those who simply take the Bible at face value). That the final *compilation* of these stories probably dates to the post-exilic period is not the issue; the original date of the *composition* of the traditions is. Secondly, if Kitchen assumed too much with regard to the setting and age of the stories, Thompson and Van Seters assumed too little. Some of the biblical material can be made to fit what is known of the MBA . But "can be" and "needs to be" are not the same. Thirdly, given the evidence that is now available (textual and archaeological), there seems to be no valid reason to deny a pre-monarchical (tenth century BC) date for some of the traditions. This includes those with personal names compounded with "El," as well as the biblical insistence that the Patriarchs had ties with the Amorite culture of Mesopotamia and interacted with Canaanite cities and their rulers, a situation that fits well with what we know of the MBA. However, much in these stories can be, and has been, dated later, particularly to the LBA (see the reference to Dever and Clark above). Fourthly, the final form of the stories in Genesis had little to do with the concern of the author(s) to provide absolute chronological material for biblical scholars and/or archaeologists. Their concern was one of faith, not dates; theology, not ancient history.

Until some unexpected discovery is made in the form of textual evidence that can date precisely the time the Patriarchs lived (assuming they were historical figures), the discussion will continue to be clouded with theories and conclusions that often rest more on the scholar's ingenuity and cleverness than hard evidence. Given this situation, it is not clear at all just what contributions archaeologists can make to this ongoing discussion (see Dever's conclusions in Dever and Clark 1977: 79).

Chapter 6

The Late Bronze Age
(1550–1200 BC)

> The civilization of Palestine in Late Bronze continued to be a poor relation of the much richer Canaanite culture of Phoenicia and southern Syria. Had it not been for the influence from the north, Palestine might easily have lost its own culture and have become a barbaric reflection of Egyptian civilization.
>
> (W. F. Albright, 1949)

The last 300 years or so of the long Bronze Age are characterized by new demographics which witnessed an almost total abandonment of the rural areas and a build-up in the coastal regions. The period saw increased power and control of the region, especially Palestine and Syria, by Egypt. This led to a general decline in living conditions for most of the people and at the same time a concentration of power and wealth into the hands of an elite group. This situation is reflected in the architectural remains of large "patrician" houses or "governor" mansions identified at many sites (Tell Beit Mirsim, Megiddo, Tell el-'Ajjul, for example), which probably served as domestic quarters for either an Egyptian official or a local who served at Egypt's behest. Egypt's control is also seen in the fact that, with few exceptions, most Palestinian sites during this period were unfortified. Furthermore, this concentration of power and wealth is reflected in increased trade, especially with the Mediterranean world, which brought such luxury items as carved ivories, copper, wines, oil and, especially, fine ceramics. Despite the overall decline reflected in the material remains of this period, one of the most important innovations in human history took place here: the development of the alphabet by the Phoenicians (see below). Furthermore, at the very end of the Late Bronze Age, it may be possible for the first time to speak of a people called "Israel."

Our knowledge of the Late Bronze Age in Palestine is closely tied to Egyptian history, which is illuminated considerably by the discovery and translation of many Egyptian inscriptions and texts that date to this period. Consequently, as Dever concluded more than twenty years ago (Dever and Clark 1977: 90–1), while our knowledge of the Late Bronze Age is constantly being refined by the addition of new data from ongoing excavations, this period has not seen the dramatic transformation that has been the case with the preceding Middle Bronze Age.

However, that does not mean that there are no controversial or debated issues. There is still considerable disagreement among archaeologists and historians over the absolute dates for both the beginning and ending of this phase of the Bronze Age, as well as over the number and dating of sub-phases. Furthermore, questions concerning the cause(s) of the swift end of this period and the origin of a new social/political/ethnic entity in Palestine called "Israel" have hardly been answered to everyone's satisfaction.[1]

Chronology

As already mentioned, the history of the Late Bronze Age in Palestine (as well as elsewhere in the Levant) is tied closely to that of Egypt, the latter history of which has been greatly illuminated by the discovery of texts, inscriptions, seals and stelae (Weinstein 1981; Leonard 1989: 6–7; Dever 1992b: fig. 1). In general, this period parallels the Eighteenth and Nineteenth Dynasties of Egypt. The Eighteenth Dynasty began with Ah-mose during the sixteenth century BC, and the Nineteenth Dynasty ended with the reign of Tewosret at the end of the thirteenth or early in the twelfth century. However, the absolute chronologies for the pharaohs of both dynasties are still being debated.[2]

In addition, there is still no unanimity among archaeologists on either the beginning or the ending of the LBA (Bunimovitz 1995: 330), as well as on the number of sub-phases of the period (Dever, in Dever and Clark 1977: 90–1; on the end of the LBA see Ussishkin 1985). The issues are real and complex, and cannot be dealt with here in any detail. To try to avoid confusion and to be as consistent as possible, most of the dates used in this chapter will once again follow those suggested by the editors of the *OEANE*. There the LBA is broken down into the following sub-phases and dates:[3]

LB IA: 1550–1450 BC
LB IB: 1450–1400 BC

LB IIA: 1400–1300 BC
LB IIB: 1300–1200 BC

In general, the beginning of the Late Bronze Age is linked to the destruction that brought an end to the Middle Bronze Age. Part of the problem, however, is that not all MBA cities/settlements suffered destruction at this time. Examples include Lachish, Gezer, Megiddo, Beth Shean and Hazor. Furthermore, the destruction that did take place cannot be linked to a single event (Bunimovitz 1995: 322). Similar problems exist for the ending of the LBA. At the end of the thirteenth century BC, much of the Near Eastern as well as the Mycenaean worlds witnessed major disruptions and collapse. This disintegration can be seen in Palestine, where many sites were destroyed (for example, Hazor and Bethel). On the other hand, Egypt's control over Palestine did not come to a complete end until sometime during the first half of the twelfth century BC. In addition, several sites (such as Megiddo, Lachish, Beth Shean and Ashkelon) were not destroyed at the end of the thirteenth century. Furthermore, the two hallmarks of the Iron Age I period – the spread of the Philistine material culture and the widespread use of iron – do not seem to have occurred until the latter half of the twelfth century (Ussishkin 1985; Gonen 1992b: 216). Under such conditions it is difficult to argue for an absolute chronology that will be accepted by all interested authorities. These issues, for the present at least, must remain open questions and subject to modification as new data are discovered.

Population

The transition from the Middle Bronze Age to the Late Bronze Age resulted in a decline in both the population in general and the density of settlements in various regions. In a recent summary of the LBA, Gonen (1992b) concluded that a "drastic change" took place in Palestinian urban areas that witnessed the abandonment of many sites in the Central Hill country with new sites established in the coastal plains and valleys (for a map of LBA sites, see Gonen 1992b: 215, map 7.2). In an earlier study Gonen (1984) estimated that some 272 Middle Bronze Age sites were known in Palestine from surveys. This number dropped to 101 during the LBA (1984: 66; table 2). Not only was there a drop in number and a shift of location of inhabited areas, the size of the Late Bronze settlements was also dramatically reduced. During the MB II period, only 11 percent of known sites were 2.5 acres or less in size. By the end of the LBA, this figure jumped to 43 percent. If sites up to 12.5 acres are included, this number increases to 95 percent!

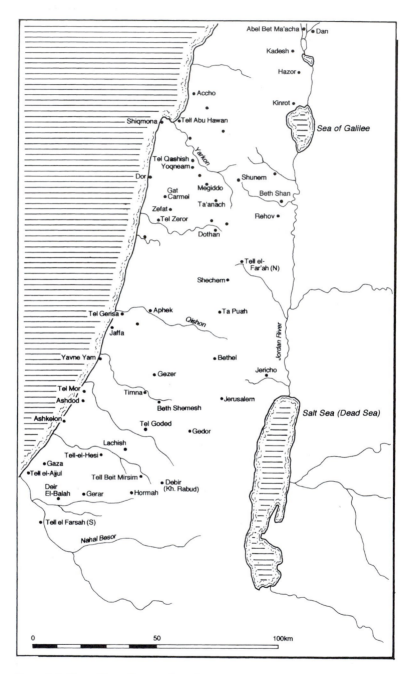

Figure 6.1 Map of Late Bronze Age sites

Of Gonen's large sites (50 acres or more), the number dropped from twenty-eight in MB II to six in the LBA. Of these six, only Lachish (50 acres) and Hazor (200+ acres – Hazor is the largest ancient site ever discovered in Palestine) existed throughout the entire Late Bronze Age (Gonen 1984: 66–7; fig. 2). Furthermore, the total area estimated to have been occupied dropped from over 1050 acres during the MB II to barely 500 acres by LB II (Gonen 1984: 68, table 4; Gonen 1992b: 216–17). Especially significant for understanding the "Israelite" occupation of Palestine at the beginning of the Iron Age (see below) is the fact that the Central Hill country, as well as the Galilean hills, were sparsely occupied during this period. Important exceptions to this observation are cities such as Shechem, Tell el-Far'ah (N), Bethel and Jerusalem.[4]

Many of the new, small sites built particularly in the coastal region are believed to have served as Egyptian outposts or official residences (probably for the protection of commercial interests). Other sites also served Egyptian interests such as Beth Shean, which guarded the eastern end of the Jezreel Valley. In fact, the Egyptian presence in Palestine during this period may account for one of the most surprising characteristics of the LBA occupied settlements: the absence of defensive walls.

Architectural remains

Domestic

Discussions of LBA architectural remains known from excavations in Palestine usually center on remains identified as "temples" and "patrician houses" or "governors' residences." This is because very little of typical private dwellings is known due to the lack of exposure at most LBA sites (for a general description of the architecture, see Gonen 1992b; Oren 1992). Most of the evidence that has been recovered has come from such sites as Megiddo and Hazor. The remains uncovered at these sites suggest that there was continuity with the domestic architectural styles of the preceding MBA, including the ubiquitous courtyard surrounded by small rooms. However, details such as windows, roofs, second stories and method of construction are often missing due to the poor state of preservation of the material remains.

Temples

Architectural remains identified as "temples," however, have been more plentiful. In fact, Gonen concluded that the temple is the most common public structure recovered from the LBA (1992b: 219). The remains of such identified structures have been found at many sites. In some cases, such as at Hazor, Megiddo, Beth Shan and Lachish, multiple examples have been found. The most outstanding physical characteristic of these structures is their diversity. There does not seem to have been any set type or style (for a general discussion of temples, see Biran 1981; A. Mazar 1990: 248–57; A. Mazar 1992a: 169–80; Gonen 1992b: 222–31; Nakhai 1997a; Ottosson 1980). It is impossible to go into detail here, but these structures range from "open-air" cult sites, such as were found in Area F at Hazor and on a hill in northern Samaria, to "monumental" buildings found at Shechem, Hazor and Megiddo (these structures have also been called *migdal*, or "fortress" temples). The building discovered at Shechem deserves special mention. If indeed it was a temple it is the largest yet discovered in Palestine. Originally constructed during the MBA (see above, Chapter 5), this building measured some 70 x 86 feet with walls 16 feet thick. Going through several phases, it was used throughout the LBA and on into Iron Age I. The excavator, G. E. Wright, suggested that this building was the temple of El Berith ("God of the Covenant") mentioned in the story recorded in Judges 9: 46–49 (Wright 1965: 80–102; see also Campbell 1983). Also associated with this temple were standing stones called *massebot*.

Other temples are tripartite in structure and reflect Syrian influence. One of the best preserved was discovered at Hazor, where it had gone through at least three phases of use (Figure 6.2; cf. A. Mazar 1992a: 171–2). Other temples, such as have been found at Beth Shean, reflect Egyptian influence. Still others seem to defy classification and are said to be "irregular." Among these is a structure at Beth Shean dated to the fourteenth century BC (Gonen 1992b: 229–31). Among other interesting finds here were a stela of the god Mekal and a relief carved in stone depicting a fight between a lion and another animal usually identified as either a lioness or a dog (A. Mazar 1990: 267, fig. 7.17). Also belonging to this category of "irregular" temples is the famous "Fosse" temple at Lachish (A. Mazar 1992a: 179; 174, figs. 21, 22).[5] This temple went through at least three phases of use before being destroyed for the last time at the end of the LBA. Perhaps the most interesting shrine identified as "irregular" from this period is one discovered at Hazor in Area C of the Lower City (A. Mazar 1990: 253–4; Gonen 1992b: 231). The remains from this structure include eleven standing stones, or *massebot*, as well as the statue of a seated figure. A. Mazar interpreted these remains, especially the *massebot*, as evidence of the link between such open cult

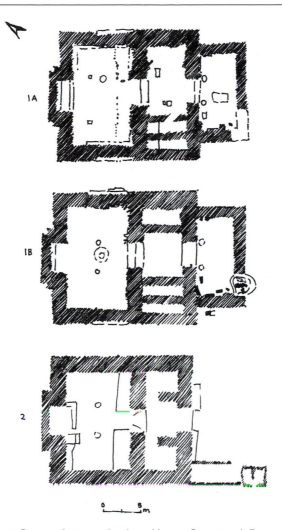

Figure 6.2 Late Bronze Age temple plans, Hazor. Courtesy, J. Fitzgerald

places of the MBA and similar practices during the time of the Monarchy (1990: 254). Other such "temples" have been found in the Jordan Valley, the northern Negev and perhaps at the airport in Amman, in Jordan (Herr 1997c).

Whereas there is an abundance of architectural evidence for temples during this period, there is almost none with regard to what rituals or beliefs the people engaged in when practicing their religion. Beyond suggesting complex, plural religious practices that seem to have included polytheism (the *massebot*) and "demographic heterogeneity" (A. Mazar 1990: 257), little more can be said.

Palaces-patrician houses

Other material remains from the LBA have been identified as royal residences or palaces and patrician houses (Oren 1992: 114–20). While there is a problem with terminology ("patrician," "governor," and so on – see Oren, ibid.), the remains belonging to these structures have been found at such sites as Tell el-Far'ah (S), Beth Shan, Tel Sera', Tell Jemmeh, Tell el-Hesi and Tell Beit Mirsim (Oren 1992: 119, figs. 18–23). Such buildings imply that each town had its own local official who could have been an Egyptian, as seems to have been the case at Beth Shean (Gonen 1992b: 221). These "residences" give solid material evidence for the concentration of wealth and power into the hands of relatively few people during this time (see Joffe 1997b).

Late Bronze Age Pottery

Despite the cultural decline reflected in the material remains of many LBA sites, this period experienced a flourishing trade, especially in the later stages, with the Mediterranean world as well as with other countries. Along with locally made Canaanite pottery, which evolved from the MBA, much imported pottery has been recovered. For analysis of the ceramic corpus see the following: Amiran 1970b: 124–90; Gonen 1992b: 232–40; A. Mazar 1990: 257–64.

The "Amarna Age"

The political situation in the Near East during the Late Bronze II period (1400–1200 BC) has been remarkably illuminated by a group of clay tablets which first came to light in 1887.[6] These tablets, written mostly in Akkadian, were found by locals[7] digging for fertilizer (decomposed mudbrick) on the ruins of a site built by Akhenaton (Amenophis IV) sometime during the first half of the fourteenth century BC.[8] This site, now called Tell el-Amarna, is located on the east bank of the Nile River some 190 miles south of Cairo. The name "Amarna" is a hybrid word coming apparently from the name of a local tribe, Beni Amran, combined with that of a village, El Till. The name is something of a misnomer since the site is not really a tell.

No one knows for sure how many tablets were ultimately found which were subsequently lost or destroyed. Today some 382 tablets are known (Moran 1992) and are held in museums in London, Berlin (more than 200), and Cairo.[9] Of these known tablets, 350 are letters of correspondence between various kings and vassals to the pharaoh. Although some of these letters are from Near Eastern powers independent of Egypt (Babylonia, Mittani, Alasia [probably Cyprus], Assyria, Arzawa and Hatti [the Hittites]), most are from vassal chiefs or rulers living in Syria-Palestine. Some 150 of the letters come from Palestine proper (Albright in *ANET*: 483; see Na'aman 1992). A small minority of the letters originated in Egypt. Why they were in the same archive as the foreign correspondence is not clear (Moran 1992: xvii).

The letters from the Palestinian vassals, as aptly put by Moran, describe "a scene of constant rivalries, shifting coalitions, and attacks and counterattacks among the small city-states" (1992: xxxiii). For example, Lab'ayu, the ruler of Shechem (Harrelson 1975) is accused by Biridiya of Megiddo of trying to destroy the latter's city (*EA* 244). In another letter (*EA* 289), this time from 'Abdu-Heba of Jerusalem, Lab'ayu is accused of giving the "land of Shechem" to the 'Apiru, who themselves are accused of plundering "all the lands of the king" (EA 286). The letters, then, if not totally exaggerated beyond all reality, paint a picture of political deterioration with local rulers fighting one another, sometimes abetted by a group of people identified as the "'Apiru."[10]

These references to the 'Apiru (originally spelled "Hab/piru"), immediately attracted the attention of biblical scholars, many of whom thought the 'Apiru were related somehow to the Hebrews of the Old Testament (Bruce 1967: 11–14; Lemche 1992a). Some even went so far as to equate the 'Apiru attacks described in the Amarna correspondence with Joshua's invasion of Canaan as told in the Bible (Campbell 1960). The question of how, if at all, the 'Apiru mentioned in the Amarna letters are related to the Hebrews of the Bible is complex. While definite answers are lacking, it can be said that up to now, no one has proven conclusively that the two terms (i.e. "'*Apiru*," and "*ibri*"= "hebrew") are etymologically related (but see Lemche 1992b), nor that the Hebrews were ever part of the 'Apiru movement. In the first place, the people to whom the term 'Apiru applies existed all over the Near East throughout the second millennium BC (M. Greenberg 1955). Consequently, it is certainly true to say that not all 'Apiru were Hebrews. Whether any Hebrews were ever 'Apiru is, at the moment, an open question (see Fritz 1981: 81, who thought they were related).

Furthermore, the exact meaning of the term *'Apiru* has also been difficult to determine. Does it refer to an ethnic group, a social group, an economic class or all of them? Chaney (1983: 72–83) concluded from his study that the best paradigm (borrowed from Landsberger 1973) with which to describe the 'Apiru in the Amarna letters, as well as in other texts, is that of "social banditry" (1983: 79). Stopping short of identifying 'Apiru as Hebrews, Chaney argued that there was social/political continuity between the Amarna Age 'Apiru and the pre-monarchic "Israelites" of Iron Age I who occupied the same territory of Palestine previously inhabited by the 'Apiru. Citing I Samuel 22: 1–2 as a "classic" example of an early Israelite tradition that parallels the 'Apiru activity of the Amarna letters, Chaney then asks:

> Can there have been no continuity, therefore, between the social dynamic of Amarna-Age Palestine and that of the formations of Israel, when premonarchic Israel's primary areas of strength, its enemies, and its forms of social organization were all congruent with those of the Amarna *'apiru* and their allies?
>
> (1983: p. 83)

What this seems to mean is that while "'Apiru" and "Hebrew" cannot be two different terms for the same people, the political and military turmoil associated with the 'Apiru in the Amarna letters certainly helped to create the social and political upheaval that made the emergence of "Israel" possible 200 years or so later (see Lemche 1992b).

The problem of the "Exodus" out of Egypt

Certainly one of the most, if not the most important story in the Hebrew Bible, at least from the perspective of the biblical writers themselves, is that of the miraculous escape from Egypt by the twelve tribes of Israel under the leadership of Moses (Exod. 1–12). Told and celebrated in song and feast (Deut. 26: 5–11; Exod. 15: 1–18; I Sam. 12: 7–8; Hos. 11: 1; Mic. 6: 4; and so on), this story, along with those of the covenant at Sinai or Horeb (Exod. 19–24) and the entry into the Land of Canaan under Joshua (Josh. 1-12), became the *sine qua non* of Israel's existence. In fact, this story (or stories) is so essential to the Bible's self-understanding that biblical scholars, and especially "biblical" archaeologists, until recently took for granted that at its core there must have been some "historical" event, however much it might have been embellished by later generations of Israelites.

The questions and issues raised by the story of the Exodus, both from a literary as well as an archaeological point of view, are many. However, in the past ten to fifteen years there has been a steady increase of archaeological data that have raised very serious doubts about the historicity of this story, as well as that of Joshua's "conquest" of Canaan (see below, Chapter 8). At the center of this discussion is the question of the ultimate origin of the Israelites. Although there are still those who would argue for some sort of "historical event" standing behind the biblical story,[11] it is becoming more and more apparent that such arguments are becoming less and less convincing. The reason why is evidence, or more to the point, the lack of evidence, both literary and archaeological.

Literary evidence

Except for the biblical story there is no literary evidence that there was ever an Egyptian Sojourn and Exodus as described in the Bible. This is true regardless of the date one assumes for the event, if there was such an "event" at all.[12] In the past (as well as the present), much discussion has been given to an Egyptian stele (or stela) dated to the time of the pharaoh Merneptah (whose revised dates are usually given as *ca.* 1213–1203 BC), who ruled at the end of the thirteenth century (on the stela, see now Hasel 1994, with references). Made of black granite and standing some 7.5 feet high, the stela was found in Merneptah's temple in Thebes in 1896 by Petrie (Figure 6.3).

Dated to the fifth year of Merneptah's reign (*ca.* 1208–7, according to the low chronology), the stela contains a hymn or a series of hymns celebrating the pharaoh's victory over his enemies (for a translation of the hymn see Pritchard 1969: 376–8). Toward the end of the inscription is a hymn that mentions enemies in Canaan. These include Ashkelon, Gezer and Yanoam. But the name that has received the most attention from biblical scholars is that of "Israel" (because of this reference, the entire inscription is sometimes referred to as the "Israel stela"). It was immediately pointed out by language experts that the name "Israel" is preceded by an Egyptian hieroglyphic sign that indicates a people as opposed to a city or region. This is the earliest reference to "Israel" as a community known from any ancient text (for occurrences of the word "Israel" as a personal name, see Hasel 1994). The inscription reads:

> The princes are prostrate, saying: "Mercy!" Not one raises his head among the nine bows. Desolation is for Tehenu; Hatti is pacified;

Figure 6.3 Merneptah stela; a) "Israel stela" of Merneptah. Photo: © Jürgen Liepe

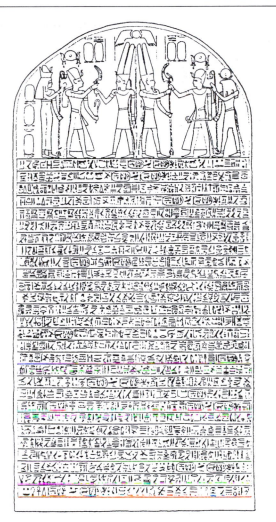

b) Drawing of Merneptah's stela and the name "Israel" in detail. From
Ancient Inscriptions: Voices from the Biblical World, P. Kyle McCarter, Jr.,
Biblical Archaeology Society, 1996, Washington, D.C.

> Plundered is the Canaan with every evil; Carried off is Ashkelon; seized upon is Gezer; Yanoam is made as that which does not exist; Israel is laid waste, his seed is not; Hurru is become a widow for Egypt! All lands together, they are pacified.
>
> (Wilson, *ANET*: 376)

For all the ink this reference to "Israel" has generated, what does it really tell us about the origin and nature of the "Israel" of the Bible? Not much. The attempts by some (for example, Yurco 1997; de Vaux 1978: 390–1, 490–2)[13] to link "Israel" on the stela with the "Israel" in the Bible that supposedly came out of Egypt under Moses have been unsuccessful. Without assuming the biblical story in advance, there is absolutely nothing in the stela inscription itself to suggest to anyone that this "Israel" was ever in Egypt. All that can be reasonably inferred from it is that an Egyptian scribe at the end of the thirteenth century BC could list among the enemies defeated by the pharaoh a group of people living in Canaan known collectively as "Israel" (see Miller and Hayes 1986: 68). How this "Israel" was organized; what deity or deities it worshiped; and most of all, from where this "Israel" originated and in what way or ways, if any, it is to be related to the "Israel" that emerged 200 years later under Saul and David is nowhere mentioned nor even suggested (see the discussions by the following: Dever 1997b; Weinstein 1997b; Ward 1997). Thus the Merneptah stela, as well as other Egyptian texts sometimes brought into the discussion,[14] are ultimately irrelevant to the question of whether or not there was ever an Israelite "exodus" from Egypt as told in the Bible. Some textual evidence, such as the Papyrus Anastasi V (Wilson, *ANET*: 259), might allow one to hypothesize that a few Egyptian slaves could have slipped out of Egypt from time to time, but all of the known Egyptian texts put together do not even remotely hint at an "Exodus" as described in the Bible. The Merneptah stela is simply irrelevant to this question.

The archaeological evidence (see Dever 1997b; Weinstein 1997b)

When one turns to the archaeological evidence vis-à-vis the Exodus, the picture, if anything, is even bleaker than that presented by the literary evidence. Despite repeated efforts by some (Malamat 1997, 1998; Sarna 1988; Yurco 1997) to defend the biblical story, "were it not for the Bible, anyone looking at the Palestinian archaeological data today would conclude that whatever the origin of the Israelites, it was not Egypt"

(Weinstein 1997b: 98). This candid conclusion by Weinstein clearly draws the line between those who interpret the archaeological evidence negatively with regard to an Egyptian background to Israel's origin and those who would interpret it otherwise. The issues here are many and complex. Furthermore, it is only for convenience that this discussion of the "Exodus" is separated from the question of the "Conquest," to be discussed in the next chapter. Any serious doubts regarding the historicity of the "Exodus" also impact upon an understanding of the "Conquest."

Although total objectivity is more an ideal than a reality, I will start by attempting to separate archaeological "facts" as they are now known from any interpretation of them. Any effort to support the biblical story of the "Exodus" substantively will have to explain the following: first, if the inhabitants of the Central Highlands of Palestine in the Iron Age I period came from a people who had an extended sojourn (over 400 years according to the Bible, I Kings 6:1) in Egypt, why have excavations and surveys of these villages yielded so little evidence of Egyptian influence (see Weinstein 1997b: 88)? Second, according to biblical tradition, several million people (cf. Exod. 12: 37; Num. 1: 45–6) wandered around the Sinai Peninsula for "forty" years. Yet not a single trace of such a group has ever been recovered.

Most telling in this regard is the archaeological history of Tell el-Qudeirat, identified as ancient Kadesh-Barnea. The excavations of this site, which is located in the northern Sinai, have recovered nothing pre-dating the tenth–ninth centuries BC (M. Dothan 1977; Cohen 1997). Kadesh-Barnea played a major role in the biblical traditions of the Exodus and wilderness wanderings (Num. 13: 26; 20: 1, 14). But the lack of material remains at this site that can be dated any earlier than the tenth century raises serious questions regarding the historicity of these traditions (cf. Dever 1997b: 72–3). Trying to explain this lack of evidence as what one should expect of a group *wandering* around a desert is more question begging than a valid objection. Furthermore, such a solution ignores the fact that according to the Bible *millions* of people were involved! Surely, if this event as described in the Bible actually happened, *something* of the presence of so many people would have turned up by now, if nothing more than camp sites with datable pottery. My point is, such an event might have taken place, but there is absolutely no indisputable archaeological evidence to support such a conclusion.

When the archaeological problems surrounding the "Conquest" traditions in the biblical books of Numbers and Joshua are added to the above evidence, the argument for a historical exodus of biblical proportions becomes even less convincing. The scholarly paradigm for understanding the origin of ancient Israel has changed dramatically in the last few years, thanks to both recent archaeological data and newer literary approaches to the biblical texts (for an example of the latter, see Exum and Clines 1993). While final conclusions concerning an Israelite exodus from Egypt need to be left open, and some new evidence yet to be discovered could change the current picture, it is becoming more and more obvious that if there is any "historical kernel" to a story about some "Israelites" coming out of Egypt at the end of the thirteenth (or any other) century BC, it bears little resemblance to the biblical version – cf. Redford (1997), who argued that the entire biblical story dates to the Persian period. One of today's leading Near Eastern archaeologists, W. G. Dever, has recently declared that the question of the historicity of the Exodus is a "dead issue" (1997b: 81). Whether one agrees with Dever or not, it is simply no longer possible to harmonize (as Malamat and others have tried to do) or to reconcile the biblical and archaeological versions of what happened (Ward 1997).

Chapter 7

Iron Age I (*ca.* 1200–1000 BC)

> The problem raised by the settlement of the Israelites in Canaan and the growth of the system of the twelve tribes is the most difficult problem in the whole history of Israel.
>
> (P. de Vaux, 1978)

The Iron Age in Palestine is conveniently divided into two major periods of disproportionate lengths: Iron Age I (IA I) from around 1200 – 1000 BC; and Iron Age II (IA II), from 1000 to 587/40 BC. Iron Age II will be discussed in the next chapter. While the absolute chronology for Iron Age I is still debated by archaeologists and historians, and different dates are still proposed, the date given above will be assumed for this discussion. Both archaeological and historical arguments can be presented to support this date – at least, in part.

During this 200-year period, major socio-political changes took place in Palestine. These changes included the weakening, and ultimate withdrawal, of the Egyptian presence in the region; the appearance in the coastal regions of the Sea Peoples, especially the Philistines; and the construction of hundreds of small villages and hamlets in the Central Highlands by peoples whose descendants 200 years later would be forged into the political state of "Israel" by David. Accordingly, some experts would consider the Iron Age I period to coincide with the biblical era of the "Judges" (for example, Stager 1985). The Iron Age II period would then begin with the founding of the United Monarchy by David. This period would end with the catastrophe in Judah brought on by the Babylonians in 587/86 BC.

Much of the absolute chronology for Palestine during the Iron Age I is linked to that of Egypt. This includes specifically the dates for the Nineteenth and Twentieth Dynasties. However, the dates assigned to the pharaohs of these dynasties are also debated by authorities. To avoid an almost endless discussion of the issues involved, I will follow here the dates recently suggested by the Egyptologist K. Kitchen, which were presented at an international colloquium on absolute chronology held at the University of Gothenberg in August 1987 (Kitchen 1987):

Nineteenth Dynasty	Twentieth Dynasty
Ramesses I: 1295–1294	Setnakht: 1186–1184
Sethos I: 1294–1279	Ramesses III: 1184–1153
Ramesses II: 1279–1213	Ramesses IV: 1153–1147
Merneptah: 1213–1203	Ramesses V: 1147–1143
Sethos II: 1200–1194	(There are other pharaohs in this
Siptah: 1194–1188	dynasty but they do not concern us.)[1]
Tewosret: 1188–1186	

For some experts the Iron Age I is the earliest period to which the term *biblical archaeology* can be applied. The reason is simple: prior to this period there are no "Israelites." This is not to prejudge the now highly debated issue of who built and lived in the Iron Age I villages which are now known to have existed in the Central Highlands of Palestine. Nevertheless, the question of "ethnicity," which has now taken a front seat in the on-going debate over the emergence of "ancient Israel,"[2] has clearly shown how presumptuous earlier studies have been in assuming that the Iron Age I peoples of the highlands belonged to one ethnic group – namely, the Israelites.[3] Suffice it to say that, as more archaeological data become available and as models for interpreting these data become more and more sophisticated, the question of the emergence of ancient Israel will be seen to be a far more complex and multifaceted process than has been heretofore assumed. Here the role of archaeologists will become, if anything, even more important, since the biblical texts recounting Israel's early history are believed by most critics to be late and, in any event, concerned with theological, not historical, questions.

This is not to say that archaeologists who specialize in this area are agreed on the meaning of the material data (see below). That sometimes diametrically opposed conclusions are reached by competent scholars can be a source of frustration and confusion for anyone interested in the subject, especially the beginning student. These differences of opinion should come as a warning that interpretations of archaeological data do not proceed by some fixed formula. Assumptions, personalities, intuition and prior experiences all figure in the equation. "Historical and cultural interpretation of archaeological finds is a vexed and complicated task. Any interpretation involves inferences and deductions, and the same set of data may yield various conclusions" (Finkelstein and Na'aman 1994: 15).

The end of the Late Bronze Age and the beginning of Iron Age I: terminology and dates

Some archaeologists (for example, Aharoni 1978: 153ff.; M. Dothan 1989: 63) have referred to the period under discussion as "Israelite," in contrast to the preceding Bronze Age which is called "Canaanite." To do so is very misleading. Even if it could be concluded, and this is debatable,[4] that the Israelites of the Bible appeared in Canaan for the first time during Iron Age I, many other "ethnic" groups were also there. Among these were Egyptians, Hurrians, Hittites and Sea Peoples, especially the Philistines. Other groups were in the Transjordan (see A. Mazar 1990: 295–6; 1992b: 258–60). Consequently, to refer to the Iron Age I period as "Israelite" is to highlight a bias warranted neither by the archaeological nor the literary evidence.

As mentioned above, the absolute date for the beginning of the Iron I period is debated. While 1200 BC is arbitrary in some respects, it can be justified in part by the fact that by the end of the thirteenth century BC, major political upheavals had occurred or were occurring throughout the ancient Near East. The Hittite empire had collapsed and the Sea Peoples were on the move throughout the Mycenaean world. Ultimately reaching the shores of Canaan, they left a trail of destruction in their wake. During this period many Canaanite cities were destroyed (A. Mazar 1992b: 260–2; cf. Dever 1990a). Furthermore, Cypriot and Mycenaean pottery imports to Canaan ceased, signaling an end to the international trade so prominent during the last stages of the Late Bronze Age.

On the other hand, the material culture known from the first half of the twelfth century BC indicates that the transition to the Iron I period did not take place at the same rate in all parts of the country. Beth Shan, a prominent Egyptian administrative center, was destroyed at the end of the thirteenth century but quickly rebuilt. Finds from this latter stage of occupation include Egyptian material that has been dated to the time of Ramesses III. Using the lower chronology, this would indicate that Egyptian influence continued at this site until at least the middle of the twelfth century. Other sites, such as Lachish and Tell el-Far'ah South also seemed to have been under Egyptian influence during this period. In contrast to these cities, Megiddo, which was also destroyed at the end of the thirteenth century, was rebuilt as a Canaanite city (A. Mazar 1992b: 260–2). Such considerations as the above have prompted some archaeologists to date the last gasp of the Late Bronze Age later than 1200 BC (cf. Dever 1995c: 206). Others have divided the Iron Age I into two subperiods: Iron Age Ia (*ca.* 1200–1150), and Iron Age Ib (*ca.* 1150–1000) (cf. A. Mazar 1992b: 260). For our purposes, we will refer to these 200 years or so simply as Iron Age I. Also it is not possible here, due to space limitations, to describe adequately the Iron I period in terms of its overall material culture. For such descriptions several recent summaries are available. See particularly the following: Finkelstein (1995); Fritz (1987a); Finkelstein and Na'aman (1994); A. Mazar (1990: 295–367; 1992b).

Rather, I will focus on two of the major social/political realities that emerged in Palestine during this period: the arrival and establishment of the so-called "Sea Peoples," especially the Philistines; and the emergence of many villages and hamlets in the Central Highlands. The discussion of this latter Iron I phenomenon will allow us to face squarely the much debated, as well as disputed, notion of a "conquest" of Canaan by the "Israelites."

"Sea Peoples"/Philistines

Much has been written concerning the arrival and settlement of the "Sea Peoples" in the coastal region of Palestine. It is usually argued that they came in two waves, the first during the first quarter of the twelfth century. Their arrival is earmarked by the presence of a particular kind of pottery called Mycenaean IIIC:1B, which has been discovered at such sites as Akko, Ashdod and Tell Miqne-Ekron (T. Dothan 1989, 1990; M. Dothan 1989; Stager 1995; Gitin and T. Dothan 1987). From wherever they came – the Aegean and/or Anatolian regions are usually suggested (T. Dothan 1982: 21–3) – they were stopped from invading Egypt by Ramesses III in the eighth year of his reign (*ca.* 1175 BC). This battle was recorded on Ramesses III's temple walls at Medinet Habu in Thebes, where five different groups of Sea Peoples are identified: Philistines, Tjeker, Shekelesh, Denye (Danaoi) and the Weshesh (Wilson, *ANET*, p. 202; fig. 6.1). Of these five groups, the most famous, and the only one mentioned in the Bible, is the Philistines. However, according to the story of Wen-Amon (*ANET*, pp. 25–9), which has been dated to *ca.* 1100 BC, the Tjeker settled at Dor, which is located on the northern coast of Palestine. Furthermore, M. Dothan has argued (1989) that the Shardina (Sherden), also among the Sea Peoples, arrived in Palestine as early as the fourteenth century and occupied the city of Akko and its vicinity. Apparently the Tjeker and the Shardina were no match for the Philistines and soon were either absorbed by them or by the local Canaanite population (cf. Singer 1994: 298; T. Dothan 1982: 1–2).

The Philistines[5]

Beginning sometime during the first half of the twelfth century BC, the Philistines began to dominate the coastal region of Palestine. For more than 100 years they would be the military and political force to be reckoned with, as the emerging clans of "Israelites" in the Central Highlands would discover. While the ultimate origin of the Philistines is still unknown,[6] they were part of the larger movement of Sea Peoples discussed above. There are three primary sources for reconstructing their history: Egyptian records, the Bible and archaeological discoveries.

Textual Evidence

According to the Egyptian texts at Medinet Habu, the Philistines were among the Sea Peoples defeated by Ramesses III around 1175 BC. The reliefs on the walls have been interpreted as depicting both a land and sea battle, assuming that the Sea Peoples arrived in Canaan by both routes (see Figure 7.1). After his victory, Ramesses III supposedly recruited many of the survivors as mercenaries, many of whom were stationed in garrisons in Palestine at such sites as Beth Shan and Tell el-Far'ah South. This tactic by Ramesses has been viewed as the way the Egyptians exercised control over the major roadways of the time (see T. Dothan 1982: 1–13, including reproductions of the scenes from the temple's walls; cf. Singer 1994: 290ff.).

This traditional interpretation has recently been challenged (Stager 1995, with full references; cf. Wood 1991) by studies which have concluded that the Philistines, as well as other Sea Peoples, came by ship only. Furthermore, it is not clear to what extent, if any, the Philistines and others were stationed in Palestine as Egyptian mercenaries. What seems now more likely to have been the case was the establishment of a Philistine center of influence in southern Canaan emanating from the five Philistine city-states. Here they remained a major power until defeated by David at the beginning of the tenth century BC. This more recent interpretation raises serious questions regarding the historical

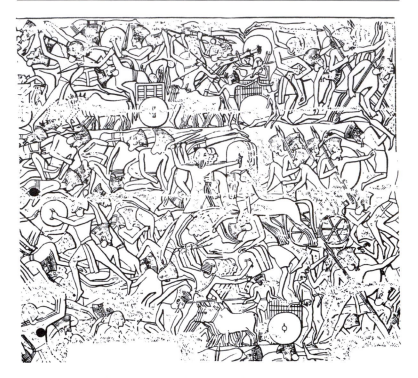

Figure 7.1 Scene showing the battle between Ramesses III and the Sea Peoples. From T. Dothan, *The Philistines and their Material Culture*, Israel Exploration Society

validity of the Medinet Habu wall scenes. If the Philistines, as well as other Sea Peoples, were devastated by the Egyptians as the inscriptions at Medinet Habu and elsewhere (see "Papyrus Harris I" in *ANET*, p. 262) indicate, how is it that in such a short period of time the Philistines became the major political power in Canaan as both the biblical texts and the archeological data suggest?

In the Bible, the Philistines, for the most part, are treated contemptuously. This contempt is most vividly displayed in passages that describe them as "uncircumcised" (Judg. 14: 3; 15: 18; I Sam. 17: 26; 18: 25), as well as in the story of Ahaziah (a son of Jezebel?) in 2 Kings 1, where the god of Ekron, Baal-zebul ("princely Lord"), is mocked as "Baal-zebub" ("lord of the flies"). But in spite of the low esteem in which the Philistines were held by the Israelites, the biblical references to these people do furnish some clues concerning Philistine culture.

Political organization

The Philistine political structure centered around the five city-states of Ashkelon, Ashdod, Gaza, Gath and Ekron (cf. Josh 13: 3; Figure 7.2). The reference in Judges 3: 3 (cf. I Sam. 6: 4, 16) to the "five lords of the Philistines" is an apparent reference to the rulers of each of these cities. Furthermore, while the details of the procedure are not clear, according to I Samuel 29: 1–7, these "lords" could sit in council and override the decision of a single lord or tyrant. The word translated *lord* in the Hebrew text is the plural of the word סרן (*seren*) and is believed to be a Philistine loan word (Singer 1994: 335). The term is used in the Bible only in reference to the Philistines and may have in its background the Doric Greek word τυραννος (*turannos*), which was applied to anyone who had made himself king by force. If this derivation is true, it would be another bit of evidence pointing to the Aegean origin of the Philistines.[7] The lack of any substantial Philistine inscriptions may indicate the rapidity with which they began to adopt the Canaanite language as their own. This may be one of the reasons for their cultural decline (Singer 1994: 335ff.).

Military organization

It is also from the Bible that clues regarding their military makeup and strength are found. According to I Samuel 13: 5, the Philistine army was composed of charioteers and horsemen (however, the numbers given may be an exaggeration). Elsewhere (I Sam. 31: 3) archers are mentioned and, of course, there would have been foot soldiers. If the description of Goliath's armor (I Sam. 17: 5–7) was typical of others, the Philistine warriors were also well armed. According to this description (the literary nature of the story notwithstanding), all of the metal in Goliath's armor was made of bronze, except for the head of his spear, which is described as weighing 600 shekels of iron, or about 15 pounds! It has been commonly held that the Philistines had a monopoly on ironwork, especially in light of I Samuel 13: 19–22. However, recent studies have called this conclusion into question (Singer 1994: 314).

Religion

What is known of the Philistine cult from the material remains so far discovered will be examined below. Little information is given in the Bible. This little, however, would lead one to conclude that they quickly

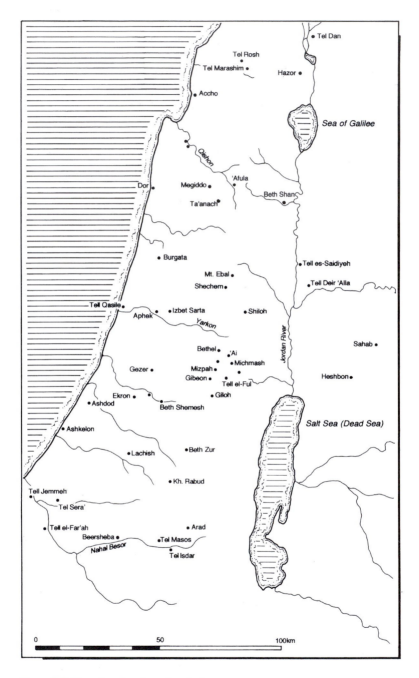

Figure 7.2 Map showing Iron Age I sites

adopted local Canaanite cults, for all of their gods mentioned in the Bible have Semitic names. In addition, different deities seem to have been worshiped in different city-states. Dagon is said to have been worshiped at Ashdod (I Sam. 5: 1–5) but Baal Zebub (Zebul) at Ekron (2 Kings 1: 1–4). However, the archaeological evidence clearly indicates that they also brought at least some of their indigenous religious practices with them (see below).

Thus, however biased it might be in some respects, the Bible presents the Philistines as well organized politically and militarily and as a people who quickly adapted to their new homeland. This adaptation also apparently included both Canaanite religion and language. The Bible, of course, is not concerned with the cultural achievements of the Philistines but with the political and military threat which they represented with respect to the Israelites. The extent of their cultural superiority, at least during most of the Iron Age I period, is made abundantly clear by the archaeological remains.

Archaeological remains

The body of archaeological remains identified as Philistine is constantly expanding due to on-going excavations (see note 6). In her 1982 study, T. Dothan identified some forty sites in Palestine known to contain Philistine remains (for a map of these sites see T. Dothan 1982: 26). Among their most distinctive cultural products is their pottery.

Philistine pottery

Clearly, one of the most distinctive material remains of these people is their pottery (Figure 7.3). It should come as no surprise, therefore, that this material has received much attention from archaeologists (see now esp. T. Dothan 1982: chap. 3). This bichrome ware (usually black and red) contains many interesting motifs, including friezes with spirals, interlocking semicircles and checkerboards. But perhaps the most distinctive feature is birds, very often portrayed with their heads turned backwards. The ceramic repertoire includes bowls, kraters, stirrup jars, amphoriskoi, pyxis, jugs made with strainer-spouts, juglets, cylindrical bottles and horn-shaped vessels.

These pottery remains, as well as others, are attributed to the Philistines for three reasons (T. Dothan 1982: 94–6). First, the geographical distribution of this pottery accords well with what is known of the Philistine settlement pattern. The ceramic remains are concentrated in

Figure 7.3 Philistine pottery. From T. Dothan, *The Philistines and their Material Culture*, © Israel Exploration Society, 1982

the coastal region and on the borders of the Hill Country, but appear only sporadically in the Central Hill Country (see T. Dothan's map in 1982: 26). Second, the stratigraphy of the sites associated with this pottery clearly indicate that it first appeared on the Palestinian coast during the first half of the twelfth century BC. This date parallels the Egyptian date of Ramesses' confrontation (however much it may have been exaggerated) with the Sea Peoples. Third, a comparison of the ceramic styles that make up much of the corpus links it to the Aegean area from which the Philistines are believed to have come. At the same time, neutron activation analysis of the clay has conclusively shown that the pottery was locally made. This implies that the pottery was made by local craftsmen who knew the styles, and that it was not imported (for the pottery from Ekron, see Gunneweg *et al.* 1986).

The ceramic corpus of the Philistines is also very eclectic, reflecting Mycenaean (Aegean), Cypriot, Egyptian and local Canaanite influence (for a complete description, with many illustrations of all of these influences, see T. Dothan 1982: 132–55). One of the styles attributed to local Canaanite culture is the so-called "beer jug." This vessel has a strainer or sieve built into the vessel which was thought to have served the purpose of straining out the grains used in beer manufacturing. However, it has recently been argued that these vessels were used to serve wine, not beer (Stager 1995: 345).

Burial practices

When burials associated with the Philistines first began to be found at such sites as Beth Shan and Tel el-Far'ah South, it was assumed that the distinctive anthropoid clay coffins (Figure 7.4) found in these burials originated with them (see T. Dothan 1982: 252–88; A. Mazar 1990: 326–7; Dothan and Dothan 1992: 57–73). However, more recent excavations, especially at Deir el-Balah, located on the coast some 25 miles south of Ashkelon, have shown that the tradition of burial in anthropoid clay coffins came from Egypt and preceded the arrival of the Sea Peoples (Dothan and Dothan 1992: 202–8, see esp. 207; Stager 1995: 341–2; for a map of sites where such coffins have been found see T. Dothan 1982: 253). All of this implies that the Philistines adopted this burial practice very quickly, just as they did other aspects of the local culture.

Architectural remains

The clearest examples of Philistine architecture have come from the excavations at Tell Qasile, Ashdod, Ashkelon and Ekron. Although final conclusions must be made with caution due to limited exposure of Philistine strata, enough has been found to conclude that the Philistines imposed upon their new homeland building styles which they brought with them (Stager 1995: 345–8). At Ashkelon, Stager has discovered a public building that went through several phases, similar to such buildings found at Ashdod, Tell Qasile and Ekron (1995: 346). He has

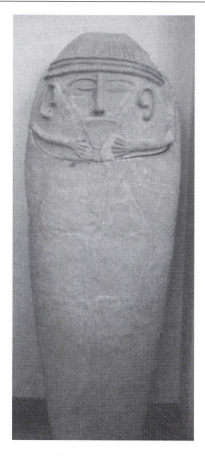

Figure 7.4 Anthropoid clay coffin. Photo J. Laughlin

tentatively associated this building with a weaving industry because of more than 150 clay spool weights found in it.

At Ekron (Figure 7.5), the site reflecting the clearest example of Philistine architectural planning, public buildings have been found in the center of the site (T. Dothan 1990; T. Dothan and Gitin 1990; Gitin and T. Dothan 1987). What has been described as a "well-planned monumental building" and identified as possibly a governor's residence or palace (Gitin and T. Dothan 1987: 205) was found in Field IV, located in the center of the city. This building contained several rooms, two of which have been associated with cultic practices. Of particular interest are the remains of a round hearth that were found in a courtyard

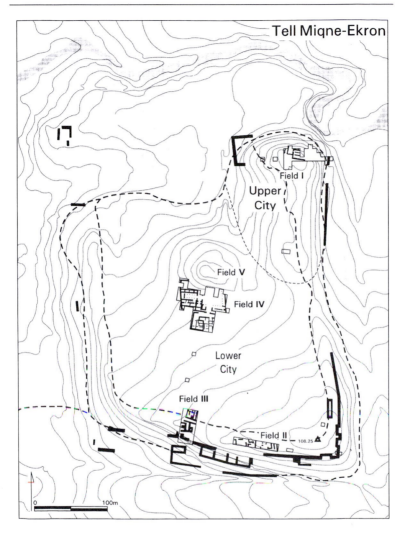

Figure 7.5 Topographic map of Tell Miqne-Ekron. © Tell-Miqne-Ekron
Excavations, J. Rosenberg

connected to the above two rooms. Such hearths are thought to have
been the main architectural feature of megaron buildings found in the
Aegean world (Figure 7.6; T. Dothan 1990: 35; Dothan and Dothan
1992: 242–4 and plates 24, 25, 26). Only in two other Philistine sites
have such hearths been discovered: Tell Qasile (A. Mazar 1985) and
Ashkelon (T. Dothan 1982: 205).

Figure 7.6 Reconstruction of a Greek hearth. Courtesy of J. Fitzgerald

What have been identified as remains of private houses have been discovered at several sites, including Ashdod and Tell Qasile. They were built of mudbrick and consisted of several rooms each. At Tell Qasile there is evidence of a pillar building (A. Mazar 1990: 319). Because this site was first occupied by the Philistines, such an architectural style may have been brought with them. Similar pillar buildings have been found at other sites not normally associated with the Philistines, such as 'Ai, Bethel, Raddana and Gibeon. 'Ai and Raddana are of particular importance since both sites are sealed loci stratigraphically, with no preceding Late or Middle Bronze Age remains. Such evidence, along with other artifacts (see below) imply that the occupants of these Iron Age I Central Highland villages had more in common with the Philistine inhabitants of the coastal region than with desert nomads from the east.

Philistine religion

Except for the brief and inconclusive biblical texts mentioned above, the only other evidence for Philistine religion is in the archaeological evidence, especially evidence from Ashdod, Tell Qasile and Ekron. From Ashdod comes the now famous "Ashdoda," a small female figurine attached to a table (throne?) representation (Figure 7.7; Dothan and Dothan 1992: 153–7; M. Dothan 1971; T. Dothan 1982: 234–7). This object, along with other broken heads and chairs of similar figurines, led the excavator to conclude that during the first half of the twelfth century BC, the Philistines still worshiped the so-called "Great Mother" of the Mycenaean world. Other finds are clay figurines interpreted as "mourning" women (A. Mazar 1990: 323, fig. 8.16). How such items

Figure 7.7 The "Ashdoda". Courtesy of J. Fitzgerald

were actually used, if at all, in Philistine cultic practices is not known. From Tell Qasile comes the only completely excavated *temenos* (sacred area) of a Philistine site (A. Mazar 1997: 374–6). During the 12th–11th centuries (Strata XII–X), the buildings in the sacred area underwent constant changes. What has been identified as a large temple (25.5 feet by 28 feet outer dimensions) in Stratum XI consisted of several rooms and a large courtyard (Figure 7.8). In the courtyard was found a pit that contained many bones as well as discarded vessels, many of which were characterized as "cultic." The excavator concluded that the architectural styles involved in this complex are unknown in Canaanite structures.

Among the cult objects recovered is a plaque with representations of what have been identified as goddesses, an anthropomorphic female libation vessel, a lion-shaped cup, cylindrical stands decorated with animal and human motifs, as well as offering bowls decorated with images of birds (A. Mazar 1990: 325, figs. 8.17, 18). However, there was no trace of the "Ashdoda" cult found at Tell Qasile (Dothan and Dothan

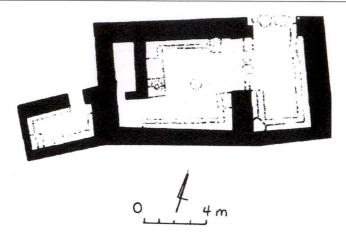

Figure 7.8 Plan of the Philistine temple from Tell Qasile. Courtesy of
J. Fitzgerald

1992: 232). Another interesting object is a bimetal knife (the blade is
of iron, while the rivets that are attached it to its handle are of bronze)
with an ivory handle. A similar knife has been discovered at Ekron
(T. Dothan 1990: 31, 33; Dothan and Dothan 1992: plates 29, 30). With
the destruction of Stratum X, perhaps by David, the heyday of Tell
Qasile came to a close.

At Ekron (Tel Miqne) a major Philistine city has come to light (Figure
7.5). Fortified with a mudbrick wall over 10 feet thick (Dothan and
Dothan 1992: 239), the city covered over 50 acres and included an
industrial zone; an area with public buildings, including one identified
as a sanctuary; and a domestic area (for a general description with
photos and drawings, see T. Dothan 1987; 1990; Dothan and Dothan
1992: 239–57). In the sanctuary building, which went through two
phases, was found the hearth, mentioned above, and many small objects,
some of which have been linked to the Philistine cult. Among these
objects are three bronze wheels with spokes and part of a frame with
a loop interpreted as a hole for an axle (T. Dothan 1990: 30–5; Dothan
and Dothan 1992: 248–50). Unique among finds in Palestine, such
objects have been discovered in Cyprus. T. Dothan has pointed out
that the description of the laver stands made for Solomon by Hiram,
King of Tyre (I Kings 7: 27–33) includes a reference to "bronze wheels
and axles of bronze" (v. 30). Another important discovery is a bimetal
knife similar to that from Tell Qasile mentioned above. What cultic or
ceremonial significance it may have had is not clear. Three other handles

dated to the first half of the twelfth century BC were also found. During the last phase (Stratum IV – late eleventh to early tenth century BC) of this building, the hearth was no longer used and many small finds point to increased Egyptian influence. By the time of its destruction in the first half of the tenth century, Ekron had already lost much of its Philistine distinctiveness (T. Dothan 1990: 25–36; Dothan and Dothan 1992: 250–3).

The end

From the textual and archaeological evidence, it can be concluded that the Philistines were a highly organized, militarily superior and economically sophisticated people for 150 years whose cultural achievements far exceeded that of any other known group in Palestine during Iron Age I. Their ceramic, architectural and industrial remains testify to a highly industrious and artistic people, which once and for all should destroy the popular connotation of crudeness and cultural unsophistication associated with the word "Philistine." Furthermore, what is known of their burial practices and domestic remains indicate that they often achieved wealth and status, for only such people could have afforded the kind of houses they lived in and the tombs they were buried in.

Even though it is now known both archaeologically and textually (Jer. 25: 20; Zeph. 2: 4; Zech. 9: 5–8) that the Philistines existed throughout the Iron Age II period (see now Stone 1995), by the middle of the tenth century, if not earlier, they seemed to have lost most of their cultural uniqueness. As they began with such wealth, craftsmanship and political and military superiority, how did this happen? Part of their demise, no doubt, was brought about by their defeat by the Israelites. But this in itself seems insufficient to explain their rapid decline. The clue, I think, lies in the two things known the least about them: their original language and religion. While ethnic identity is a complex subject, certainly language and religion play a role. The Philistines seem to have been as eclectic in these areas as they were with their pottery styles. This eclecticism enabled them to assimilate fairly rapidly to Canaanite culture, but such assimilation also robbed them of much of their original identity. The land which they shared with the Israelites ultimately became their cultural grave. Fittingly enough, the name by which this land has been known for at least 2000 years, "Palestine," stands today as their epitaph.

The emergence of early "Israel"

Of all the problems facing archaeologists and biblical historians, none has been more difficult and vexing, controversial and debated, than that of the "conquest of Canaan" by the people the Bible calls "Israelites." For the most part, the story told in the Bible primarily in the books of Numbers and Joshua, is straightforward and matter-of-fact.

After their exodus from Egypt under the leadership of Moses and their miraculous escape from the Reed ("Red") Sea, the Israelites were terrified by the reports of spies who were sent out to reconnoiter Canaan. Told that giants were in the land (Num. 13–14), the people rebelled against Moses and Aaron and made plans to return to Egypt. Finally, they agreed to invade Canaan from the south, only to be defeated by the Amalekites and Canaanites (Num. 14: 45). Condemned to wander around the desert for "forty years," they encountered various groups of people with whom they had armed conflict. Among these were the King of Arad, the Amorites and the King of Bashan (Num. 21). By the end of the book of Numbers, the Israelites are said to have been massed in the Transjordan opposite Jericho. Following the death of Moses, and under the leadership of Joshua, they invaded the land of Canaan (Josh. 1–12), organizing their attack into three phases: (1) the Central Hill Country, including Jericho and 'Ai (Josh. 6–10); (2) a southern campaign, defeating Libnah, Eglon, Hebron and Debir (Josh. 10: 29–43); and (3) a northern assault that resulted in the destruction of Hazor (Josh. 11: 1–15). Thus we are told that within a space of five years (Josh. 14: 7, 10): "Joshua defeated the whole land, the Hill Country and the Negev and the lowland and the slopes, and all their kings; he left no one remaining , but utterly destroyed all that breathed, as the LORD God of Israel commanded" (Josh. 10: 40).

The clear impression one gets from this story is that a united Israel attacked Canaan from the east and that the defeat of its inhabitants, at least in the Central Highlands, was sudden, swift and complete. That something is seriously wrong with this picture is an understatement.

Because of space limitations, it is impossible to present here an in-depth discussion of the many problems and proposed solutions facing the serious student of this biblical scenario. Furthermore, any attempt to simplify such a complex issue is done so at the risk of considerable distortion. Nevertheless, such a risk must now be taken.

There are two totally separate issues here. First, there are the biblical stories themselves. The textual compilations of Numbers, Joshua and Judges have long, complex histories according to most literary critics.

The overriding consensus is that these texts were written late in Israel's history (most likely during the post-exilic period, including Judges 1; see P. K. McCarter, Jr 1992: 119–22), are primarily theologically motivated and must therefore be used with extreme caution, if at all, in any attempt to reconstruct the early history of Israel. Nevertheless, the stories of "Israel's" sojourn in Egypt, its miraculous escape under Moses, the covenant forged at Sinai/Horeb and the forceful entry into the land are the *sine qua non* of the biblical authors' presentation of their history.

However, new archaeological data that have come to light over the past several years have raised serious questions concerning the historicity of this central biblical story. It is with these data that I will be primarily concerned here. As always, readers should remind themselves constantly that any and all attempts to evaluate these sources, both textually and archaeologically, with the goal of reconstructing the actual process by which "Israel" came to occupy the land of Canaan involves significant amounts of subjective judgments regardless of the final interpretation one chooses to embrace (see now the programmatic essay by Dever 1992c).

Models for interpreting "Israel's" occupation of Canaan

Before the mid-1980s

Prior to the 1980s there were basically three models touted for interpreting the "conquest." Since these views are so well known, they will be given the briefest of summaries here.

ALBRIGHT'S MILITARY MODEL

One of the most influential theories put forth to explain the "conquest" is that of the late W. F. Albright. A professor for many years at Johns Hopkins University, Albright knew there were inconsistencies and other problems in the biblical stories. Nevertheless, he believed that these stories were essentially historical in character, and he used what was beginning to be known from archaeological excavations to support his interpretation. In particular, he cited such evidence as was then known from Lachish (Josh. 10: 31–32), Bethel (Judg. 1: 22f.), and Tell Beit Mirsim, which he identified with ancient Debir (Josh. 10: 38–39 – an identification which is disputed today), to support his interpretation. All of these sites were destroyed at the end of the Late Bronze Age, or in the case of Lachish, in the middle of the twelfth century BC. If Tell Beit Mirsim is not ancient Debir, then it is an unidentified site that also suffered destruction at this time.

Albright's reconstruction has had wide-ranging influence, especially in America, because it seemed as if he had demonstrated that archaeology could be used to support the biblical stories. For reasons to be discussed below, there is virtually no part of his reconstruction that is still taken seriously by archaeologists and historians today. To quote one well-known American archaeologist: "a decade of intensive, multidisciplinary field excavation and survey, mostly carried out by Israeli archaeologists, has swept away 'conquest models' completely. . . . Today no reputable Biblical scholar or archaeologist anywhere would espouse Albright's views" (Dever 1993c: 33;[8] see also Dever's comments in 1992c).

ALT'S MIGRATION MODEL

While Albright and his students, particularly G. E. Wright (1957) and John Bright (1981), were formulating and defending the "military conquest" model in America, an entirely different approach was being advocated in Germany by Albrecht Alt (1968: 173–221) and his students, the most notable of whom was M. Noth (1960: 68–84). These scholars were not archaeologists but skilled literary critics. They concluded that the stories of the conquest in Joshua and elsewhere were for the most part aetiological legends with little historical value. Israel emerged in the land of Canaan through peaceful infiltration of pastoral groups or nomads over a long period of time. One of the major strengths of this theory is its recognition that the "Israelite" settlement was a long, complicated and multifaceted process. However, Alt's theory of the origin of these "Israelites" has been seriously questioned (for a critique of this, and the other theories presented here, see, with references, Finkelstein 1988: 295–314; 1995: 363;[9] see also Dever 1992c for critiques of all of these models).

THE "PEASANTS' REVOLT" OF G. MENDENHALL

In 1962, Mendenhall, of the University of Michigan, wrote what has become a widely read and debated article, entitled "The Hebrew Conquest of Palestine." In this essay he argued that the so-called conquest of Palestine by Israel was actually a "peasants' revolt against the network of interlocking Canaanite city-states" (1970: 107). According to Mendenhall, this revolt was triggered by a small group of slaves who had escaped from Egypt to Canaan bringing with them the worship of a deity named YHWH. This small religious group was then able to polarize the indigenous population of Canaan – namely, the peasants – who in the main joined forces with this group, and attacked the city-state kings who opposed them. In the end, the peasants won, and the kings and their supporters were either driven out of the land or killed.

This seminal essay, while receiving support from some quarters, has not been accepted by many authorities. For one thing, it is known that many Canaanite cities located in the coastal region of the country were not destroyed at this time but should have been if there had occurred a universal revolt of the masses. For another, of the cities which were destroyed, many are believed to have been done so by the Philistines or even the Egyptians. In addition, the general breakdown and disruption of societies at the end of the Late Bronze Age resulted in the movements of any number of other peoples besides the Sea Peoples. Thus none of the destructions in Canaan needs to be assigned to a revolt of peasants (see Dever in Shanks 1992: 29–30). Furthermore, this "internal revolt" model does not explain at all the biblical emphasis that the "Israelites" came from outside the land. Nevertheless, in many respects, this model can be supported by current archaeological data (see Dever 1992c: 553).

After the mid-1980s

What has happened since about the mid-1980s as a result of regional surveys, archaeological excavations, and demographic and ethnographic studies is nothing short of a revolution in the understanding of the emergence of early "Israel." In fact, these developments are so recent and so "revolutionary" for understanding Israel's origins, with profound implications for understanding the biblical story, that they have not, to my knowledge, been integrated into the mainstream of scholarly discussion. However, there is anything but scholarly agreement on some of the key issues.[10]

The catalyst for starting much of this discussion was the publication of I. Finkelstein's book, *The Archaeology of the Israelite Settlement*, in 1988 (see Dever's review 1991c). Using new data from excavations, surveys and demographic studies, Finkelstein showed that there were hundreds (more than 300, p. 333) of new villages or hamlets that had sprung up in the Central Hill Country of Canaan during the Iron Age I

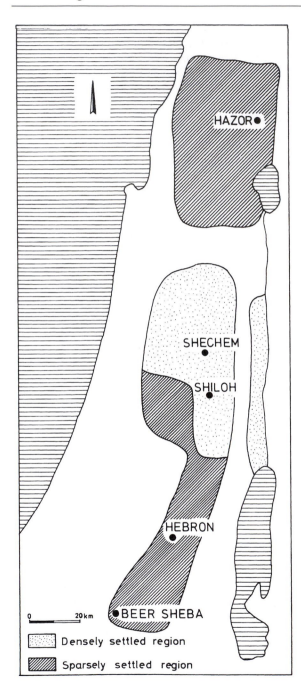

Figure 7.9 Map of the "Israelite" settlement, end of Iron Age I. From Israel Finkelstein, *The Archaeology of the Israelite Settlement,* © Israel Exploration Society, Jerusalem, 1988

(Figure 7.9). Furthermore, the major settled area was the northern part of the Hill Country, located between Jerusalem and the Jezreel Valley. Judah, at the beginning of the period (*ca.* 1200 BC) was virtually uninhabited and remained so until the tenth century BC (Finkelstein 1988: 326ff.). Furthermore, Finkelstein estimated the entire population of the Hill Country peoples to be no more than 50,000, if not fewer (p. 333), a remarkably small number when compared with the millions who supposedly left Egypt with Moses only "forty" years earlier (Exod. 12: 37; Num. 1: 45–46).

Other studies (Stager 1985; Coote 1990: 13–139) have also argued that the people who moved into the highlands were farmers and horticulturists, not nomadic raiders from the east. Architectural structures, especially the famous "four-room house," which only a short time ago was identified as "Israelite," are now known to have few or no ethnic implications (Finkelstein 1988: 254–9; 1996: 200, 204; D. R. Clark 1996; London 1989: 47–8). The same can be said for the equally famous "collared rim store jar," once thought to be a distinctive Israelite ceramic form.[11] Other technological remains, such as plastered water cisterns and hillside terracing, have been interpreted to mean that a non-nomadic population inhabited these Iron I villages. These, and other archaeological data, have led Dever to conclude that the Iron I inhabitants of these Central Hill villages were anything but invading nomads from the desert, as portrayed in the Bible. Rather, they "appear to be skilled and well-adapted peasant farmers, long familiar with local conditions in Canaan" (Dever 1992c: 549–50).

This does not mean that all archaeologists are agreed on what all of this means. The question seems to be whether these technologies should be interpreted as innovations that made the settlement of the Central Hill Country possible, or as outcomes of the settlement process.[12] In any event, whether one interprets these new data as innovations, outcomes or both, the important point is that the people(s) who built, lived and worked in these Central Hill villages during Iron Age I were not nomadic invaders from the desert.

This new evidence raises many questions regarding these people(s), not the least of which being who they were and from where they came. Until recently it was assumed by most scholars that the Iron I inhabitants were Israelites. A cursory look at even recent publications will reveal this uncritically held assumption (For example, T. Dothan 1985: 165; Stager 1985; London 1989; Gal 1992: 84–93). But thanks to the pioneering efforts of archaeologists such as Dever and Finkelstein, this is no longer acceptable. The ethnic identity of these peoples must be proven by evidence, not simply assumed to be "Israelites" based upon a non-critical reading of the biblical texts.

Finkelstein has shown that the occupation of the Central Highlands beginning in Iron Age I was but the third period for the occupation of this region, the other two having occurred during the Early Bronze I period (*ca.* 3200–2900 BC), when some eighty-eight sites were occupied , and during the Middle Bronze II period (*ca.* 2000–1550 BC) when some 248 sites were inhabited (1994; 1995; 1996: 199ff.). From this long-term perspective, Finkelstein has concluded that throughout the late fourth millennium to the end of the second millennium BC, pastoral groups had become sedentarized in the highlands. Thus, the people who settled there (including the Transjordan) during Iron Age I were involved in a process which "was part of a cyclic mechanism of alternating processes of sedentarization and nomadization of indigenous groups in response to changing political, economic, and social circumstances" (1996: 208). In other words, the inhabitants of these Iron I villages were resedentarized pastoral nomads, with no or little connection with the lowland Canaanite populations (1995: 363). Who these resedentarized people were ethnically is difficult to say, according to Finkelstein. In his earlier work (1988), he too referred to them as "Israelites." Of late, however (1994; 1995; and esp. 1996), he has used the term "proto-Israelite," first suggested, as far as I can tell, by Dever (in Shanks 1992c and elsewhere). Except for vague references to "pastoral nomads" or "transhumant groups," Finkelstein did not suggest who exactly these "proto-Israelites" might have been (1996: 208). For him, the "real Israel" does not emerge before the ninth–eighth century BC (1996: 209). Furthermore, the only material remains Finkelstein thought may have ethnic implications are pig bones, or rather the lack of them, in the case of the Central Hill villages (1995: 365). What does all of this have to do with the biblical story of Israel's entry into Canaan?

> It is therefore evident that the emergence of Israel was not a unique, meta-historical episode in the history of a chosen people, but rather part of a much broader historical process that took place in the Ancient Near East, a process that brought about the destruction of the *ancien régime* [emphasis his] and the rise of a new order, of national, territorial states.... *The combination of archaeological and historical research demonstrates that the biblical account of the conquest of Canaan is entirely divorced from historical reality* [emphasis mine]. The late date and literary-theological character of the biblical accounts calls for a cautious, critical and multi-faceted preliminary analysis, before

any conclusion may be drawn about their possible contribution to deciphering of the early history of Israel.

(Finkelstein and Na'aman 1994: 12–13; see also
Finkelstein 1996: 203)

Although Dever (1993b: 26*; 1995c – both with earlier references) has agreed with Finkelstein that the Iron I village people were not nomads invading from the east, he has disagreed with Finkelstein completely on the question of their origin. For Dever, most of the Iron I Central Hill villagers came from the already sedentary Canaanite population (Dever 1992c; 1993b: 26*ff.; 1995c), not from non-sedentarized pastoralists.[13] It is these Hill Country newcomers whom Dever has labeled "Proto-Israelites," who were "the ancestors of later Israel" (1993b: 31*; but cf. his comments in 1995c). From other defining characteristics of the Hill Country culture – such as their settlement types (small rural villages and hamlets); an increase in population that cannot be accounted for by natural growth alone; an economy based on farming and animal husbandry; a village layout that included the four-room courtyard house, often with plastered cisterns for water storage; the use of silos to store grain; and hillside terracing – Dever concluded that these people were "mostly not invaders, political refugees, revolutionaries, 'social bandits,' or the like, but simply immigrants from elsewhere in Canaan, most of them apparently experienced farmers and stockbreeders" (1995c: 208).[14] For Dever, using the ethnic term *Israelite* (or at least *proto-Israelite*) to refer to the Iron I century Hill Country people is as justifiable as using other ethnic terms such as *Canaanite*, *Egyptian* and *Philistine* (1995c: 209).

It is not likely that the issues in this debate between Dever and Finkelstein (as well as others) will be resolved to everyone's satisfaction, especially since they themselves seem unable to agree on one of the most basic of the questions: What counts for an ethnic marker and what doesn't? Although Dever has admitted the impasse caused by experts who cannot agree on the meaning of the evidence, he has offered little in the way of solving it except to bemoan the fact that there are no "agreed upon ground rules" (1993b: 30*). Until such ground rules are specified and adhered to, no agreement among qualified experts seems likely.

Conclusions

While there may never be total agreement among scholars on the question of the emergence of "Israel" vis-à-vis the material remains of the Central Hill villages of Palestine now known to have existed during the Iron Age I period, there is enough at least to point to some conclusions regarding the biblical version of Israel's occupation of the land.[15] First, all interpretations of a full-scale military invasion by desert nomads, be they "Israelites" or any other group, have been proven false. Thus, any attempt to interpret the biblical stories literally is doomed to failure. The cost in human suffering and death through the millennia by those who have literally interpreted this "holy war" mentality to support wars of their own is incalculable.

Second, if it can be reasonably assumed that the Iron I inhabitants of the Central Hill country formed the gene pool from which the later "biblical Israel" arose, then Israel's direct ancestors were a diverse lot, not only in terms of ethnic identity but probably also religiously. The implications of this for the formation of the state of "Israel" has been succinctly stated by Callaway: "Their [that is, Iron I tribes'] emergence into a nation with a national religion was the result of a long process of struggle shaped internally by dynamic leaders we know as Judges, and externally by political pressures exerted primarily by the Philistines" (1988: 77–8).[16]

Third, the religious practices of these Iron I peoples are virtually unknown. The question of a people's religion is always complex and easily distorted by over-simplification. But the material evidence of these highland villages hardly lends itself to the Yahwistic monism of later Israel (Callaway 1988: 81–3; Dever 1995c: 211; A. Mazar 1990: 348–52; 1992b: 292–4). The theological implications of this fact as well as the question of the origin(s) of Israel's "Yahwism" must be faced squarely by anyone seeking to deal honestly with the evidence now available.

Chapter 8

Iron Age II (1000–550 BC)

In one's enthusiasm for archaeological research, one is sometimes tempted to disregard the enduring reason for any special interest in Palestine – nearly all the Hebrew Old Testament is a product of Palestinian soil and Israelite writers.

(W. F. Albright, 1949)

Introduction: Archaeology and the Bible

With the move away in recent years from so-called "Biblical Archaeology," Albright's observation of fifty years ago seems quaint and dated. However, I believe he has raised here a very valid issue for all students of Palestinian archaeology and the Bible. I doubt seriously that much of what has been published through the years about this peculiar piece of real estate would have been done so at all were it not for the simple fact that Palestine is the home of the Bible. This is not in any way to denigrate the contemporary emphasis, most of which has been embraced in this volume, among archaeologists and biblical historians to produce a "secular" history of Israel. It is to raise, in my judgment, the very necessary and important question once again of the relationship of archaeological data to biblical texts and vice versa.

While the question of how archaeology and the Bible might, should or can be related has been in the background throughout this volume, here it moves to the front and center. If there is an archaeological period deserving of the description "biblical," it is Iron Age II.[1] This is the time of David and Solomon (at least for those who still believe that they existed as more than figments of some post-exilic writer's imagination). It is the time of the kings of Israel and of Judah; of the prophets and of the first temple. It is also the time of the destruction of Israel by the Assyrians

(722 BC), and of Judah by the Babylonians (587/86 BC). Iron Age II is the main time of the Hebrew Bible.

This hardly means that one can now excavate with the "Bible in one hand and a spade in the other," as "Biblical Archaeology" has sometimes been practiced and characterized. As has been argued throughout this book, the direct application of archaeological data to biblical texts can be done, if at all, only after both the archaeological data and biblical texts have been critically understood on their own terms. However, the contemporary dogma now accepted in some scholarly circles that there is no historical validity in the Bible prior to the post-exilic period seems to me to be as extreme as it is unwarranted. As J. M. Miller has consistently argued (most of it falling upon deaf ears, as far as I can tell), it is not a question of "*whether* we should use the Hebrew Bible in historical research but *how* we should use it" (1991: 100, emphasis in the original). Miller has rightly pointed out the frequent circular reasoning and question begging that characterize much of the scholarly discussion.[2]

A classic example of Miller's point is the recent article by J. Holladay, Jr (1995). Holladay began with the claim that he would produce a history of "early Hebrew monarchies" "solely on the basis of the archaeology itself . . . and accepting as *historical evidence only materials from contemporary sources*" (1995: 368, emphasis mine). These "contemporary sources" do not include the Hebrew Bible because, according to Holladay, it was written for the most part in the post-exilic period and is therefore unreliable as a historical source for most of Iron Age II. Having thus laid out his methodology, he immediately began a discussion of "David" and "Solomon" and identified the Iron Age I inhabitants of the Central Hill Country as "early Israel."[3] To quote Miller again:

> From the artifactual, non-verbal evidence alone . . . one would never even surmise that the people known as Israel appeared on the scene in ancient Palestine. . . . Any time historians, archaeologists, sociologists, or whoever speak of Israelite tribes in the central Palestinian Hill Country at the beginning of Iron Age I, or about the Davidic-Solomonic monarchy or about two contemporary king-doms emerging from this early monarchy, they are presupposing information that comes from, and only from, the Hebrew Bible.
>
> (1991: 94, 95)[4]

None of the above should be taken as an attack upon the contemporary literary critical understanding of the Bible. For the most part, the critics are probably right. The Bible, as we know it, is a product of the post-exilic period, written primarily by a relative few *literati* (Dever 1995a: 73) who had their own agenda which was mostly theological. None of the "historical" information in the Bible should be taken at face value (cf. Miller 1991). The point, however, is that it is now fashionable, in some circles, simply to *dismiss* this information rather than to attempt to use it *critically* in historical reconstruction (cf. the comments by Schniedewind 1996). As Dever has pointed out (1995a: 61), such critics assume that biblical texts are late not only in edited form, but also in content, and thus "unhistorical." Unfortunately, such unsupported assertions have now become, for some, scholarly conclusions. I hope the discussion that follows will be a balanced treatment of the basic issues involved.

Iron Age II – General Introduction

While disagreement over the chronology and terminology for this period still exists,[5] the following dates and terminology will be used:

- Iron Age IIa: 1000 *ca.*–923 BC (tenth century BC – the period of the "United Monarchy")
- Iron Age IIb – 923–722/21 BC (ninth–eighth centuries BC – beginning of "divided" monarchies and the destruction of Israel in 722/21 BC)
- Iron Age IIc: 722–540 BC (Late eighth–mid-sixth centuries BC - this period includes the destruction of Jerusalem and other Judean sites by the Babylonians in 587/86 BC and the Babylonian Exile, 587–540 BC)

There are three primary sources for critically reconstructing the history of this period: archaeological data, biblical traditions and non-biblical written sources. The latter include Egyptian, Assyrian and Babylonian inscriptions; Hebrew ostraca, bullae, stelae and inscriptions. Most of these written sources date to the eighth–seventh centuries, thus giving testimony to the growing literacy among the general population.

Israel's neighbors

The Iron II period not only witnessed the rise of the states of Israel and Judah but also several other nation-states that were their neighbors. These include Edom, Moab and Ammon, all located in the Transjordan; Phoenicia and Aram to the north and northeast; and Philistia to the west.

A complete description and discussion of the Iron Age II would need to include these other states, since they all impacted upon the histories of Israel and Judah. However, due to space considerations, they will be referred to only when crucial to an understanding of our discussion. The reader is referred to the bibliography.[6]

Iron Age IIa – the United Monarchy (*ca.* 1000–923 BC)

The difficulty of relating archaeological data to biblical traditions is clearly apparent when studying the Iron Age IIa period. Biblically speaking, this is the time assigned to David and Solomon and the United Monarchy. It includes the massive building program credited to Solomon by the Deuteronomic editors (I Kings 6–9), and widespread destruction of many sites that brought the period to a close at the end of the century.

But there remain many unresolved problems and unanswered questions. While many sites have been excavated that contain material dated to the tenth century (Figure 8.1; Herr lists some sixty-one sites, 1997b: 121), in many cases little horizontal exposure has been achieved, limiting both the number and kinds of material discovered. Among these sites are such well-known biblical cities as Arad, Beersheba, Beth Shan, Dan, Gezer, Hazor, Jerusalem, Lachish, Megiddo, Samaria and Ta'anach.[7]

For the time of David, however, there is little that can be assigned archaeologically. In fact, until the remarkable discovery of the so-called "Tel Dan Stela" (see below) in the summer of 1993 (Biran and Naveh 1993), no reference to "David" was known outside of the Bible, with the possible exception of the Meshe Inscription ("Moabite Stone"). The Tel Dan inscription, as well as the Meshe Stela, are both dated to the end of the ninth century BC. Here I would simply point out that while the translation, "House of David," on the Dan stela has been hotly disputed by a few scholars, the majority of experts who have examined the inscription have confirmed this reading. However, even assuming that the authenticity of this reading proves nothing about a supposedly tenth-century BC monarch, its date (late ninth century) provides what, in archaeology, is known as a *terminus post quem* (the earliest date that can be assigned to an event or material remains based upon *archaeological evidence alone*). What it does prove is that by the end of the ninth century BC, a political entity known as the "House of David" could be referred to in a public inscription and its referent be expected to be understood by passers-by. However, the connection of the "David" on this stela with the

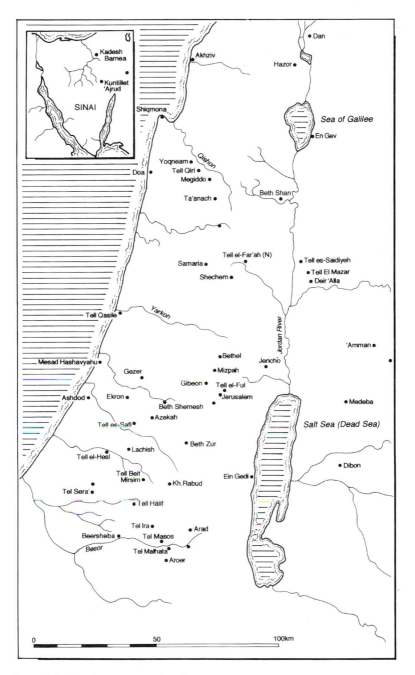

Figure 8.1 Map showing Iron Age II sites

"David" in the Bible is a matter of interpretation, not archaeology (cf. Knoppers 1997). Furthermore, this reference to "David" proves nothing about a "Solomon."

In fact, there is very little in the overall archaeological picture of the tenth century BC that can be connected with David (for a discussion on what little evidence there may or may not be, see now Cahill 1998; Na'aman 1998; Steiner 1998). The evidence for this period is limited, often controversial, and rarely, if at all, can be directly related to any biblical story concerning this figure.[8] Even the geographic boundaries of David's empire are ambiguous (cf. Herr 1997b: 130). While the total population of this period is also unknown, most people are thought to have lived in small villages and hamlets. On the other hand, the evidence from some sites, such as Megiddo and Hazor, indicates the presence of an upper class (Herr 1997b: 124). The economy, well documented by O. Borowski (1987), was based primarily on agriculture and the raising of sheep and goats.

One of the most obvious archaeological characteristics of this period, usually assigned to the time of Solomon, is the remains of massive fortifications, especially walls and gates. A lot has been written about the so-called "Solomonic six-chamber" gates (Figure 8.2) , some of it very controversial (for a brief discussion, with plans, see A. Mazar, 1990: 380–7). They have been discovered at such sites as Hazor, Gezer, Megiddo (the most controversial site, due to the way it was excavated), Beth-Shemesh, Ashdod and Lachish. Other important remains, that indicate a move toward urbanization and centralization during this period, are what have been identified as "palaces" (Megiddo, Hazor). Other structures include the more normal domestic dwellings, including the ubiquitous "four-room house" found throughout the Iron II period (for an artist's reconstruction of such a house, see Herr 1997b: 125).

Although the biblical tradition (I Kings 10: 28–29) recounts the importation of horses and chariots by Solomon, there is little archaeological evidence for trade during this time. However, studies have shown that Palestine could have produced agricultural surpluses during the Iron IIa period which could have been used as trade goods. While it is reasonable to assume that Solomon's government participated in trade, direct evidence of such activity has not been unambiguous in the archaeological record (cf. Herr's comments, 1997b: 127).

Another important development that was taking place was the spread of literacy. The Northwest Semitic alphabet (of which Hebrew is a variant) was well developed by this time, but so far almost no surviving examples from the tenth century have been found. The most notable

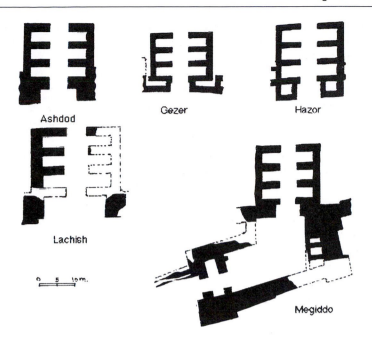

Ashdod

Gezer

Hazor

Lachish

0 5 10 m.

Megiddo

Figure 8.2 Plans showing "Solomonic" gates of the 10th century BC. Courtesy of J. Fitzgerald

exception is the famous "Gezer Calendar," which has usually been interpreted to be a schoolboy's writing exercise (for a translation see Albright, *ANET*, p. 320).

Jerusalem (Figure 8.3)

Because of its importance in the Bible, Jerusalem deserves special mention.[9] According to the tradition in 2 Samuel (5: 6–10), David captured the city by intrigue, made it his capital and "built the city all around from the Millo inward" (2 Samuel 5: 9, NRSV). Solomon, we are told (1 Kings 6–9), engaged in a major building project that included a palace and, of course, the famous temple. Archaeologically speaking, there is no non-controversial evidence for any of these building projects.

Among all Palestinian sites, Jerusalem stands out as one of the most, if not *the* most, difficult site to understand archaeologically. There are several reasons for this. First, the site has been excavated by many different people through the years, beginning with F. de Saulcy in 1860. Reports on these excavations are scattered about in a wide assortment

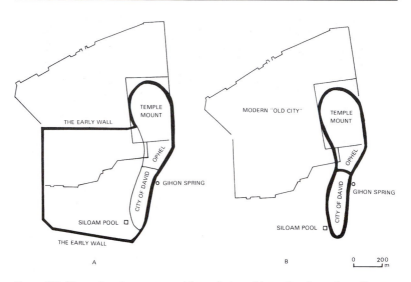

Figure 8.3 Maps showing suggested boundaries of Iron Age Jerusalem. From A. Ben-Tor, ed. *The Archaeology of Ancient Israel*, Yale University Press, © 1992

of publications in various languages. Second, Jerusalem is still a "live" city, not an abandoned tell. In many instances contemporary structures cover desirable excavation areas.[10] In addition, the city has been destroyed and looted many times throughout its history, no doubt resulting in the loss of incalculable material. Finally, one of the areas of most interest archaeologically, the so-called "Temple Mount," is off limits to archaeologists.

Despite these conditions, some twenty-one archaeological strata in the "City of David" have been identified, ranging from the Chalcolithic (fourth millennium BC) to the late Medieval periods (fourteenth–fifteenth centuries AD) (Cahill and Tarler 1994). However, very few of these remains can be dated with certainty to the tenth century BC. This includes the famous stepped-stone structure (Figure 8.4), excavated by Shiloh, which has been dated as early as the Late Bronze/Iron I period (Cahill and Tarler 1994: 35); Shiloh himself dated it to the tenth century (1985: 454). Whether this structure has anything to do with the "Millo" mentioned in the Bible (2 Sam. 5: 11; 1 Kings 9: 15) is anything but certain.

Figure 8.4 City of David excavations. Photo: J. Laughlin

The Solomonic Temple (Figure 8.5)

By far the most famous and most discussed building supposedly built by Solomon is the First Temple.[11] Despite all of the archaeological work conducted in this city, not one piece of this building has ever been found.[12] Nevertheless, the description of Solomon's temple (1 Kings 5: 16–6: 38; cf. 2 Chron. 4) compares best with what is known of similar buildings dating for the most part to the second millennium BC. The description is so precise that C. Meyers called it a "blueprint" (1992b: 352). The point has also been made that these details could not have been known by a post-exilic writer who had never seen such a building unless he had access to authentic traditions concerning its description (Dever 1995a: 33; cf. A. Mazar 1990: 377).

This description is important for another reason also. Tenth-century BC Palestine is lacking in what can be called "art work." If the description of such things as "cherubim" (1 Kings 6: 29), "palm trees," "open flowers" (1 Kings 6: 29), door-post carvings (1 Kings 6:31f.), and other objects associated with the Temple (cf. 1 Kings 7: 13–50) are accurate, it provides literary evidence for the existence of monumental art work during this period (Herr 1997b: 128–9). Nevertheless, it still remains true that no part of this temple has ever been discovered.

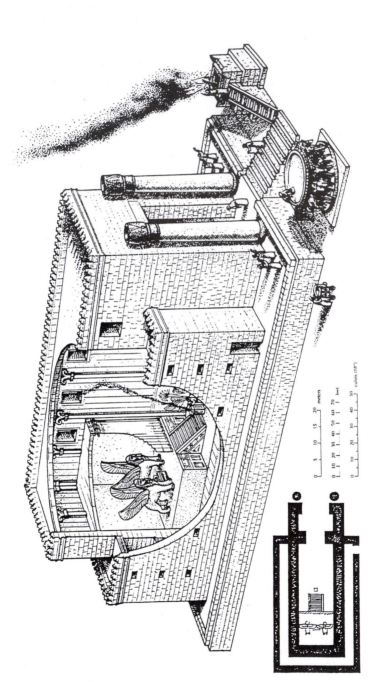

Figure 8.5 Reconstruction of "Solomonic" temple. Courtesy of M. Lyon

Negev settlements

An often overlooked aspect of the material culture of the Iron Age IIa is the many settlements that appeared in the Negev after an abandonment of most of the second millennium BC (A. Mazar 1990: 390–7). More than fifty of these sites have been called "fortresses" and are believed to have been built by the government to protect trade routes to the Red Sea. There is some disagreement over the identity of the peoples who lived here, but the ceramic evidence suggests that maybe there were at least two different groups.

One group is associated with what is called "Negebite ware," which is characterized by rough, handmade vessels thought perhaps to be associated with nomads. The other ware is common to tenth-century Judean forms (for a discussion of the latter, see Amiran 1970b: 191–265 – note that my "Iron Age IIa" is called "Iron IC" by Amiran), and is thought to indicate the presence of outsiders who moved here to man the fortresses. In any event, these sites were short-lived, most of them destroyed at the end of the period. This destruction is usually accredited to Shishak of Egypt, who claimed to have destroyed seventy Negev sites.[13] The destruction evident in the Negev can be duplicated elsewhere in Palestine at the end of the tenth century and is also usually associated with Shishak (*ca.* 935–914 BC). However, the archaeological evidence itself for such extensive *Egyptian* destruction is ambiguous.

Iron Age II b–c (923–550 BC)

Following the split of the United Monarchy, Judah and Israel became separate states, each with its own government, as well as social and religious organizations. Israel, with its capital at Samaria (from *ca.* the mid-ninth century), and other royal cities such as Dan, Hazor and Megiddo, survived for some 200 years until they were abandoned or destroyed by the Assyrians in 722/21 BC. Judah, on the other hand, managed to survive until 587/86 BC, when it was devastated by the Babylonians. This period, Iron Age II b–c, corresponding to the main period of the Bible, has probably been more intensively studied than any other in Palestinian history. Thus the amount of secondary sources dealing with relevant issues is immense. As more and more sites are surveyed and/or excavated , it can only be expected that these sources will increase. Here, only a brief summary can be offered.

The material remains from the excavated sites include defensive systems (walls, gates, guard towers), domestic and public architecture, water systems, tombs, streets, cultic installations, ceramics, jewelry and innumerable other small finds. Perhaps the most important "artifact" from this time, especially Iron IIc, are the thousands of inscriptions of one sort or another that are now known. Their importance for understanding many aspects of Israelite and Judean history, especially their religion(s), is enormous (see below).

Israel (923–722/21 BC)

Dozens of Iron IIb Israelite sites have been excavated (see Herr 1997b: 135 for a list) though no complete plan of a site is known. Among the more important are Dan, Hazor, Megiddo and Samaria. Surveys in this region have also located numerous small villages and hamlets (see, for example, Gal 1992).[14] The overall population of Israel during Iron IIb has been estimated to be between 250,000 and 350,000 (Broshi and Finkelstein 1992; cf. Herr 1997b: 137). Due to space limitations, only Dan and Samaria will be surveyed here.

Tel Dan (Figure 8.6; Biran 1994)

One of the most impressive Iron II sites yet excavated in Palestine is the 50-acre mound of Tel Dan. Located at the northern end of the Hula Valley, Dan was no doubt a major economic, political and religious center throughout the Iron II period. Discoveries from this period include a massive fortification system and a large cult site.

THE IRON AGE GATE-SYSTEM (Figure 8.7)

Strata IV–II have been dated to the Iron IIb period (ninth–eighth centuries).[15] From this time dates one of the largest fortification systems yet discovered in Palestine. While an earlier defensive system built at the end of the tenth century was identified by the excavator, the gate site (Areas A and B) was greatly enlarged during the first half of the ninth century (attributed to the activities of Ahab [ca. 871–852], Biran 1994: 247). The Iron IIb city-gate was approached by a stone pavement that led up to an outer gate. Inside this gate, a paved courtyard led to the main gate-system: a four-chambered structure with two guard towers. This massive structure measures some 96 feet by 58 feet and was destroyed by the Assyrians during the last third of the eighth century BC.[16] Beyond this gate, a paved road led the traveler up into the city. An upper gate found on top of the mound is dated to the time of Jeroboam

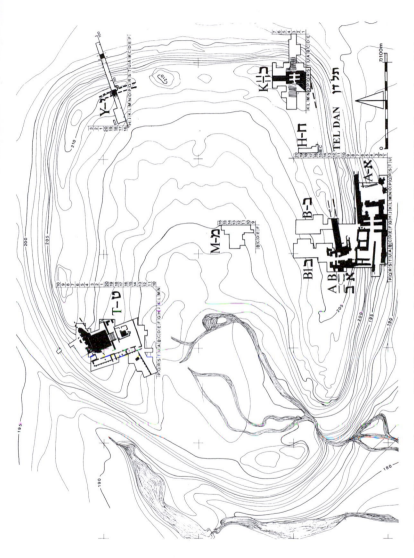

Figure 8.6 Topographic map of Tel Dan. From *Dan I*. Courtesy of A. Biran, Tel Dan Excavations, Hebrew Union College, Jerusalem

Figure 8.7 Tel Dan iron gates. From *Dan I*. Courtesy of Tel Dan Excavations, Hebrew Union College, Jerusalem Union College, Jerusalem

II (*ca.* 784–748), indicating that at that time the lower defenses were not considered sufficient for the city's protection. This gate was also of the four-chambered type.

A most interesting find associated with this gate-system is five standing stones (*massebot*) discovered to the right of the outer gate, against the defensive wall (Figure 8.8). (As this work is going to press, Biran has reported the discovery of three other sets of *massebot*. See Biran 1998.) Along with the stones, ceramic remains of oil lamps, incense bowls and other pottery remains were found. This installation would appear to be cultic in nature, though what deity or deities might have been involved is not known. While some biblical traditions speak positively of the use of sacred stones or pillars (For example, Gen. 28:18, 22; 31:13, 45; 35:14), others clearly show it was a practice associated with Baalism and was condemned, particularly by the Deuteronomic editors (2 Kings 10: 26; 17:10; Deut. 16:22; Hos. 10:1; see Dever 1994: 149). Other discoveries at the gate complex include Proto-Aeolic capitals and an architectural fragment thought to be a base for some type of canopied structure. Associated with this structure is a limestone bench, measuring about 15 feet long (Figure 8.9; Biran 1994: 239).

However, the most sensational discovery from this gate area is the now famous "Tel Dan Stela" fragment mentioned above (Figure 8.10). It

Figure 8.8 Five standing stones – *massebot*, at Tel Dan. Iron Age gate.
Courtesy of Tel Dan Excavations, Hebrew Union College, Jerusalem

Figure 8.9 Podium with limestone bench, Tel Dan. Photo: J. Laughlin

was found in secondary usage as part of an Israelite wall located on the eastern side of the pavement leading up to the outer gate.[17] Discovered in July 1993, this fragment was part of a larger memorial stone set up by a conqueror of Dan – believed to be either Ben-Hadad of Aram (Biran 1994 and Halpern 1994; cf.1 Kings 15: 20), or by Hazael (Schniedewind 1996). It is written in Aramaic and dated to the last half of the ninth century BC. It contains the first clear literary reference to David found outside the Bible, though a similar claim has now been made for the so-called "Moabite Stone," which is dated to the same time as the Dan Stela (Lemaire 1994).

The historical importance of this reference (it also contains the words "king of Israel" in line 8) is difficult to overestimate. This inscription clearly demonstrates that the expression "House of David" was a political term used to refer to Judah (assuming its existence as a monarchy at this time) at the end of the ninth century BC (Schniedewind 1996: 86). This does not, of course, "prove" the historicity of the biblical stories about David, but it does lend considerable weight to those who argue that he did, after all, exist (see above and the discussion by Knoppers 1997).

Figure 8.10 Aramaic stele, Tel Dan. Courtesy of Tel Dan Excavations, Hebrew Union College, Jerusalem. Photo: Zev Radovan

THE SACRED PRECINT – AREA T (see Figure 8.6).

A significant cultic area has also been discovered at Dan (Biran 1994: 159–233), and is located in the northwestern corner of the mound, close to a spring. The archaeological evidence, including broken pieces of statuettes dating to the Late Bronze Age, indicates that the area served a cultic function long before the time of the Israelites. However, during the Iron IIb period, monumental cultic structures were built, including what the excavator has identified as a *bamah*[18] (Figure 8.11; on the idea of bamahs, see Nakhai 1994). This area apparently went through several phases of construction which have been dated to the periods of Jeroboam I (*ca.* 928–907), Ahab (*ca.* 871–852) and Jeroboam II (*ca.* 784–748). Other finds from this area include altars, figurine offerings, various pottery remains including seven-spout oil-lamps, pithoi (large jars) with snake reliefs, and incense stands. An amazing discovery is an altar or chamber room (*lishkah*) dated to the time of Jeroboam II that was found about 50 feet southwest of the *bamah* (Figure 8.12; Biran 1994: 194). In addition to the altar itself, the room contained incense shovels (the earliest so far found in ancient Israel), and a jar used to deposit ashes. A spectacular discovery was found buried under the altar. It is a bronze and silver object identified as a mace or scepter head, used perhaps by the priests, although for what purpose is unknown (Figure 8.13; Biran 1987; 1994:

Figure 8.11 Tel Dan, Area T, *bamah*. Photo: J. Laughlin

Figure 8.12 Tel Dan, Area T, the *lishkah*. Photo: J. Laughlin

plates 32–4; Shanks 1987). One of the most controversial discoveries from Area T is an installation dated to the late tenth–early ninth century BC. It has been interpreted as a water libation structure by the excavator. Others have identified it as an olive press (Figure 8.14).[19]

The importance of these discoveries, as well as those from other sites, for understanding the religion(s) of ancient Israel seems to have received little attention as yet from biblical scholars as a whole (cf. Dever 1991c). But the physical evidence clearly indicates that throughout its history, the inhabitants of Dan engaged in religious practices which were considered apostate by the biblical editors (1 Kings 12: 25–31). In fact, when the evidence from Dan is added to other discoveries, such as the cult stand from Ta'anach (on cult stands in general, see DeVries 1987); the hundreds of 'Asherah fertility figurines; evidence of solar worship (Taylor 1994) and the *marzeah* (see below); serpent imagery on ceramic vessels;

Figure 8.13 Bronze and silver scepter head. Courtesy of Tel Dan Excavations, Hebrew Union College, Jerusalem. Photo: Zev Radovan

massebot from Dan and elsewhere; other cultic paraphernalia; and religious texts from el-Qom and Kuntillet 'Ajrud (see below), Dever's conclusion that Israelite religion developed gradually out of Late Bronze Age Canaanite fertility cults seems well justified (1983: 578–9; see also 1987b; 1994b, all with references).[20]

While many Iron IIb Israelite sites were destroyed by the Assyrians and were abandoned in the following period (Iron IIc; see Gal 1998), such was not the case with Dan. During the seventh century the city

Figure 8.14 Tel Dan, Area T, stone-plaster installation. Photo: J. Laughlin

experienced a time of expansion that included international trade. However, the makeup of the population is not clear and, in any event, the city would have been under the control of the Assyrians. The end finally came in the first quarter of the sixth century BC when the site was abandoned, most likely as the people fled the approach of the Babylonians.[21]

Samaria

Located about 35 miles north of Jerusalem, Samaria was the capital city of the Israelite kingdom for nearly 150 years.[22] Most of the finds here have been associated with a monumental palace (Figure 8.15) that has been interpreted as hard archaeological evidence of a separate political organization during the time of the so-called "Divided Monarchy" (Herr 1997b: 137). The city, according to biblical tradition (1 Kings 16: 21–24), was built by Omri (*ca.* 882–871 BC) and his son, Ahab. By the time of the prophet Amos (*ca.* 750 BC), the city had reached its final era of greatness. Now ruled by Jeroboam II, he, along with other wealthy and powerful inhabitants of the city, was attacked by the prophet for their social, economic, and legal exploitation of the poor and powerless, as well as for their corrupt religion (Amos 2: 7; 4: 1; 5: 21–24; 8: 4–8).

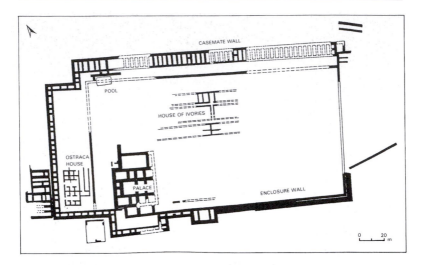

Figure 8.15 Plan of the Samaria acropolis. From A. Ben-Tor, ed. *The Archaeology of Ancient Israel*, Yale University Press, © 1992

While there is evidence that some sort of activity took place here prior to Iron Age IIb (Stager 1990), the major archaeological discoveries date to this latter period. The most important find has been identified as a royal acropolis which enclosed an area nearly 4 acres (over 17,000 square feet) in size. Finds associated with this enclosure include walls and storehouses. In addition to the monumental architectural remains, two other major discoveries were made.

THE OSTRACA

More than 100 ostraca[23] have been found (Figure 8.16) of which sixty-three were legible enough to publish.[24] These sherds, along with the Tel Dan stela, are the most important written remains known from the kingdom of Israel. While the absolute date(s) of the sherds, as well as their function, are still debated (Kaufman 1982; Rainey 1988), a date sometime during the eighth century BC seems to be the most accepted. It is also generally believed that they served as records for goods, such as oil and wine, delivered to Samaria, perhaps as taxes (A. Mazar 1990: 410). These inscriptions are not only important for what they reveal about the ancient Hebrew script and taxation system. They also contain information about the topography around Samaria, mentioning towns with names such as "Yasith," "Yashub" and "Qosoh," which are not

Figure 8.16 Samaria ostraca. Photo: J. Laughlin

mentioned in the Bible. Furthermore, some of the ostraca contain personal names compounded with the word "Baal" (such as "Abibaal," "Meribaal"). Such practices clearly indicate the continued involvement of the Israelites with the worship of the Canaanite god Baal, so condemned in the Bible by the prophets (for example, Hosea 2: 16–17). If the names on the sherds refer to the recipients of the goods, it may mean that they were receiving provisions from their country estates. Such practices may have contributed to the exploitation of the poor so roundly condemned by Amos (cf. 2: 6–8).

THE IVORIES

The material wealth enjoyed by at least some of the inhabitants of this city is also indicated by the hundreds of ivory fragments which have been recovered from the site. Again, due to the circumstances of their discovery (they were found in an ancient dump), their dates are unclear. Nevertheless, most are thought to come from the ninth–eighth centuries BC. Described as "the most important collection of miniature art from the Iron Age discovered in Israel" (Avigad 1993: 1304), the fragments are believed to have been parts of items imported, probably from Phoenicia.[25] The ivories portray various motifs, including Egyptian

Figure 8.17 Samaria ivory, "Woman in the Window". Courtesy of
J. Fitzgerald

myths, animals in mortal combat, and what is perhaps the best known
theme, the "woman in the window" (Figure 8.17). It is believed that they
were used as inlays decorating the furnishings of the king's palace as
well as the homes of the wealthy. Ahab is remembered as having built a
"house of ivory" (1 Kings 22: 39; cf. Ps. 45: 8); and the prophet, Amos,
a hundred years later, announced that the "houses of ivory" (3: 15) of his
day would be torn down. The prophet also accused the wealthy and
powerful of lying on "beds of ivory" while participating in a festival called
a *marzeah* (Amos 6: 4–7).[26] This festival seems to have involved feasting,
drinking and perhaps sexual intercourse, all the while accompanied by
music and song. It often took the form of a funerary cult (cf. Jer. 16:5).
The studies of these ivories by King and Beach (see note 24) are excellent
examples of how archaeological discoveries, when properly used, can
greatly illuminate the context of biblical texts (cf. Dever 1994b).

As was the fate of Dan, Samaria was captured by the Assyrians towards
the end of the eighth century and became an Assyrian administrative

center. The site was occupied at least up until the Byzantine period. But, with few exceptions, the archaeological remains from these later periods are scarce.

Judah in Iron Age IIB–C (*ca.* 923–550 BC)

For over 350 years (*ca.* 923–587/86) Judah existed as a separate political entity in the southern Levant. This is one of the longest continuous monarchies known from the ancient Near Eastern world. During this time, especially during the late eighth–seventh centuries, Judah, along with its neighboring states, enjoyed a period of prosperity, with Jerusalem serving as the major urban, as well as capital city. Many archaeological sites have been excavated containing strata from these periods.[27] It has been estimated that the Iron IIb population for Judah was around 110,000 people (Broshi and Finkelstein 1992).

In addition to Jerusalem, other important Iron II sites include Lachish, Tell en-Nasbeh (ancient Mizpah), Tell el-Ful (Gibeah, primarily Iron IIc) and Debir (Khirbet Rabud), all in the Central Hill country. Major sites excavated in the Shephelah include Beth-Shemesh, Azekah and Tell Beit Mirsim. In the northern Negev, Arad, Beersheba, Tel 'Ira and 'Aroer have all contributed important information for this period (for a brief description of these Negev sites, see A. Mazar 1990: 438–51). Important desert sites are Jericho and En Gedi.[28] These sites, except for Lachish, which attained a size of about 20 acres, averaged about 5–8 acres, with an estimated population of around 500–1000 inhabitants each. Jerusalem, of course, was the largest city, with an estimated size by the end of the eighth century of 150 acres. No site has been excavated completely, but Nasbeh and Beersheba have yielded enough to get a general plan for these cities (Figure 8.18). For most of these sites, the Iron IIb period of occupation ended with their destruction by the Assyrians at the end of the eighth century, the most famous, as well as most documented case being that of Lachish (see below).

Writing

One of the most important developments of the entire Iron Age IIb–c periods is the spread of literacy, known from hundreds of inscriptions, most of which date between the eighth and sixth centuries BC. While the percentage of the population that was actually literate is unknown, the number and variety of written materials is so great that from at least the eighth century "basic knowledge of writing seems to have been

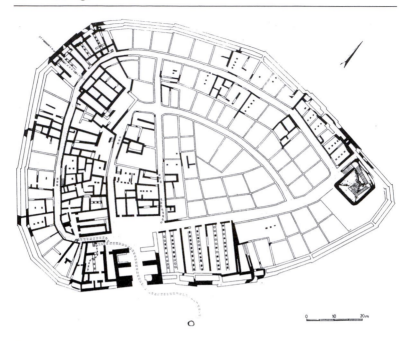

Figure 8.18 General plan of Iron Age II Beersheba, stratum II. Ze'ev Herzog,
Archaeology of the City, University of Tel Aviv monograph, no. 13

common in Israelite urban centers" (Demsky 1997: 366; cf. Herr 1997b:
145; A. Mazar 1990: 515).[29] Although papyrus might have been the most
common writing material used, it rarely survives the ravages of time.
Thus most of the inscriptions that have been found are on pieces
of pottery called "ostraca." Such inscriptions have been discovered
at Jerusalem, Arad, Samaria (see above), Lachish, Mesad Hashavyahu,
Khirbet Ghazza and elsewhere. In addition to the Tel Dan stela
discussed above, other important textual discoveries include the so-called
"Hezekiah's Tunnel Inscription," "LMLK Jar" handles and religious
inscriptions from Kuntillet 'Ajrud and Khirbet el-Qom. Here I can only
briefly summarize the material. Into the context of this literary discussion
will be placed two major cities of Judah during Iron II, Lachish and
Jerusalem.

Eighth-century BC *Judah*

HEZEKIAH'S TUNNEL INSCRIPTION (THE "SILOAM INSCRIPTION").[30]

One of the most important, as well as famous, inscriptions ever found in Judah was in a water tunnel dug in Jerusalem (Figure 8.19). Discovered in 1880, the inscription describes the meeting of the two teams of workmen who dug the tunnel, which is S-shaped and over a third of a mile long, from opposite directions. The tunnel was cut to bring water from the Gihon Spring, located on the eastern side of the so-called "City of David," to a pool inside the city wall. This inscription has been

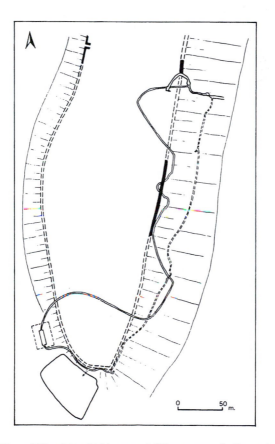

Figure 8.19 Plan of King Hezekiah's tunnel (Siloam tunnel). From A. Ben-Tor, ed. *The Archaeology of Ancient Israel*, Yale University Press, © 1992

described by A. Mazar as "one of the longest and most important monumental Hebrew texts from the period of the monarchy" (1990: 484). It has traditionally been dated toward the end of the eighth century BC and ascribed to King Hezekiah's preparation for war with the Assyrians (cf. 2 Kings 20: 20; Borowski 1995).

LMLK ("LAMELKH") JAR HANDLES (Figure 8.20)

Another group of important inscriptions from the time of Hezekiah are some 2000 stamped jar handles (Bordreuil 1997: 166; Barkay 1992: 346 says 1200). Chemical analysis has shown that all of the jars were

Figure 8.20 Stamped jar handle. The inscription reads "LMLK," Hebrew for, "Belonging to the King." Under the wings is the name of the place, Hebron. Tel-Lachish. Courtesy of the Israel Antiquities Authority

produced near Jerusalem, in the Shephelah, with all of the seals coming from some twenty-two to twenty-five stamps (Mommsen *et al.* 1984; Barkay 1992). The seals have either a four-winged beetle or a two-winged sun disk. Above the beetle or disk is the expression "lmlk," "belonging to the king." In addition, some of the seals contain one of four place names located below the beetle or disk: "Hebron," "Ziph," "Sochoh," or "mmst." The last name is not known in any other source. These stamped handles have been found at many sites, including Lachish (more than 400), Jerusalem (some 300), Ramat Rahel (near Jerusalem, 170), Tel Batash, Beth-Shemesh, Gibeon (thirty-six), and Tel en-Nasbeh (eighty-five). While there is no consensus over their precise function, many experts believe that the stamped jars were related to royal and/or military activities of Hezekiah. Under this interpretation, the place names refer to the administrative centers where military provisions for the Judean army were stored and/or dispersed (for other suggestions, see Mommsen *et al.* 1984). Why the symbols are in the form of the beetle and sun disk is still a disputed question. Also, with regard to regional distribution (the two-winged solar disk is more prevalent in Jerusalem and northern Judean sites), it has been argued that the four-winged beetle was the royal symbol for Israel, and the two-winged disk the symbol of Judah (Tushingham 1992). However, since all of the jars were apparently manufactured in the same place, and given the political realities at the end of the eighth century BC, it is more likely that both seals were royal symbols of Judah (Barkay 1992).[31]

KUNTILLET 'AJRUD AND KHIRBET EL-QOM

The site of ancient Kuntillet 'Ajrud is located about 30 miles south of Kadesh-Barnea and is thought to have been a caravanserai (a kind of ancient motel for caravans or travelers) for traders traveling between Israel/Judah and the Red Sea. It was excavated in 1975–76 (Meshel 1997), and its period of use was dated from *ca.* 950–850 BC. The discovery here that has created the most controversy, as well as literature (Chase 1982; Day 1992; Dever 1984; A. Mazar 1990: 446–50), is an inscription, with drawings, found on a large pottery jar. The transliterated inscription reads: "lyhwh smron wl'srth," and has been translated as: "To Yahweh of Samaria and His a/Asherah" (Figure 8.21) One of the main issues is whether or not the word *Asherah* refers to the Canaanite female consort of Baal, or to a cultic symbol, usually identified as a tree. Relevant to this discussion is another eighth-century BC inscription

Figure 8.21 Drawing of the Kuntillet 'Ajrud jar inscription, "To Yahweh and his Asherah." Courtesy Ze'ev Meshel, excavator, Kuntillet 'Ajrud Excavations

discovered in the late 1960s by W. G. Dever at Khirbet el-Qom, a site located about 12 miles west of Hebron. An inscription found in a tomb by Dever (1997d) reads in part: "May Uriyahu be blessed by Yahweh, for from his enemies he has been saved by his a/'Asherah" (Dever 1997d: 391; see also Zevit 1984 with references).

These references to "a/'Asherah" have created a considerable controversy among scholars concerning their exact meaning. However this debate turns out, these inscriptions and other material remains mentioned above all point to the fact that in popular religion, at least, many Israelites associated Yahweh with a female consort. Dever's conclusion concerning these literary references has implications for a critical understanding of the final edited form of the Hebrew Bible: "The 'silence' regarding 'Asherah as the consort of Yahweh, successor to Canaanite El, may now be understood as the result of the near-total suppression of the cult by the eighth–sixth century reformers" (1984: 31;

see also his comments in 1995e and 1996b; see also above and note 20). The questions and issues involved in a study of ancient Israelite religion(s) are many and complex. But from the growing amount of archaeological data – some of it, such as the Ta'anach Cult Stand (Figure 8.22), stretching back into the tenth century BC – it is becoming clearer that for most of Israelite/Judean history, Yahweh, the national deity, was believed to have had a consort, 'Asherah. While the Bible (for example,

Figure 8.22 Ta'anach Cult Stand, late 10th century BC. Collection of the Israel Antiquities Authority, © Israel Museum, Jerusalem

1 Sam. 4: 4; 2 Sam. 6: 2; 2 Kings 19: 15; Isa. 37: 16; Deut. 33: 2) clearly reflects such religious practices, it is the archaeological evidence which has pointed to their widespread reality, thus redressing some of the "silence" referred to by Dever above.

Seventh–sixth centuries BC

Many seals and ostraca are known from this time. Recently, two ostraca belonging to a private collection and dating from the second half of the seventh century BC have been made public (Bordreuil *et al.* 1998). One deals with an obligatory temple tax and the other with a widow's plea to an official following the death of her husband. Other ostraca have been found at Mesad Hashavyahu, the most important being seven sherds that belong to the same document. The text is a plea by a workman for the return of his confiscated garment (Pardee 1997b). Such texts open the window on the social and political realities of the time.

One of the largest collections of Hebrew inscriptions (more than 100) was found at Arad (Lemaire 1997). The dates, however, for these ostraca are not clear, and a wide range is given, spanning the tenth–sixth centuries. The content of these inscriptions are very varied. Some deal with military issues; others are name lists and at least two seem to be abecedaries. Nine are royal (*lmlk*) seal impressions found on jar handles and date to the eighth century. Thirteen inscribed weights dated to the seventh century were also found. The importance of these inscriptions has been succinctly stated by A. Mazar: "the Arad inscriptions comprise a wealth of varied data that reveals much about the historical geography of the region, the role of the fortress, the Judean military hierarchy, linguistic usages, the structures of private names in Judah, quantities of food consumed by troops, and aspects of daily life such as the system of numbers, measures, and distances" (1990: 441).

Lachish

One of the most important of Judean sites is Lachish, located in the Shephelah (Figure 8.23). The mound, modern Tell ed-Duweir, was first identified by W. F. Albright in 1929. It has been the location of several excavations beginning with J. L. Starkey in the 1930s. Unfortunately, Starkey was murdered in January 1938 while on his way to Jerusalem. Since his time, the site has been re-excavated, most recently by D. Ussishkin of Tel Aviv University (Ussishkin 1997, with references to earlier publications). Levels IV–II have been dated by the excavator to

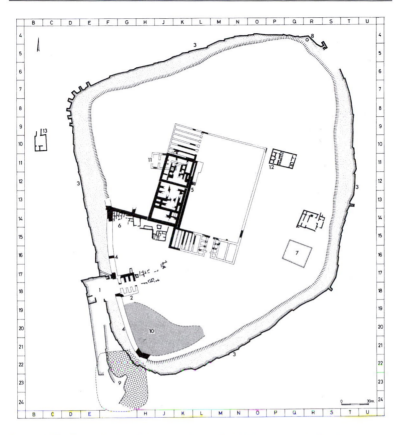

Figure 8.23 General plan of Lachish. From *Tel Aviv*, Volume 5, Fig. 1.
Courtesy of D. Ussishkin

the Iron IIb–c periods. The Level III city was destroyed by Sennacherib (704–681) in 701 BC and the Level II city by Nebuchadnezzar during the Babylonian conquest in 588–586 BC.

In the Bible, Lachish is mentioned in the context of the Assyrian war (2 Kings 18: 13–19: 37), but only incidentally so. The biblical emphasis is upon the miraculous deliverance of Jerusalem. Here is a classic example of how archaeological data can tell the "rest of the story," as it were. According to Assyrian texts (cf. Oppenheim in *ANET*, pp. 287–8) and reliefs; (for discussion and photo of one of the details of the reliefs see Ussishkin 1997a), as well as destruction debris at Lachish, the city was violently destroyed at the end of the eighth century BC. This convergence of evidence, both archaeological and literary, makes the Assyrian destruction of Lachish one of the "best documented events from the period of the Monarchy" (A. Mazar 1990: 432). In addition, the remains of some 1500 people found in nearby caves may point to a merciless massacre by the Assyrian army. The pottery remains found beneath the destruction debris have been extremely important in establishing the ceramic chronology for this period of Judah's history. Among the discoveries were the hundreds of stamped jar handles discussed above, thus settling the dispute with regard to their date.

Following the Assyrian destruction, Ussishkin concluded that the city was abandoned for some seventy years until re-inhabited during the time of King Josiah (639–609 BC). To this later period of the city's history belong the famous "Lachish Letters" (Pardee 1997c, with references). Found in the destruction debris of a guardroom, the letters reflect the last days of Judah when it was destroyed in 587/86 BC by the Babylonians. One of the best-known letters, number 4, reads in part: "And let (my lord) know that we are watching for the signals of Lachish, according to all the indications which my lord hath given, for we cannot see Azekah" (Albright in *ANET*: 322; cf. Jer. 34: 7). With Azekah having apparently already fallen into Babylonian hands, the fate of Lachish was not far behind. The site would be re-occupied down through Roman times, but it never again achieved its pre-exilic greatness.

Jerusalem in Iron Age II b–c

Few archaeological remains have been recovered from the ninth century BC. However, by the end of the eighth century, the city expanded to the west (Avigad 1985). This expansion is usually explained as a conse-quence of the influx of refugees from the north during the time of Hezekiah (727–690 BC). Archaeological remains from this time include a massive wall some 16 feet thick, a cobbled pavement and other building remains (Avigad 1985; Cahill and Tarler 1994; Shiloh 1985, 1989). Shiloh estimated that the size of Jerusalem went from around 40 acres in the tenth century to around 150 acres by the end of the eighth. He also estimated that the population increased to 25,000–40,000 people (1989: 98). The geographical expansion of the ancient city was dictated by the numerous burial caves that ring the site.[32] This fact, plus the growth in population, which would have made Jerusalem in Hezekiah's time noisy and crowded, may have been the major factors in the building of the royal palace at Ramat Rachel, located between Jerusalem and Bethlehem. The many LMLK jar handles found there (some 170) indicate its use during the time of Hezekiah.

Other important archaeological remains in Jerusalem are its water systems, especially "Hezekiah's Tunnel" (see Figure 8.19) and the so-called "Warren's Shaft." The latter was discovered by C. Warren in 1867, thus its name. This water system is sometimes connected with the biblical story of David's capture of Jerusalem (2 Sam. 5: 18; I Chr. 11: 6). However, this has never been proven. Furthermore, the date of its construction is unclear. Shiloh (1994) dated it to the late tenth–ninth century, in which case it would be later than the time of David . Others have suggested it existed long before the tenth century (Cahill and Tarler 1994: 44).

Many interesting discoveries have been made that date to the last years of Iron Age Jerusalem (Stratum 10, in Shiloh's excavation), especially in the City of David. Among these are several architectural structures interpreted as domestic quarters (Figure 8.24). One is a "four-room house," and close to it is the "House of Ahi'el," so called because of a storage jar found with this name incised on it. One of the most exciting discoveries was made in building remains just east of the Ahi'el house. It is called the "Bullae House" because of the fifty-one bullae found there.[33] Eighty-two names have been recovered from these seals, two of which mentioned in the Bible: "Gemaryahu ["Gemariah" in English] son of Shaphan" (Jer. 36: 10, 25), and "'Azaryahu son of Hilqiyahu" ("Azariah son of Hilkiah," I Chr. 9: 10–11).[34]

If the "Gemaryahu" of the bulla is indeed the same as the scribe mentioned in Jeremiah, then this external epigraphic evidence provides an important chronological reference point. The account in Jeremiah is dated to the fifth year of King Jehoiakim, or around 603 BC (Jer. 36: 9; cf. Shiloh 1989: 104). Thus the biblical and archaeological evidence converge to place the activities in the "Bullae House" immediately before the destruction of Jerusalem in 587/86 BC.

The Bible

It is sometimes overlooked in discussions of ancient Hebrew texts that the most significant literary product of Iron Age II Judea is a large part of the Bible. Though there are no extant biblical manuscripts from this period,[35] many literary critics of the Bible have argued that much of the material now found in the Pentateuch, the Deuteronomic History (Joshua, Judges, Samuel and Kings), as well as many of the pre-exilic prophets and Psalms, was first composed during the Iron IIc period.[36] That the final, edited form of all of these writings is to be dated to the post-exilic period is not the issue here.

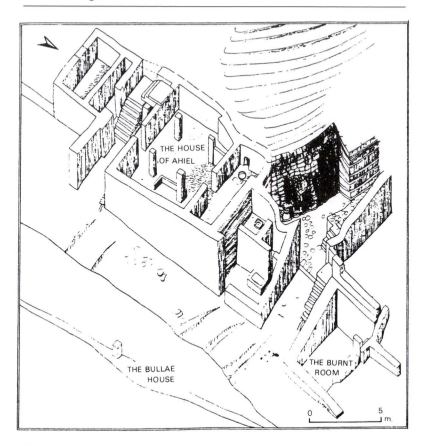

THE HOUSE OF AHIEL

THE BULLAE HOUSE

THE BURNT ROOM

0   5
                      m.

Figure 8.24 Domestic quarters, "City of David" excavations. A. Ben-Tor, ed., *The Archaeology of Ancient Israel*, Yale University Press, © 1992

Epilogue

It has been a long journey from the hovels of the Neolithic people to the ruins of Israel and Judah left behind in the military catastrophes of the Iron Age II. During this approximately 8000-year period countless people lived and died, most leaving little evidence of their meager existence. The archaeological landscape left by these ancient folk is strewn with countless publications, many technical and not easily accessible to the interested non-specialist. Nevertheless, it is to these ancient people, especially to those we know as "Hebrews" or "Israelites," that we stand in debt for one of the world's great religions. Fragments of their existence also lie buried beneath the soil of Palestine, often over the very remains of their Neolithic ancestors! It has been the purpose of this short study to try to shed some light on this amazing story, many pieces of which are still missing, and others only partially understood. Furthermore, many other important pieces have, of necessity, been omitted.

Despite these omissions, I hope one thing has been very clear throughout this journey: archaeology matters. It matters a lot. It matters because it is the one bridge that can truly take us back to the distant past and let us actually stand where our ancestors were born, lived, loved, feared and died. It is the one discipline that can provide us with contemporary evidence of the culture out of which the Bible came. This evidence never has, and never will, "prove" the Bible "true," if one means by such a statement proving true the theological interpretations that the biblical writers gave their own history. Archaeology is a humanistic study, not a theological one. But on occasion, it can greatly illuminate the context in which biblical stories were placed by their authors and can give us a different perspective from that preserved in the sacred text. Furthermore, in excavating the ruins of the past, we come face to face with ourselves. For we are the children of our ancestors whose cities and towns, hovels and palaces, graves and tombs we seek to find and study. Whether or not we are the better for it, is, I suppose, a verdict that is still out. In this day of excessive excavation expenses, countless hours of physical toil, and for many of us, separation from our loved ones and friends, questions of the value of archaeological excavations naturally arise. Of all the justifications one could give for this activity, no one, in my judgment, has said it any better than the late Paul Lapp:

> Perhaps the discoveries of Jerusalem are even more important than those of Cape [Canaveral]. The discoveries at Cape [Canaveral] are concerned with the expansion of man's world. The discoveries in Jerusalem concern man himself. Perhaps historians have more to contribute to our society than cosmic theoreticians. Perhaps archaeological discoveries in Palestine will enlighten men more than finds from an excavation on the moon. Perhaps it is more important for man to understand himself than to expand his world. Perhaps men need more desperately to understand each other than to discover new creatures out in space. If such should be your conviction, ancient and biblical history and archaeology offer stimulating opportunities to expand your horizons.
>
> (1969: 113)

Notes

I Introduction: archaeology and the Bible

1 Cf. King (1985: 49): "The pace of archaeological activity since the Arab–Israeli war of 1967 has accelerated so rapidly on both sides of the Jordan River that it is difficult even to name all the field projects underway in Israel and Jordan, as well as in adjacent countries."

2 A brief history

1 Concerning Smith's discovery, see Lloyd (1955: 176ff.); Moorey (1991: 11–12). This story, known as "The Epic Gilgamesh," can be read in translation in the *ANET*, pp. 42–4.

2 See Tadmor (1985: 260–8). In recent years there has emerged a controversy over the term *Biblical Archaeology*, led mainly by W. G. Dever of the University of Arizona. Among many publications where he discusses this issue see (1985a, 1985b, 1988, 1992a, 1996a, 1996b, 1997a). See also Moorey (1991) for a concise, but informative summary of the history of "Biblical Archaeology."

3 On Robinson's life and contributions to biblical studies, see Moorey (1991: 14–17); and esp. King (1983c). Also, brief biographies on many of these early pioneers, as well as other significant Near Eastern archaeologists, can be found in the *OEANE*.

4 Attributed to Titus Tobler. Quoted in Albright (1949: 25).

5 See, *inter alia*, Dever 1980a, 1985a, 1992a; cf. Moorey's analysis (1991); and Miller (1987). Since Dever's analysis of this history is widely known among archaeologists, the following discussion will follow his basic outline. He calls these stages in the development of archaeology "revolutions."

6 Dever (1985a); see the very helpful summaries of the histories of the various national "schools" in the opening chapters in *BTC*.

7 Space limitations prohibit an adequate assessment of Albright's contributions to, and influence upon, the development of "Biblical Archaeology." The beginning student need only become familiar with the literature in the field to see how widespread and persuasive Albright's shadow was, and perhaps still is. For brief assessments, see Moorey (1991: 67–75); King

(1983a). While it is impossible to list all of Albright's writings here, the following two works by him are highly recommended for introducing the student to the depth and magnitude of his thought: *From the Stone Age to Christianity* and *The Archaeology of Palestine*. For an assessment of his life and contributions, see also the entire issue of *BA* 56 (1) (March) 1993.

8 Dever (1982a, 1985a, 1990a, 1992a). For an interesting informal dialogue with Dever concerning this controversy as well as other issues, see Shanks (1996a,b).

9 As of 1998, there is not, to my knowledge, a single trained field archaeologist teaching any more in any of the seminaries owned and operated by my church tradition.

10 A classic example of such a dispute is the discussion now taking place over the existence of Jerusalem before and during the time of the "United Monarchy." See Cahill (1998); Na'aman (1998); Steiner (1998).

11 Cf. the histories of Israel and Judah by J. A. Soggin (1984), and J. M. Miller and J. Hayes (1986). Note the latters' conclusion that the biblical stories prior to the time of David are an "artificial and theologically influenced literary construct" (p. 78). Note also the similar conclusion by Lemche (1985: 414). The issues and complexities of Israelite historiography deserve a full discussion, which is impossible here. Among an ever growing literature on the subject, in addition to the above-mentioned works, the reader will benefit from the following studies as well as their bibliographies: M. Z. Brettler (1995); R. B. Coote (1990); B. Halpern (1983); J. Van Seters (1983).

3 How it's done: an introduction to field work

1 Much of popular "newspaper archaeology," which can be very confusing and misleading to an unsuspecting public, is oftentimes the result of "excavators" whose field methods are questionable at best. See the critique of V. Jones's search for the ashes of the "Red Heifer" by Daniel C. Browning, Jr (1996). See also L. Davidson (1996).

2 Digging techniques, and even what to call them, have their own evolutionary history. Archaeologists are constantly striving to improve these methods. The literature on this subject is too vast to list here. But the following works will contain helpful discussions as well as bibliographic references: Dever (1974, 1985b); R. L. Chapman III (1986); G. W. Van Beek (1988). In addition, the following field manuals will introduce the reader to terminology, field techniques, recording systems and so on: Blakely and Toombs (1980); Dever and Lance (1978); Joukowsky (1980).

3 See now the discussion by W. Dever (1996a); M. B. Schiffer (1987). While Schiffer refers only rarely to Near Eastern tells, his discussion is very relevant to the questions concerning tell formation, their disturbance and deterioration. Helpful too are the various chapters under the heading: "Archaeological Methodology: the Techniques," in *BTC*. On the problem of stratigraphy, see J. Holladay (1997a,b). See also the brief article by A. M. Rosen (1997). A little noted essay by G. E. Wright (1974) is worth reading in this context.

4 See Schiffer (1987: 199–234), for a discussion of disturbance processes that

can cause the mixing of soils and materials belonging to a tell. This activity is called "pedoturbation."

5 Strange (1988). See also Longstaff (1997). For further study on the development and practice of computer use by archaeologists see the bibliographies accompanying both articles.

6 Cf. Dessel (1997).

7 On some excavations it is the area and/or field supervisor's responsibility to produce section drawings. See Dever (1978:164–72).

8 The scandal of publication vis-à-vis archaeology in Israel is well known. See Shanks (1996c). It has been reported that, since 1967, 30,000 coins have been found in the excavations carried out in Jerusalem. As of July 1996, not one of these coins had been published. See *BAR* (July/August) 22/4 (1996: 9).

9 Lance (1981:57). For more detailed, recent discussions of important issues involved in the problem of archaeological publications, see Shanks (1996c). Cf. also the helpful discussion by Boraas (1988).

10 Two prominent examples are the publications now being prepared for the separate excavations of Jerusalem conducted by K. Kenyon and Y. Shiloh.

4 The rise of civilization: the Neolithic through the Early Bronze Age (*ca.* 8500–2000 BC)

1 See now the relevant chapters in *ASHL*.

2 The general as well as specialized studies on both of these periods are large and growing. For the Neolithic, the following surveys, all of which contain full bibliographies can guide further study: A. Gopher (1995); A. M. T. Moore (1982); O. Bar-Yosef (1992, 1995). For the Chalcolithic, see R. Gonen (1992a); T. Levy (1986, 1995a).

3 For older treatments, see Lapp (1970); G. E. Wright (1971); R. de Vaux (1971); K. Kenyon (1979:84–118); R. Amiran (1970a). For more recent perspectives, see Richard (1987); A. Mazar (1990: 91–150); A. Ben-Tor (1992).

4 W. F. Albright seems to have been the first archaeologist to coin the phrase "Early Bronze Age." See Richard (1987, with bibliography). G. E. Wright as early as 1937 divided the period into EB I–EB IV. Most archaeologists use this terminology today. However, a few Israelis use the ethnic term "Canaanite," or "Early Canaanite," to refer to the same period; see M. Dothan (1985).

5 Cf. *OEANE*, vol. 4: 412–13; for a slightly different assignment, see S. Richard (1987) and the *NEAEHL*, vol. 4, under "Chronological Tables."

6 P. Gerstenblith (1980: 66); see also her endnotes, nos 6 and 7. Cf. S. Richard (1987: 23).

7 In his 1987 article, J. F. Ross identified some 102 excavated EB sites and more than 550 that had been surveyed. He also included major bibliographies for each site listed. For a study of settlement patterns in Palestine during the EB II and EB III, see Broshi and Gophna (1984); see also Finkelstein and Gophna (1993). For a study of settlement patterns in southern Palestine and the southern Sinai during the third millennium BC, see I. Beit-Arieh (1981).

M. Haiman has reported some 1000 known EB IV sites that have been found in the Sinai Desert (1996). Palumbo, on the other hand, has catalogued more than 3000 such sites from the same period. The older work, by T. Thompson (1979), should be used with caution. See critiques by Ross (1987: 316) and W.G. Dever (1980b: 53ff.).

8   P. Lapp (1970); De Vaux identified the "founders" of the Early Bronze Age as "Canaanites" who migrated from the north (1971:234). K. Kenyon argued, based on her pottery studies from the tombs at Jericho, that three groups of "migrant tribesmen" coming from the east, and also, perhaps, from the north, were responsible for the EB I culture, which she called the "Proto-urban Period" (1979: 66). All of these theories have now been discredited by newer evidence and better understanding and interpretation of the older data. See esp. J. W. Hanbury-Tenison (1986), for a full discussion of the Late Chalcolithic–EB I horizon in Palestine and the Transjordan with summaries of several standard views by leading archaeologists from the pre-1945 era through the 1980s.

9   For a more detailed discussion of the EB I economy see Hanbury-Tenison (1986: 72–103).

10 In the past, some have included a third division, EB IC. See, for example, Paul Lapp (1970), and J. A. Callaway (1978). For the position that there is no EB I, see S. Richard (1987: 25; cf. Schaub (1982:69).

11 Broshi and Gophna (1984: 41); According to Finkelstein and Gophna's study (1993), the average size of the 35 EB I sites surveyed in northern Samaria is *ca.* 5 acres; for the 29 sites in southern Samaria and Judea, 2.5 acres.

12 A. Mazar and de Miroschedji (1996: figs. 4–15). Space does not allow for even a minimal discussion of *massebot*, which have been traced back as far as the Neolithic period. They were widespread in the ancient world and often condemned in the Bible because of their association with Canaanite practices. Nevertheless, there is much archaeological evidence from sites such as Tel Dan, that these stones played a prominent role throughout the period of Israelite religion. See the discussion and bibliography in Mazar and de Miroschedji (1996), and Chapter 8, below.

13 While R. Amiran's classic study, *Ancient Pottery of the Holy Land* (1970b), is in need of revision, it is still a very useful resource for the ceramic history of ancient Canaan and Israel.

14 Hanbury-Tenison (1986:104–38; figs 15 and 23). R. Amiran's (1970b) suggestion of a "southern" culture with line-painted pottery that was paralleled with the northern "gray-burnished" culture has been criticized by Hanbury-Tenison as "misleading." See the latter's comments (1986:125–6).

15 The issues involved here are highly technical. Details can be found in Amiran (1970b: 35–57) and the discussion in Hanbury-Tenison (1986).

16 For a summary of issues and a list of sites, as well as bibliography, see Hanbury-Tenison (1986: 231–250).

17 Among the ever-increasing publications on Egyptian–Palestinian relations during the EB period, see the following: W. A. Ward (1991); I. Beit-Arieh (1984); J. M. Weinstein (1984); M. Wright (1985).

18 For the argument that the emergence of these walled settlements of EB II were due more to social and economic factors, see Hanbury-Tenison (1986: 102).

19 It is impossible here to give detailed treatment that all of these sites deserve. For Dan, see Biran (1994: 33–45); R. Greenberg (1996); R. Greenberg and Porat (1996). For 'Ai, see Callaway (1972, 1978, 1980b, 1987). For Arad, see Amiran *et al.* (1978); Amiran (1985a); Amiran and Ilan (1996). Much shorter summary articles, with fuller bibliographies, can be found in the *NEAEHL* and the *OEANE*.

20 The following works contain either summaries or specialized studies of this period. All contain helpful bibliographies. S. Richard (1980); W. G. Dever (1980b, 1995b); S. Richard and R. Boraas (1984, 1988); R. T. Schaub and W. E. Rast (1984); G. Palumbo (1991); R. Gophna (1992); G. Palumbo and G. Peterman (1993); Y. Goren (1996); M. Haiman (1996).

21 While Dever has argued that the pottery may serve as chronological indicators, he has also suggested that in some cases the assemblages may overlap and represent regional differences only (1995b:296, n. 21).

22 For a brief critique of these models see Dever (1995b).

5 The Middle Bronze Age (2000–2550 BC)

1 The nomenclature can be especially confusing. Some scholars (Israelis, in particular) refer to the first part of this period as "MBA II A" (cf. the *NEAEHL*, vol. 4; B. Mazar 1968; A. Mazar 1990: 174). But even among this group there are inconsistencies. Some divide the entire period into two sub-phases: MB II A (2000–1750 BC) and MB II B (1750–1550 BC), as in the *NEAEHL*. Others (e.g., A. Mazar 1990) use the nomenclature but combine the last phase of the MBA into "MB II B–C" (cf. Kempinski 1992b: table 1.1, who questions the validity of dividing the last phase of this period into sub-phases, b c. What is common to all of these schemes is the assumption that the "MB I" should refer to the end of the third millennium BC (2200–2000 BC), and not the beginning of the second millennium.

2 Ward's conclusions need to be carefully considered in light of the past and present use of Egyptian chronology by contemporary scholars in an attempt to establish absolute dates. His conclusion that modern scholars have imposed on the ancient Egyptians "a modern precision" that they (i.e., the Egyptians) "did not need or care about" (p. 60) needs to be especially noted.

3 The questions surrounding the origin, meaning and use of the terms "Canaan" and "Canaanite" are far beyond the scope of this study. See J. C. H. Laughlin (1990), and A.F. Rainey (1996).

4 The problem of identifying "ethnic" groups based upon archaeological remains is complex and difficult. See Kamp and Yoffee (1980). Note particularly their critique of the "Amorite Hypothesis." Where "Israel" is concerned, see Dever (1993b, 1995a, 1995c); Finkelstein (1996).

5 The "science" of population estimations for ancient societies is very imprecise. Different authorities use different methods and arrive at totally different numbers. For the coastal plain region, Gophna and Portugali (1988) listed around 50 MB I sites and estimated the population to be about 28,000; 60 sites for MB II with a population of some 37,000. Kempinski (1992b:194), on the other hand, estimated the population for all of Palestine during MB II (his MB IIb) to be around 200,000.

6 Once again, using the word *city* to describe these ancient settlements carries few of the connotations of the modern usage of this term, especially in regard to size. Most Palestinian "cities" were quite small even by the standards of their own time (i.e., compared with the size of cities in Syria and Mesopotamia).

7 For one set of criteria by which such remains can be assessed, see Oren (1992: 115). Among other items, he includes the proximity of "patrician" houses to other important structures such as temples, palaces and city gates; the overall dimensions and quality of the construction of the building; the presence of plastered floors, servant quarters and storerooms.

8 For a discussion of rampart construction from the perspective of an engineer, see E. Pennells (1983).

9 Terminology is always a concern. Note that A. Mazar has called the remains at Shechem, Hazor and Megiddo "monumental symmetrical temples" (1992a: 166).

10 Dever admits that there is very little archaeological evidence for Palestinian exports during this period. Neither does he suggest how cattle, or any other livestock, might have been transported, though one assumes by some type of water craft.

11 For a full discussion of the theories of collapse of ancient societies, see Yoffee and Congill (1988).

12 Albrecht Alt made this observation nearly 70 years ago in his well-known essay, "The God of the Fathers." See now the reprint in Alt (1968).

13 The history of the debate among biblical scholars, archaeologists and historians on the issue of the Patriarchs and their historical setting, including the question of whether or not the Patriarchs were real historical individuals, is far too involved and complex to go into in detail here. An excellent starting place for students is Dever and Clark's essays (1977), which include a very helpful bibliography. Other shorter but useful assessments can be found in McCarter, Jr (1988); Millard (1992).

14 This does not mean that all scholars who would argue that parts, at least, of the patriarchal traditions are older than the time of the Monarchy are agreed on dates. Clark (1977), for example, has argued for a time during the Late Bronze Age.

6 The Late Bronze Age (1500–1200 BC)

1 I am well aware that I cannot even begin to treat all of the important issues of this period in this brief overview. Thus the following summaries (primarily from a political/historical perspective) are highly recommended. Many of them also contain helpful bibliographies. Aharoni (1978: 112–52); Albright (1949: 96–109); Bunimovitz (1995: 180–211); Drower (1973); Gonen (1992b); Kenyon (1979: 180–211); Leonard (1989); A. Mazar (1990: 232–94); De Vaux (1978: 82–152).

2 The use of different dates for the same person or event by different "authorities" can quickly become confusing, especially to someone who may be studying this material for the first time. Until recently, the so-called "high" chronology used by the *Cambridge Ancient History* (see vol. II, part 2B:1038) was widely accepted. Today, some scholars argue for a "low"

chronology (see esp. P. Astrom 1987). For a convenient chart comparing both chronologies see the *NEAEHL*, vol. 4.

3 A. Mazar, in his study of the stratigraphical history of 19 LBA sites, identified three major occupational periods: LB IB; IIA and IIB (1990: 242, table 5).

4 The estimation of the number of sites, population sizes and total number of acres occupied is, of course, anything but exact. In most cases LBA archaeological sites have only been partially exposed, and others may have gone undetected. However, the general picture of this period as greatly diminished from that of the MBA has been firmly established.

5 While Ottosson (1980) concluded that this "temple" was nothing more than a pottery workshop, his suggestion has not been accepted by most other archaeologists (A. Mazar 1992a:179, n. 65). However, for a different assessment of Ottosson's conclusion, see Callaway (1982a).

6 Although 1887 is the year usually given for this discovery, there are conflicting stories. Some place the discovery in 1886; see Moran (1992: xiii, fn 1).

7 Some authorities say by a single bedouin woman (Campbell 1970: 2, fn 1).

8 The dates for Akhenaton vary considerably from scholar to scholar. According to the "high" chronology his reign would have been *ca.* 1379–1362; according to the "low" chronology, 1352–1336. See now the discussion by Moran (1992: xxxiv–xxxix).

9 As might be suspected, there is a considerable amount of secondary literature devoted to these tablets. The following, most with references of their own, are highly recommended: Aharoni (1979: 169–76); Albright (1975); Bruce (1967); Bryan (1997); Campbell, Jr (1960); Harrelson (1975); Izre'el (1997); Moran (1985, 1992); Na'aman (1992). For a map showing the Canaanite cities mentioned in the correspondence, see Aharoni (1979: 173, map 11). Twenty-five of these letters, mostly from Palestinian vassal kings, are conveniently grouped in *ANET*, 483–90.

10 The 'Apiru are mentioned in some 53 letters; see Moran (1992: 393).

11 See, for example, Sarna (1988). His arguments seem very forced to me and at times almost trivial (cf. Dever 1997b: 69); Malamat (1997) – (he summarized his main arguments in his 1998 article); Yurco (1997). The secondary literature on the subject of the Exodus is so vast that I hesitate even to begin to list references. However, for students who are being exposed to this subject for the first time I recommend two recent publications, both with sources: *The Rise of Ancient Israel* (1992) edited by H. Shanks; *Exodus: the Egyptian Evidence* (1997), edited by E. S. Frerichs and L. H. Lesko.

12 According to the tradition reflected in I Kings 6:1ff., the "Exodus" would have taken place around the middle of the fifteenth century BC, a date rejected by most scholars. For the sake of argument, my discussion will assume a date sometime during the thirteenth century BC, which is commonly held today. However, arguments for any date are irrelevant if it turns out that there never was an "Exodus" as told in the Bible.

13 The literature on this stela, and especially on the "Israel" reference, is far too vast to list. The references that are provided are done so simply as representative of various positions on the issues raised.

14 It is not a little interesting to see how creative some scholars can be in trying to salvage some "historical event" behind the biblical story. Thus, Malamat

(1997, 1998), after admitting that the Israel reference on the Merneptah Stela is immaterial to the question of the Exodus, cites other Egyptian literature to conclude that there could have been some kind of an "exodus" of Israel toward the end of the thirteenth century BC. He even suggested that there could have been several "Exoduses" that went on for several centuries. His arguments are far from convincing, and in the end even he had to admit "that none of the Egyptian sources substantiates the story of the Exodus" (1997: 15).

7 Iron Age I (1200–1000 BC)

1 Kitchen's dates are usually referred to as "lower." For the "higher" dates, long accepted by scholars, see *CAH*, vol II, part 2B, p. 1038. Cf. also the *NEAEHL*, vol. 4: 1530, where both the higher and lower dates are given.

2 While there are many scholarly participants in this debate, I will concentrate on the contributions of two of the most visible, and published: W. G. Dever, an American Syro-Palestinian archaeologist; and I. Finkelstein, an Israeli archaeologist. As a beginning, see Dever (1993b and 1995c, both with full references); Finkelstein (1988, 1994 and 1996, all with references).

3 How common this has been, and still is, in biblical/archaeological studies is illustrated by far too many publications to list here. The student need only begin to read the relevant literature to pick this tendency up. In addition to the works listed in note 3, see now Finkelstein and Na'aman (1994).

4 Cf. Finkelstein's and Na'aman's caveat that any term used to identify the "inhabitants of the Hill Country in Iron Age I will be inaccurate" (1994: 17). Out of a need to call them something, I will use the term suggested by Dever, "proto-Israelites" (see Dever 1993b and esp. 1995c). Finkelstein also used this term in his 1996 article. Furthermore, it seems to me that the term can be justified by the fact that it is reasonable to assume that these Iron I peoples, from wherever they might have come, were the direct ancestors of the people the Bible will identify as "Israel."

5 The literature on the Philistines is far too extensive to list here. The following, many with full references, will orientate the student to the pertinent issues involved. In addition, three of the five cities of the Philistine pentapolis (Ashdod, Ashkelon and Tell Miqne-Ekron) have been or, in the case of Ashkelon, is still being excavated. Gaza, identified with Tell Harube, was excavated in 1922 but the scant Philistine material has not conclusively established the identification of this site. The location of Gath is still unknown but Tell es-Safi has been suggested (T. Dothan 1982: 48, 50 and n. 133; see now esp. Schniedewind 1998). Articles on these sites can be found in the following major publications: the *EAEHL*, the *NEAEHL* and the *OEANE*. In addition, consult the following for a much fuller treatment: R. D. Barnett (1975); T. Dothan (1982). Dothan's volume is the most thorough study of Philistine culture up to around 1980. Especially noteworthy is Dothan's presentation of Philistine pottery (1985, 1989); T. Dothan and M. Dothan (1992); A. Mazar (1990: 300–34; 1992b: 262–81); I. Singer (1994); L. Stager (1995). For two popular articles see A. Raban and R. R. Stieglitz (1991); and B. Wood (1991).

On Ekron, see now T. Dothan (1990); Gitin and T. Dothan (1987);

T. Dothan and Gitin (1990); Gitin (1990). For a popular summary of the Philistine presence at Ashkelon, see Stager (1991, 1993).

The Ashdod excavations were carried out between 1962 and 1972 under the direction of M. Dothan. Many of his reports can be found in various issues of the journal *'Atiqot*, a publication of the Antiquities Authority of the State of Israel. For a good summary of the archaeological data from this site, see M. Dothan (1993).

6 Stager's suggestion (1991: 14) that the Philistines were none other than the Mycenaean Greeks has not met with wide acceptance .

7 At present, the entire known Philistine vocabulary consists of two words: *seren* and *k/qoba*, which is usually translated into English as "helmet" (I Sam. 17: 5, 38; of interest is the fact that most usages of *k/qoba* are late: Isa. 59: 17; Jer. 46: 4; Ezek. 23: 24; 27:10; 38: 5; 2 Chr. 26: 14). Of course, the word in Egyptian to refer to these people, Peleset, may also be a Philistine word.

8 For critical assessments of other aspects of Albright's scholarship, see the entire issue of *Biblical Archaeologist* 61(1) (March 1992). On the "Israelite" settlement in Israel, see further Dever (1990a: chap. 2).

9 One of Finkelstein's reasons, however, for discounting Alt's views – namely, that camels, which are necessary for desert nomads, had not been domesticated yet – has been contradicted by other studies. See particularly R. D. Barnett (1985).

10 The literature now emerging on this subject is voluminous. Here I can only mention what seem to me to be some of the most important and helpful for beginning students. For a good starting point for where the discussion was around 1980 see the section, "Session II: Archaeology, History and the Bible – the Israelite Settlement in Canaan: a Case Study," *BAT* (1985). For two different interpretations of this new evidence and its implications for writing a history of early Israel, see the following works by W. G. Dever and I. Finkelstein: Dever (1990a, 1990b, 1991b, 1992c, 1993b, 1995a, 1995c). For Finkelstein, 1988, 1994, 1995, 1996. See also the volume edited by Finkelstein and Na'aman (1994). For secondary sources exploring the implications of the new data for writing a history of early Israel, all with references, see Coote (1990); Shanks (1992); Lemche (1985); cf. Halpern (1983).

11 As early as 1978, Ibrahim had argued that this ceramic type could not be assigned to any particular "ethnic" group. See his article for references to earlier scholars (Albright, Aharoni, Amiran and others) who did interpret the jar as "Israelite." See also Finkelstein (1996: 204); London (1989: 43–5); Yellin and Gunneweg (1989).

12 Finkelstein has argued for the latter (1996; Finkelstein and Na'aman 1994), and accused Dever of the former. Dever, while referring (rightly so) to these technologies has, in my judgment, gone far beyond looking at these technologies in isolation (1992c, 1993b, 1995c) to placing them into the larger question of culture change and "material correlates."

13 The on-going debate between Dever and Finkelstein over the meaning of the archaeological data serves as a timely warning that all of these issues are complex and open to more than one interpretation. Their "disagreement" also extends to the ceramic evidence, which is technical and meaningful only to specialists. Here I will only note that Dever has argued for continuity

between the pottery forms of Late Bronze Age Canaan and that of the Central Hill villages (1993b: 27*, 30*; see esp. figs. 3.1, 2; 1995c: 201–7), while Finkelstein has disputed the similarity (1996). Stay tuned!

14   Interestingly, Dever did not mention the lack of pig bones in the faunal remains of the Hill Country culture, a fact Finkelstein emphasized (Finkelstein 1996: 206).

15   A full-scale treatment of the implications of the recent archaeological data and contemporary literary studies is far beyond the scope of this brief overview. In addition to the works by Dever and Finkelstein, see now Coote (1990); Lemche (1995). Regrettably, in some instances the debate has become personal and even bitter. See Thompson's attack on Dever in Fritz and Davies (1996: 26–43); and cf. Dever's comments in Dever (1995c: 212 and n. 15 – which should be changed to n. 14).

16   Cf. Dever: "The inescapable conclusion . . . is that the Israelite settlement in Canaan was part of the larger transition from the Late Bronze to the Iron Age. It was a gradual, exceedingly complex process, involving social, economic, and political – as well as religious – change, with many regional variations" (1990a: 79; see also his conclusion in 1992c: 548).

8   Iron Age II (1000–550 BC)

1   Cf. Barkay's comment: "The term 'biblical archaeology' . . . is most appropriate when confined to the Iron Age II–III" (1992: 302).

2   Among his examples is W. Dever, who seems to have become more cautious. See now Dever (1995c).

3   Holladay's quip that "purists" could substitute "Pre-Red Burnished King Number I (and possibly II or III)" for David and "Red-Burnished King" for Solomon (1995: 368) hardly matters. The fact is, based "solely" upon archaeological evidence, ceramics included, it is impossible to argue for a Hebrew United Monarchy in Palestine during the tenth century BC under the rule of any king(s). Furthermore, while questioning the historical validity of the Bible, Holladay, like many others, seems to have taken at face value the historical credibility of other written sources such as Shishak's list of supposedly destroyed Palestinian sites. For the latter, cf. the far more cautious comments of J. Wilson, in *ANET*: 263–4; see also pp. 242–3. Cf. also the comments by Barkay (1992: 306–7).

4   Cf. A. Mazar: "The Bible is the only written source concerning the United Monarchy and it is therefore the basis of any historical presentation of the period" (1990: 369). Cf. Dever (1995a, with bibliography). See also the interesting observations of D. N. Freedman (1985).

5   For a helpful summary of the issues with an accompanying chart, see Herr (1997b: 116–18); for an alternative scheme, see Barkay (1992); for recent archaeological overviews of the Iron II period, see Barkay (1992); Herr (1997b); A. Mazar (1990: 368–530). For specialized studies of parts of the period, see Dever (1995d; Holladay, Jr 1995).

6   For a detailed study of the theory of state formation, see Frick (1985); for summaries of the archaeological histories of the above-mentioned states, see Herr (1997b), *inter alia*; in addition, for the archaeology of Moab see now the entire issue of the *BA*, 60(4) (December 1997). For the Ammonites, see in

addition to the above, Herr (1993); for Ammon, Moab and Edom, see La Bianca and Younker (1995).

7   For excavation histories of these and other sites mentioned in this chapter, see the relevant articles in the *NEAEHL* and the *OEANE*.

8   The archaeological evidence for "Saul" is even more negligible. For a discussion of what little there is, see A. Mazar (1990:371–4).

9   The scholarly publication on this city is enormous. The reader is referred to the articles in the *NEAEHL* and the *OEANE*; see also Geve (1994); Kenyon (1974).

10 In 1984, the late Y. Shiloh pointed out to me a house on Ophel Hill from whose owner he had to gain permission to dig through the house's basement floor!

11 See now the articles by Fritz (1987b) and C. Meyers (1992b) both with bibliographies.

12 The only object yet discovered which may have come from the First Temple is a small inscribed pomegranate dated to the eighth century BC. See Avigad (1994).

13 A topographical list of sites claimed to have been conquered by Shishak is preserved on his temple walls at Karnak. Cf. Herr (1997b: 134).

14 It is impossible to review here all the archaeological data now available from so many excavation reports and other publications. The reader is again referred to the summary articles, with bibliographies, in the *NEAEHL* and the *OEANE*.

15 The excavator, A. Biran, also concluded that the site was occupied after the Assyrian onslaught. This period of occupation has been identified as "Stratum I," and dated from the end of the eighth to the early sixth centuries BC. However, during this time (Iron IIc in this volume), Dan, while apparently heavily occupied, was controlled by the Assyrians and will not be discussed here.

16 For a plan and reconstruction of this gate, see Biran (1994: 236, 248).

17 The discussion concerning this remarkable discovery is growing. The following will orientate and guide the reader to other works: Biran and Naveh (1993); Dever (1995a); Halpern (1994); Schniedewind (1996); Shanks (1994). Two smaller fragments of the same stela were found in 1994.

18 Barkay's suggestion that this structure should be identified as the remains of a palace has not received much support (Barkay 1992: 312).

19 While an olive press seems to be the most feasible interpretation (see particularly Stager and Wolff 1981), it should be noted that the bottom of this structure is constructed of unplastered, irregularly shaped stones that would have allowed the loss of much oil through seepage. Also, while constituting an argument from silence, not one olive stone was found in association with this installation.

20 To my knowledge, most literary scholars have not yet incorporated what is now known of Israelite "popular religion" (Dever 1994b) into systematic treatments of the Hebrew Bible. But see now Albertz (1994) and Dever's review (1996b). This subject, especially in light of Dever's publications, deserves a much fuller treatment than is possible here.

21 The site was re-occupied during the Hellenistic, Roman and Byzantine periods, but the discussion of these strata lies beyond the scope of this study.

22   For brief summaries of the history of the excavations of this site, with sources, see the articles in the *NEAEHL* and the *OEANE*.
23   An "ostracon" (singular) is a pottery sherd that contains an inscription. See Lemaire (1997).
24   For examples, see *ANET*: 321.
25   For a discussion and comparison of the Samaria ivories with other such ivories known from the Near East, see Barnett (1982).
26   On this festival see King (1988b, 1988c); Beach (1993), with full references to earlier discussions. From English translations of the Bible, one would scarcely conclude that a major religious festival of some sort was involved here. In Amos 6: 7, the NRSV translates *marzeah* as "reveling," while in Jeremiah 16:5, as "mourning."
27   Herr (1997b) lists 22 primary sites for the Iron IIb period (p. 142), and 42 for Iron IIc (p. 155). Out of the 22 Iron IIb sites, 16 were also occupied during Iron IIc.
28   For summary articles on all of these sites see under individual headings in the *NEAEHL* and the *OEANE*.
29   Cf. Barkay's comment (1992: 349): "by the end of the eighth century Israelite society as a whole was literate."
30   In recent years a controversy has arisen over the date of this inscription, which is now in the museum in Istanbul. Rogerson and Davies have argued for a date in the second century BC (1996). This late date has been rejected by other experts on epigraphic (Hendel 1996; Hackett *et al.* 1997) as well as historical and archaeological grounds (Cahill 1997). For a translation of this inscription see Albright in *ANET* (1969: 321).
31   In addition to these seals from the time of Hezekiah, there has recently been published a seal claimed to be from the reign of Ahaz (733–737 BC), Hezekiah's father. See Deutsch (1998).
32   These burial practices have economic, social and artistic as well as religious significance. For orientation and description of the burial caves in Jerusalem, see the following: Barkay and Kloner (1986); Barkay (1994); Barkay *et al.* (1994); Kloner and Davis (1994); Reich (1994); Herr (1997b: 161–2). For a detailed discussion of burial practices in Judah in general, see now E. Bloch-Smith (1992).
33   The word *bulla(ae)* is derived from Latin and refers to a seal impression stamped on a lump of clay used to seal documents. Often, the bulla contains the name of the person to whom the seal belonged (see Shiloh 1985).
34   Shiloh reported finding only the name, "Gemaryahu" (1989: 104). For "Azaryahu," see Schneider (1994) and Shoham (1994).
35   The oldest biblical text yet discovered, the Levitical blessing in Numbers 6: 24–26, has been found in Jerusalem (Ketef Hinnom) on two small silver amulets dated to the late seventh or early sixth century BC (Barkay 1994).
36   A good place to begin a study of this complex and controversial issue is Friedman (1987).

Bibliography

Aharoni, Y. (1978) *The Archaeology of the Land of Israel* (Philadelphia: Westminster Press).

—— (1979) *The Land of the Bible: A Historical Geography* (Philadelphia: Westminster Press).

Albertz, R. (1994) *A History of Israelite Religion in the Old Testament Period* vol. I: *From the Beginnings to the End of the Monarchy* (Louisville, KY: Westminster/John Knox Press).

Albright, W. F. (1931) "Recent Progress in the Late Prehistory of Palestine," *BASOR*, 42: 13–15.

—— (1932) "The Chalcolithic Age in Palestine," *BASOR*, 43: 10–13.

—— (1949) *The Archaeology of Palestine* (London: Penguin Books).

—— (1957) *From the Stone Age to Christianity* (Garden City, NY: Doubleday Anchor Books) (first published in 1940).

—— (1974) *The Archaeology of Palestine and the Bible* 3rd edn (Cambridge: ASOR).

—— (1975) "The Amarna Letters from Palestine," in: *CAH*, vol. II/2: 98–116.

Alon, D. (1977, May) "A Chalcolithic Temple at Gilath," *BA*, 40(2): 63–5.

Alt, A. (1968) *Essays on Old Testament History and Religion* (Garden City, NY: Doubleday & Co.).

Amiran, R. (1970a) "The Beginnings of Urbanization in Canaan," in: James A. Sanders (ed.) *Near Eastern Archaeology in the Twentieth Century* (Garden City, NY: Doubleday), pp. 83–100.

—— (1970b) *Ancient Pottery of the Holy Land* (New Brunswick, NJ: Rutgers University Press).

—— (1985a) "The Transition from the Chalcolithic to the Early Bronze Age," in: *BAT*, pp. 108–12.

—— (1985b) "A Suggestion to See the Copper 'Crowns' of the Judean Desert Treasure as Drums of Stand-like Altars," in: *PBIA*, pp. 10–14.

Amiran, R. (1978) *Early Arad: The Chalcolithic Settlement and Early Bronze City I First–Fifth Seasons of Excavations, 1962–1966* (Jerusalem: Israel Exploration Society).

Amiran, R. and Ilan, O. (1996) *Early Arad II: The Chalcolithic and Early Bronze I B Settlements and the Early Bronze II City – Architecture and Town Planning, Sixth to Eighteenth Seasons of Excavations, 1971–1978, 1980–1984* (Jerusalem: Israel Exploration Society).

Astroms, P. (ed.) (1987) *High, Middle or Low? Acts of an International Colloquium on Absolute Chronology Held at the University of Gothenburg 20th–22nd August 1987* (Gothenburg: Paul Astroms).

Avigad, N. (1985) "The Upper City," in: *BAT*, pp. 469–75.

—— (1993) "Samaria (City)," in: *NEAEHL*, vol. 3: 1300–10.

—— (1994) "The Inscribed Pomegranate from the 'House of the Lord'," in: *AJR*: 128–37.

Banning, E. B. (1996) "Highlands and Lowlands: Problems and Survey Frameworks for Rural Archaeology in the Near East," *BASOR*, 301: 25–45.

Bar-Adon, P. (1980) *The Cave of the Treasure: The Finds from the Caves in Nahal Mishmar* (Jerusalem: Israel Exploration Society).

Bar-Yosef, O. (1992) "The Neolithic Period," in: *AAI*, pp. 10–39.

—— (1995) "Earliest Food Producers – Pre-pottery Neolithic (8000–5500)," in: *ASHL*, pp. 190–204.

Barkay, G. (1992) "The Iron Age II–III," in: *AAI*, pp. 302–73.

—— (1994) "Excavations at Ketef Hinnom in Jerusalem," in: *AJR*, pp. 85–106.

Barkay, G. and Kloner, A. (1986, March/April) "Jerusalem Tombs from the Days of the First Temple," *BAR*, 12(2): 22–39.

Barkay, G., Kloner, A. and Mazar, A. (1994) "The Northern Necropolis of Jerusalem during the First Temple Period," in: *AJR*, pp. 119–27.

Barnett, R. D. (1975) "The Sea Peoples," in: *CAH*, vol. II/2, pp. 359–78.

—— (1982) *Ancient Ivories in the Middle East* (Jerusalem: Institute of Archaeology).

—— (1985) "Lachish, Ashkelon and the Camel: A Discussion of its Use in Southern Palestine," in: *PBIA*, pp. 15–30.

Baumgarten, J. J. (1992) "Urbanization in the Late Bronze Age," in: *AAIPP*, pp. 143–50.

Beach, E. F. (1993, June) "The Samaria Ivories, Marzeah, and Biblical Text," *BA*, 56(2): 94–104.

Beck, P. and Zevulun, U. (1996) "Back to Square One," *BASOR*, 304: 64–75.

Beit-Arieh, I. (1981) "A Pattern of Settlement in Southern Sinai and Southern Canaan in the Third Millennium B.C.," *BASOR*, 243: 31–55.

—— (1984) "New Evidence on the Relations between Canaan and Egypt during the Protodynastic Period," *IEJ*, 34: 21–3.

Ben-Dor, M. (1992) "Middle and Late Bronze Age Dwellings," in: *AAIPP*, pp. 99–104.

Ben-Tor, A. (1978) *Cylinder Seals of Third-millennium Palestine*, *BASOR* Supplement Series 22 (Cambridge, MA: ASOR).

—— (1991) "New Light on the Relations between Egypt and Southern Palestine during the Early Bronze Age," *BASOR*, 281: 3–10.

—— (1992) "The Early Bronze Age," in: *AAI*, pp. 81–125.

—— (1994) "Early Bronze Age Cylinder Seal Impressions and a Stamp Seal from Tel Qashish," *BASOR*, 295: 15–29.

Betts, A. V. G. (1997) "Jawa," in: *OEANE*, vol. 3: 209–10.

—— ed. (1991) *Excavations at Jawa, 1972–1986* (Edinburgh: Edinburgh University Press).

Bienkowski, P. (1989) "The Division of Middle Bronze II B–C in Palestine," *Levant*, 21: 169–79.

Bietak, M. (1991) "Egypt and Canaan during the Middle Bronze Age," *BASOR*, 281: 27–72.

—— (1997) "Avaris, Capital of the Hyksos Kingdom: New Results of Excavations," in: *HNHAP*, pp. 87–139.

Binford, L. (1989) *Debating Archaeology* (New York: Academic Press).

Biran, A. (ed.) (1981) *Temples and High Places in Biblical Times* (Jerusalem: Nelson Glueck School of Biblical Archaeology Hebrew Union College–Jewish Institute of Religion).

—— (1987) "Prize Find: Tel Dan Scepter Head: Belonging to Priest or King?" *BAR*, 15 (1): 29–31.

—— (1994) *Biblical Dan* (Jerusalem: Israel Exploration Society, Hebrew Union College–Jewish Institute of Religion).

—— (ed.) (1996) *Dan I: A Chronicle of the Excavations, the Pottery Neolithic, the Early Bronze Age and the Middle Bronze Age Tombs* (Jerusalem: Nelson Glueck School of Biblical Archaeology, Hebrew Union College–Jewish Institute of Religion).

—— (1998) "Sacred Spaces of Standing Stones, High Places and Cult Objects at Tel Dan," *BAR* Sept.–Oct., 24/5: 38–45, 70.

Biran, A. and Naveh, J. (1993) "An Aramaic Stela Fragment from Tel Dan," *IEJ*, 43: 81–98.

Blakely, J. A. (1997) "Site Survey", in: *OEANE*, vol. 5, pp. 49–51.

Blakely, J. A. and Toombs, L. E. (1980) *The Tell El-Hesi Field Manual* (Cambridge, MA: American Schools of Oriental Research).

Blau, J. (1997) "Hebrew Language and Literature," in: *OEANE*, vol. 3, pp. 5–12.

Blenkinsopp, J. (1995) *Sage, Priest, Prophet: Religious and Intellectual Leadership in Ancient Israel* (Louisville, KY: Westminster/John Knox Press).

Bloch-Smith, E. (1992) *Judahite Burial Practices and Beliefs about the Dead* (Sheffield: Journal for the Study of the Old Testament).

Boraas, R. S. (1988) "Publication of Archaeology Reports," in: *BTC*, pp. 325–33.

Bordreuil, P. (1997) "Northwest Semitic Seal Inscriptions," in: *OEANE*, vol. 4, pp. 166–9.

Bordreuil, P. Israel, F. and Pardee, D. (1998, March) "King's Command and Widow's Plea: Two New Hebrew Ostraca of the Biblical Period," *NEA*, 61(1): 2–13.

Borowski, O. (1987) *Agriculture in Iron Age Israel* (Winona Lake, IN: Eisenbrauns).

—— (1995, September) "Hezekiah's Reforms and the Revolt against Assyria," *BA*, 58(3): 148–55.

Brandl, B. (1992) "Evidence for Egyptian Colonization in the Southern Coastal Plain and Lowlands of Canaan during the EB I Period," in: *NDT*, pp. 441–7.

—— (1997) "'Erani, Tel," in: *OEANE*, vol. 2, pp. 256–8.

Braun, E., Rosen, S. A. and Horwitz, L. K. (1985) *En Shadud Salvage Excavation at a Farming Community in the Jezreel Valley, Israel* (London, Oxford: *BAR*).

Braun, E. and Gibson, S. (1984) "'En-shadud: An Early Bronze I Farming Community in the Jezreel Valley," *BASOR*, 253: 29–40.

Brettler, M. Z. (1995) *The Creation of History in Ancient Israel* (London: Routledge).

Bright, J. (1981) *A History of Israel*, 3rd edn (Philadelphia: Westminster).

Bronowski, J. (1973) *The Ascent of Man* (Boston: Little, Brown & Co.).

Broshi, M. and Finkelstein, I. (1992, August) "The Population of Palestine in Iron Age II," *BASOR*, 287: 47–60.

Broshi, M. and Gophna, R. (1984) "The Settlements and Population of Palestine during the Early Bronze Age II–III," *BASOR*, 253: 41–53.

—— (1986) "Middle Bronze Age II Palestine: Its Settlements and Population," *BASOR*, 261: 73–90.

Browning, D. C., Jr (1996) "The Strange Search for the Ashes of the Red Heifer," *BA*, 59(2): 74–89.

Bruce, F. (1967) "Tell el-Amarna," in: D. Thomas (ed.) *Archaeology and Old Testament Study* (Oxford, Clarendon Press), pp. 3–20.

Bryan, B. M. (1997) "Amarna, Tell El," in: *OEANE*, vol.1, pp. 81–6.

Bunimovitz, S. (1992) "The Middle Bronze Age Fortifications in Palestine as a Social Phenomenon", *Tel Aviv*, 19(2): 221–34.

—— (1995) "On the Edge of Empires – Late Bronze Age (1500–1200 BCE)," in: *ASHL*, pp. 320–31.

Bunimovitz, S. and Lederman, Z. (1997, January/February) "Beth-Shemesh: Culture Conflict on Judah's Frontier," *BAR*, 23(1): 42–9; 75–7.

Cahill, J. M. (1997, September) "A Rejoinder to 'Was the Siloam Tunnel Built by Hezekiah?'," *BA*, 60(3): 184–5.

—— (1998, July/August) "It is There: The Archaeological Evidence Proves It," *BAR* 24 (4): 34–41, 63.

Cahill, J. M. and Tarler, D. (1994) "Excavations Directed by Yigal Shiloh at the City of David, 1978–1985," in: *AJR*, pp. 31–45.

Callaway, J. A. (1961) "Biblical Archaeology," *Review & Expositor*, 58: 155–72.

—— (1972) *The Early Bronze Age Sanctuary at Ai (et-Tell): No. 1* (London: Bernard Quaritch).

—— (1978) "New Perspectives on Early Bronze III in Canaan," in: R. Moorey and P. Parr (eds) *Archaeology in the Levant: Essays for Kathleen Kenyon* (Warminster: Aris & Phillips Ltd), pp. 46–58.

—— (1980a) "Sir Flinders Petrie: Father of Palestinian Archaeology," *BAR*, 6(6): 44–55.

—— (1980b) *The Early Bronze Age Citadel and Lower City at Ai (Et-Tell): A Report of the Joint Archaeological Expedition to Ai (Et-Tell): No. 2* (Cambridge, MA: American Schools of Oriental Research).

—— (1982a, December) A Review of *Temples and Cult Places in Palestine* by M. Ottosson, *JBL*, 101(4): 597–8.

—— (1982b) "A Review of Arad 1," *BASOR*, 247: 71–9.

—— (1985) "A New Perspective on the Hill Country Settlement of Canaan in Iron Age I," in: *PBIA*, pp. 31–49.

—— (1987) "Ai (Et-Tell): Problem Site for Biblical Archaeologists," in: *ABI*, pp. 87–99.

—— (1988) "The Settlement in Canaan: The Period of the Judges," in: H. Shanks (ed.) *Ancient Israel – A Short History from Abraham to the Roman Destruction of the Temple*, pp. 53–84 (Englewood Cliffs, NJ: Prentice-Hall).

Cameron, D. O. (1981) *The Ghassulian Wall Paintings* (London: Kenyon-Deane Ltd).

Campbell, E. F., Jr (1960, February) "The Amarna Letters and the Amarna Period," *BA*, xxiii/1: 2–22; reprinted in *BA Reader*, 3 (1970): 54–75.

—— (1983) "Judges 9 and Biblical Archaeology," in *WLS*, pp. 263–71.

Chaney, M. L. (1983) "Ancient Palestinian Peasant Movements and the Formation of Premonarchic Israel," in: D. N. Freedman and D. F. Graf (eds) *Palestine in Transition: The Emergence of Ancient Israel* (Sheffield, The Almond Press), pp. 39–90.

Chapman III, R. L. (1986) "Excavation Techniques and Recording Systems: A Theoretical Study," *PEQ*, 118: 5–26.

Charlesworth, J. H. and Weaver, W. P. (eds) (1992) *What Has Archaeology to Do with Faith?* (Philadelphia: Trinity Press International).

Chase, D. A. (1982, Spring) "A Note on an Inscription from Kuntillet 'Ajrud," *BASOR*, 246: 63–7.

Christopherson, G. L. (1997) "Computer Mapping," in: *OEANE*, vol. 2, pp. 55–7.

Clark, D. L. (1978) *Analytical Archaeology* (New York: Columbia University Press).

Clark, D. R. (1996, December) "Early Iron I Pillared Building at Tell al-'Umayri," *BA*, 59(4): 241.

Cohen, R. (1997) "Qadesh-Barnea," in: *OEANE*, vol. 4, pp. 365–7.

Conrad, D. (1984) "An Introduction to the Archaeology of Syria and Palestine on the Basis of the Israelite Settlement," in: *A History of Ancient Israel From the Beginnings to the Bar Kochba Revolt, AD 135*, by J. A. Soggin (Philadelphia: Westminster Press), pp. 357–67.

Coote, R. B. (1990) *Early Israel: A New Horizon* (Minneapolis, MN: Fortress Press).

Davidson, L. (1996) "Biblical Archaeology and the Press," *BA*, 59(2): 104–14.

Davies, G. I. (1988) "British Archaeologists," in: *BTC*, pp. 37–62.

Day, J. (1992) "Asherah," in: *ABD*, vol. 1, pp. 483–7.

Demsky, A. (1997) "Literacy," in: *OEANE*, vol. 3, pp. 362–9.

Dessel, J. P. (1997) "Excavation Strategy," in: *OEANE*, vol. 2, pp. 293–4.

Deutsch, R. (1998, May/June) "First Impression: What We Learn from King Ahaz's Seal," *BAR*, 24(3): 54–6, 62.

de Vaux, R. (1971) "Palestine in the Early Bronze Age," in: *CAH*, I/2: 208–37.

—— (1978) *The Early History of Israel* (Philadelphia: Westminster Press).

Dever, W. G. (1970) "The 'Middle Bronze' Period in Syria and Palestine," in: J. A. Sanders (ed.) *Near Eastern Archaeology in the Twentieth Century: Essays in Honor of Nelson Glueck* (Garden City, NY: Doubleday & Co.), pp. 132–63.

—— (1973) *Archaeology and Biblical Studies: Retrospects and Prospects* (Evanston, IL: Seabury).

—— (1974) "Two Approaches to Archaeological Method – the Architectural and the Stratigraphic," *Eretz-Israel*, 11: 1–8.

—— (1978) "Field Surveying and Drafting for the Archaeologist," in: W. G. Dever and H. D. Lance (eds) *A Manual of Field Excavation* (New York, Hebrew Union College–Jewish Institute of Religion), pp. 138–74.

—— (1980a) "Archaeological Method in Israel: A Continuing Revolution," *BA*, 43: 40–8.

—— (1980b) "New Vistas on the EB IV ('MB I') Horizon in Syria-Palestine," *BASOR* 237: 35–64.

—— (1981) "The Impact of the 'New Archaeology' on Syro-Palestinian Archaeology," *BASOR*, 242: 14–29.

—— (1982a) "Retrospects and Prospects in Biblical and Syro-Palestinian Archaeology," *BA*, 45: 103–7.

—— (1982b) "Monumental Architecture in Ancient Israel in the Period of the United Monarchy," in: T. Ishida (ed.) *Studies in the Period of David and Solomon and Other Essays* (Winona Lake, IN: Eisenbrauns), pp. 269–306.

—— (1983) "Material Remains and the Cult in Ancient Israel: An Essay in Archaeological Systematics," in: *WLS*, pp. 571–87.

—— (1984, Summer) "Asherah, Consort of Yahweh? New Evidence from Kuntillet 'Ajrud," *BASOR*, 255: 21–37.

—— (1985a) "Syro-Palestinian and Biblical Archaeology," in: D. Knight and G. M. Tucker (eds) *The Hebrew Bible and Its Modern Interpreters* (Philadelphia: Fortress), pp. 31–74.

—— (1985b) "Archaeology, Methods of," in: *HBD*, pp. 53–9.

—— (1985c) "From the End of the Early Bronze Age to the Beginning of the Middle Bronze," in: *BAT*, pp. 113–35.

—— (1985d) "Relations between Syria-Palestine and Egypt in the 'Hyksos' Period," in: *PBIA*, pp. 69–87.

—— (1987a) "The Middle Bronze Age: The Zenith of the Urban Canaanite Era," *BA*, 50 (3): 148–77.

—— (1987b) "The Contribution of Archaeology to the Study of Canaanite and Early Israelite Religion," in P. D. Miller, Jr, P. D. Hanson and S. D. McBride (eds) *Ancient Israelite Religion: Essays in Honor of Frank Moore Cross* (Philadelphia: Scholars Press).

—— (1988) "Impact of the New Archaeology," in: *BTC*, pp. 337–52.

—— (1989) "Archaeology in Israel Today: A Summation and Critique," in: *REI* (Winona Lake, IN: Eisenbrauns), pp. 143–52.

—— (1990a) *Recent Archaeological Discoveries and Biblical Research* (Seattle, WA: University of Washington Press).

—— (1990b, February/May) "Of Myths and Methods," *BASOR*, 277/278: 121–30.

—— (1991a) "Tell el-Dab'a and Levantine Middle Bronze Age Chronology: A Rejoinder to Manfred Bietak," *BASOR*, 281: 43–79.

—— (1991b, November) "Archaeological Data on the Israelite Settlement: A Review of Two Works", *BASOR*, 284: 77–90.

—— (1991c) "Archaeology, Material Culture and the Early Monarchical Period in Israel," in: D. V. Edelman (ed.) *The Fabric of History, Text, Artifact and Israel's Past* (Sheffield: *Journal for the Study of the Old Testament*), pp. 103–15.

—— (1992a) "Archaeology, Syro-Palestinian and Biblical," in *ABD*, vol. 1, pp. 354–67.

—— (1992b) "The Chronology of Syria-Palestine in the Second Millennium BCE: A Review of Current Issues," *BASOR*, 288: 1–25.

—— (1992c) "Israel, History of (Archaeology and the 'Conquest')," *ABD*, vol. 3, pp. 545–58.

—— (1993a) "Biblical Archaeology: Death or Rebirth?" *BAT 90*, pp. 706–22.

—— (1993b) "Cultural Continuity, Ethnicity in the Archaeological Record and the Question of Israelite Origins," *Eretz-Israel*, 24: 22*–33*.

—— (1993c, March) "What Remains of the House that Albright Built?" *BA*, 56(1): 25–35.

—— (1994) "The Silence of the Text: An Archaeological Commentary on 2 Kings 23," in: M. D. Coogan, J. C. Exum and L. E. Stager (eds) *Scripture and Other Artifacts; Essays on the Bible and Archaeology in Honor of Philip J. King* (Louisville, KY: Westminster/John Knox Press).

—— (1995a) "'Will the Real Israel Please Stand Up?' Archaeology and Israelite Historiography: Part 1," *BASOR*, 297: 61–80.

—— (1995b) "Social Structure in the Early Bronze IV Period in Palestine," in: *ASHL*, pp. 282–96.

—— (1995c, December) "Ceramics, Ethnicity, and the Question of Israel's Origins," *BA*, 58(4): 200–13.

—— (1995d) "Social Structure in Palestine in the Iron II Period on the Eve of Destruction," in: *ASHL*, pp. 416–31.

—— (1995e, May) "'Will the Real Israel Please Stand Up?' Part II: Archaeology and the Religions of Ancient Israel," *BASOR*, 298: 37–58.

—— (1996a) "The Tell: Microcosm of the Cultural Process," in: J. D. Seger (ed.) *Retrieving the Past: Essays on Archaeological Research and Methodology in Honor of Gus W. Van Beek* (Starkville, MS: Cobb Institute of Archaeology, Mississippi State University), pp. 37–45.

—— (1996b, February) "Archaeology and the Religions of Israel", A Review of *A History of Israelite Religion in the Old Testament Period*, vol. I: *From the Beginnings to the End of the Monarchy*, by Rainer Albertz, 1994 (Louisville, KY: Westminster/John Knox Press), *BASOR*, 301: 83–90.

—— (1997a) "Biblical Archaeology," in: *OEANE*, vol.1, pp. 315–19.

—— (1997b) "Qom, Khirbet El-," in: *OEANE*, vol. 4, pp. 391–2.

—— (1997c) "Is There any Archaeological Evidence for the Exodus?" in: E. S. Frerichs and L. H. Lesko (eds) *Exodus: The Egyptian Evidence* (Winona Lake, IN: Eisenbrauns), pp. 67–86.

—— (1997d) "Settlement Patterns and Chronology of Palestine in the Middle Bronze Age," in: *HNHAP*, pp. 285–301.

—— (1998, March) "Archaeology, Ideology, and the Quest for an 'Ancient' or 'Biblical' Israel," *NEA*, 61(1): 39–52.

Dever, W. G. and Clark, W. M. (1977) "The Patriarchal Traditions," in: J. H. Hayes and J. M. Miller (eds) *Israelite and Judaean History* (Philadelphia: Westminster Press), pp. 70–148.

Dever, W. G. and Lance, H. D. (1978) *A Manual of Field Excavation* (New York: Hebrew Union College–Jewish Institute of Religion).

De Vries, B. (1997) "Architectural Drafting and Drawing," in: *OEANE*, vol. 1, pp. 197–200.

DeVries, L. F. (1987, July/August) "Cult Stands – a Bewildering Variety of Shapes and Sizes," *BAR* 12 (4): 26–37.

Dornemann, R. H. (1981, Winter) "The Late Bronze Age Pottery Tradition at Tell Hadidi, Syria," *BASOR*, 241: 29–47.

Dothan, M. (1971) "Ashdod II–III," *'Atiqot*, 9–10.

—— (1977) "Kadesh-Barnea," in: *EAEHL*, vol. III, pp. 697–8.

—— (1981) "Sanctuaries along the Coast of Canaan in the MB Period," in: A. Biran (ed.) *Temples and High Places in Biblical Times* (Jerusalem: Nelson Glueck School of Biblical Archaeology, Hebrew Union College–Jewish Institute of Religion), pp. 74–81.

—— (1985) "Terminology for the Archaeology of the Biblical Periods," in: *BAT*, pp. 136–41.

—— (1989) "Archaeological Evidence for Movements of the Early 'Sea Peoples' in Canaan," in: *REI*, pp. 59–70.

—— (1993) "Ashdod," in: *NEAEHL*, vol. 1, pp. 93–102.

Dothan, T. (1982) *The Philistines and their Material Culture* (Jerusalem: Israel Exploration Society).

—— (1985) "The Philistines Reconsidered," in: *BAT*, pp. 165–76.

—— (1989) "The Arrival of the Sea Peoples: Cultural Diversity in Early Iron Age Canaan," in: *REI*, pp. 1–22.

—— (1990, January/February) "Ekron of the Philistines Part I: Where They Came from, How They Settled Down and the Place They Worshiped in," *BAR*, 16(1): 26–36.

—— (1994) "Tel Migne-Ekron: The Aegean Affinities of the Sea Peoples' (Philistines) Settlement in Canaan in the Iron Age I," in: S. Gitin (ed.) *Recent Excavations in Israel: A View to the West*, Archaeological Institute of America, Conference and Colloquium Series, No. 1, chap. 3 (Boston: Archaeological Institute of America).

Dothan, T. and Dothan, M. (1992) *People of the Sea: The Search for the Philistines* (New York: Macmillan Publishing Co.).

Dothan, T. and Gitin, S. (1990, January/February) "Ekron of the Philistines," *BAR* 16(1): 20–5.

Drower, M. S. (1973) "Syria *c.* 1550–1400 BC," in: *CAH*, II/1: 467–525.

Emerton, J. (1982) "New Light on Israelite Religion: the Implications of the Inscriptions from Kuntillet 'Ajrud," *ZAW*, 94: 2–20.

Epstein, C. (1977) "The Chalcolithic Culture of the Golan," *BA*, 40(2): 56–62.

—— (1985) "Laden Animal Figurines from the Chalcolithic Period in Palestine," *BASOR*, 258: 53–62.

Exum, J. C. and Clines, D. J. A. (eds) (1993) *The New Literary Criticism and the Hebrew Bible* (Valley Forge, PA: Trinity Press International).

Finkelstein, I. (1988) *The Archaeology of the Israelite Settlement* (Jerusalem: Israel Exploration Society).

—— (1992) "Middle Bronze Age 'Fortifications': A Reflection of Social Organization and Political Formations," *Tel Aviv*, 19: 201–20.

—— (1994) "The Emergence of Israel: A Phase in the Cyclic History of Canaan in the Third and Second Millennia BCE," in: *FNM*, pp. 150–78.

—— (1995) "The Great Transformation: The 'Conquest' of the Highlands Frontiers and the Rise of the Territorial States," in: *ASHL*, pp. 349–65.

—— (1996, December) "Ethnicity and Origin of the Iron I Settlers in the Highlands of Canaan: Can the Real Israel Stand Up?" *BA*, 59(4): 198–212.

Finkelstein, I. and Gophna, R. (1993, February) "Settlement, Demographic, and Economic Patterns in the Highlands of Palestine in the Chalcolithic and Early Bronze Periods and the Beginning of Urbanism", *BASOR*, 289: 1–22.

Finkelstein, I. and Na'aman, N. (1994) "Introduction: From Nomadism to Monarchy – the State of Research in 1992," in: *FNM*, pp. 9–17.

Fisher, C. S. (1929) *The Excavation of Armageddon* (Chicago: University of Chicago Press).

Franken, H. and Franken-Battershill, C. A. (1963) *A Primer of Old Testament Archaeology* (Leiden: E. J. Brill).

Freedman, D. N. (1985, January/February) "Remarks," *BAR*, 11(1): 63.

—— (1987, December) "Yahweh of Samaria and His Asherah," *BA*, 50(4): 241–9.

Frerichs, E. S. and Lesko, L. H. (eds) (1997) *Exodus: The Egyptian Evidence* (Winona Lake, IN: Eisenbrauns).

Frick, F. S. (1985) *The Formation of the State in Ancient Israel: A Survey of Models and Theories* (Sheffield: Almond).

Friedman, R. E. (1987) *Who Wrote the Bible?* (New York: Harper & Row).

Fritz, V. (1981, Winter) "The Israelite 'Conquest' in the Light of Recent Excavations at Khirbet el-Meshash," *BASOR*, 241: 61–73.

—— (1987a, June) "Conquest or Settlement? The Early Iron Age in Palestine," *BA*, 50(2): 84–104.

—— (1987b, July/August) "What can Archaeology Tell us about Solomon's Temple?" *BAR*, 13(4): 38–49.

—— (1994) *An Introduction to Biblical Archaeology* (Sheffield: *Journal for the Study of the Old Testament*).

Fritz, V. and Davies, P. R. (eds) (1996) *The Origins of the Ancient Israelite States* (Sheffield: Sheffield Academic Press).

Gal, Z. (1991) "A Note on the Settlement Pattern of the MB II Jezreel and Beth Shan Valleys," *BASOR*, 284: 29–31.

—— (1992) *Lower Galilee during the Iron Age* (Winona Lake, IN: Eisenbrauns).

—— (1998, May/June) "Israel in Exile," *BAR*, 24(3): 48–53.

Gerstenblith, P. (1980) "A Reassessment of the Beginning of the Middle Bronze Age in Syria-Palestine," *BASOR*, 237: 65–84.

Geve, H. (ed.) (1994) *Ancient Jerusalem Revealed* (Jerusalem: Israel Exploration Society).

Gilead, I. (1987, June) "A New Look at Chalcolithic Beer-Sheba", *BA*, 50(2): 110–17.

—— (1994) "The History of Chalcolithic Settlement in the Nahal Beer Sheva Area: The Radiocarbon Aspect," *BASOR*, 296: 1–13.

Gitin, S. (1990, March/April) "Ekron of the Philistines Part II: Olive-oil Suppliers to the World," *BAR*, 16(2): 32–42, 59.

Gitin, S. and Dothan, T. (1987, December) "The Rise and Fall of Ekron of the Philistines: Recent Excavations at an Urban Border Site," *BA*, 50(4): 197–222.

Gittlen, B. M. (1981, Winter) "The Cultural and Chronological Implications of the Cypro-Palestinian Trade During the Late Bronze Age," *BASOR*, 241: 49–59.

Glueck, N. (1940) *The Other Side of the Jordan* (New Haven, CT: American Schools of Oriental Research).

Gonen, R. (1984, Winter) "Urban Canaan in the Late Bronze Period," *BASOR*, 253: 61–73.

—— (1992a) "The Chalcolithic Period," in: *AAI*, pp. 40–80.

—— (1992b) "The Late Bronze Age," in: *AAI*, pp. 211–57.

Gopher, A. (1995) "Early Pottery-bearing Groups in Israel – the Pottery Neolithic Period," in: *ASHL*, pp. 205–25.

Gopher, A. and Goren, Y. (1995) "The Beginning of Pottery," in: *ASHL*, pp. 224–5.

Gopher, A. and Tsuk, T. (1991) *Ancient Gold – Rare Finds from the Nahal Qanah Cave* (Jerusalem: Israel Museum).

Gophna, R. (1992) "The Intermediate Bronze Age," in: *AAI*, pp. 126–58.

—— (1995) "Early Bronze Age Canaan: Some Spatial and Demographic Observations," in: *ASHL*, pp. 219–80.

Gophna, R. and Portugali, J. (1988) "Settlement and Demographic Processes in Israel's Coastal Plain from the Chalcolithic to the Middle Bronze Age," *BASOR*, 269: 11–28.

Goren, Y. (1996) "The Southern Levant in the Early Bronze Age IV: The Petrographic Perspective," *BASOR*, 303: 33–72.

Greenberg, M. (1955) *The Hab/Piru* (New Haven, CT: American Oriental Society).

Greenberg, R. (1996) "The Early Bronze Age Levels," in: A. Biran (ed.) *Dan I: A Chronicle of the Excavations, the Pottery Neolithic, the Early Bronze Age and the Middle Bronze Age Tombs* (Jerusalem: Nelson Glueck School of Biblical Archaeology, Hebrew Union College–Jewish Institute of Religion), pp. 83–160.

Greenberg, R. and Porat, N. (1996) "A Third Millennium Levantine Pottery Production Center: Typology, Petrography, and Provenance of the Metallic Ware of Northern Israel and Adjacent Regions", *BASOR*, 301: 5–24.

Grigson, C. (1995) "Plough and Pasture in the Early Economy of the Southern Levant," in: *ASHL*, pp. 245–68.

Gunneweg, J., Perlman, I., Dothan, T. and Gitin, S. (1986) "On the Origin of Pottery from Tel Miqne-Ekron," *BASOR*, 264: 3–16.

Hackett, J. A. *et al.* (1997, March/April) "Defusing Pseudo-scholarship: The Siloam Inscription Ain't Hasmonean," *BAR*, 23(2): 41–50, 68.

Haiman, M. (1996) "Early Bronze Age IV Settlement Pattern of the Negev and Sinai Deserts: View from Small Marginal Temporary Sites", *BASOR*, 303: 1–32.

Halpern, B. (1983) *The Emergence of Israel in Canaan* (Chico, CA: Scholars Press).

—— (1994, November) "The Stela from Dan: Epigraphic and Historical Considerations," *BASOR*, 296: 63–80.

—— (1998, March) "Research Design in Archaeology: The Interdisciplinary Perspective," *NEA*, 61(1): 53–65.

Hanbury-Tenison, J. (1986) *The Late Chalcolithic to Early Bronze Transition in Palestine and Transjordan* (Oxford, BAR International Series 311).

Harrelson, W. (1957, February) "Shechem in Extra-Biblical References," *BA*, xx(1): 2–10; reprinted in *BA Reader*, 2 (1975): 258–65.

Harris, M. (1978) *Cows, Pigs, Wars and Witches* (Glasgow: William Collins Sons & Co. Ltd).

Hasel, M. G. (1994, November) "Israel in the Merneptah Stela," *BASOR*, 296: 45–61.

Hayes, W. C. (1973) "Egypt: From the Death of Ammenemes III to Seqenenre II," *CAH*, vol. II/1, pp. 42–76.

Hendel, R. S. (1995, July/August) "Finding Historical Memories in the Patriarchal Narratives," *BAR*, 21(4): 52–59, 70–71.

—— (1996, December) "The Date of the Siloam Inscription: A Rejoinder to Rogerson and Davies," *BA*, 59(4): 233–7.

Herr, L. G. (1988, November) "Tripartite Pillared Buildings and the Market Place in Iron Age Palestine," *BASOR*, pp. 47–67.

—— (1993, November/December) "Whatever Happened to the Ammonites?" *BAR*, 19(6): 26–35, 68.

—— (1997a) "Periodization," in: *OEANE*, vol. 4, pp. 267–73.

—— (1997b, September) "The Iron II Period: Emerging Nations," *BA*, 60(3): 114–83.

—— (1997c) "Ammon," in: *OEANE*, vol. 1, pp. 102–3.

Herzog, Z. (1992) "Cities in the Levant," in: *ABD*, vol. 1, pp. 1032–43.

—— (1997) "Fortifications of the Bronze and Iron Ages," in: *OEANE*, vol. 2, pp. 322–6.

Hestrin, R. (1987) "The Lachish Ewer and the 'Asherah," *IEJ*, 37: 212–23.

Hodder, I. (1991) *Reading the Past: Current Approaches to Interpretation in Archaeology* (New York: Cambridge University Press).

Holladay, J.S., Jr (1995) "The Kingdoms of Israel and Judah: Political and Economic Centralization in the Iron II A–B (*ca*. 1000–750 BCE)," in: *ASHL*, pp. 368–98.

—— (1997a) "Stratum," in: *OEANE*, vol. 5, pp. 88–9.

—— (1997b) "Stratigraphy," in: *OEANE*, vol. 5, pp. 82–8.

Ibrahim, M. M. (1978) "The Collared-rim Jar of the Early Iron Age," in: R. Moorey and P. Parr (eds) *Archaeology in the Levant: Essays for Kathleen Kenyon* (Warminster: Aris & Phillips, Ltd), pp. 116–26.

Ilan, D. (1995) "The Dawn of Internationalism – the Middle Bronze Age," in: *ASHL*, pp. 297–319.

—— (1996) "The Middle Bronze Age Tombs," in: A. Biran (ed.) *Dan I: A Chronicle of the Excavations, the Pottery Neolithic, the Early Bronze Age and the Middle Bronze Age Tombs* (Jerusalem: Nelson Glueck School of Biblical Archaeology, Hebrew Union College–Jewish Institute of Religion), pp. 163–267.

Ilan, O. and Amiran, R. (1997) "Arad: Bronze Age Period," in: *OEANE*, vol. 1, pp. 169–74.

Izre'el, S. (1997) "Amarna Tablets," in: *OEANE*, vol. 1, pp. 86–7.

James, F. (1978) "Chariot Fittings from Late Bronze Age Beth Shan," in: J. N. Tubb (ed.) *Archaeology in the Levant: Essays for Kathleen Kenyon* (Warminster: Aris & Phillips Ltd), pp. 102–15.

Joffe, A. (1997a) "Far'ah, Tell el- (North)," in: *OEANE*, vol. 2, pp. 303–4.

—— (1997b) "Palestine in the Bronze Age," in: *OEANE*, vol. 4, pp. 212–17.

Joukowsky, M. (1980) *A Complete Manual of Field Archaeology: Tools and Techniques of Field Work for Archaeologists* (Englewood Cliffs, NJ: Prentice-Hall).

Kamp, K. A. and Yoffee, N. (1980) "Ethnicity in Ancient Western Asia during the Early Second Millennium BC: Archaeological Assessments and Ethnoarchaeological Prospectives," *BASOR*, 237: 85–104.

Kaufman, I. T. (1982) "The Samaria Ostraca: An Early Witness to Hebrew Writing," *BA*, 45(4): 229–39.

Kempinski, A. (1992a) "Reflections on the Role of the Egyptians in the Shefelah [*sic*] of Palestine in the Light of Recent Soundings at Tel Erani," in: *NDT*, pp. 419–25.

—— (1992b) "The Middle Bronze Age," in: *AAI*, pp. 159–210.

—— (1992c) "Urbanization and Town Plans in the Middle Bronze Age II," in: *AAIPP*, pp. 121–6.

—— (1992d) "Middle and Late Bronze Age Fortifications," in: *AAIPP*, pp. 127–42.

Kenyon, K. (1971) "An Essay on Archaeological Technique," *Harvard Theological Review*, 64(2,3): 271–9.

—— (1973a) "Palestine in the Middle Bronze Age," in: *CAH*, II/1: 77–116.

—— (1973b) "Palestine in the Time of the Eighteenth Dynasty," in: *CAH*, II/1: 526–56.

—— (1974) *Digging up Jerusalem* (London: Ernest Benn).

—— (1979) *Archaeology in the Holy Land*, 4th edn (London: Ernest Benn).

King, P. J. (1983a) *American Archaeology in the Mideast: A History of the American Schools of Oriental Research* (Winona Lake, IN: Eisenbrauns).

—— (1983b) "The Contribution of Archaeology to Biblical Studies," *Catholic Biblical Quarterly*, 45: 1–16.

—— (1983c) "Edward Robinson: Biblical Scholar," *BA*, 45: 230–2.

—— (1985) "Archaeology, History, and the Bible," in: *HBD*, pp. 44–52.

—— (1987) "The Influence of G. Ernest Wright on the Archaeology of Palestine," in: *ABI*, pp. 15–30.

—— (1988a) "American Archaeologists," in: *BTC*, pp. 15–35.

—— (1988b, July/August) "The Marzeah Amos Denounces: Using Archaeology to Interpret a Biblical Text," *BAR*, 15(4): 34–44.

—— (1988c) *Amos, Hosea, Micah: An Archaeological Commentary* (Philadelphia: Westminster Press).

Kitchen, K. A. (1987) "The Basics of Egyptian Chronology in Relation to the Bronze Age," in: P. Astroms (ed.) *High, Middle or Low? Acts of an International Colloquium on Absolute Chronology Held at the University of Gothenburg 20th–22nd August 1987 – Part I* (Gothenburg: Paul Astroms Forlag), pp. 37–55.

—— (1993) "New Directions in Biblical Archaeology: Historical and Biblical Aspects," in: *BAT* 90: 34–52.

—— (1995, March/April) "The Patriarchal Age – Myth or History?" *BAR*, 21(2): 48–57, 88, 90, 92, 94–5.

Kloner, A. and Davis, D. (1994) "A Burial Cave of the Late First Temple Period on the Slope of Mount Zion," in: *AJR*, pp. 107–10.

Knoppers, G. N. (1997, Spring) "The Vanishing Solomon: The Disappearance of the United Monarchy from Recent Histories of Ancient Israel," *JBL*, 116(1): 19–44.

Krahmalkov, C. R. (1994, September/October) "Exodus Itinerary Confirmed by Egyptian Evidence," *BAR*, 20(5): 54–62, 79.

La Bianca, O. and Younker, R. W. (1995) "The Kingdoms of Ammon, Moab and Edom: The Archaeology of Society in Late Bronze/Iron Age Transjordan (*ca.* 1400–500 BCE)," in *ASHL*, pp. 399–415.

Lance, H. D. (1978) "The Field Recording System," in: W. G. Dever and H. D. Lance (eds) *A Manual of Field Excavation* (New York: Hebrew Union College–Jewish Institute of Religion), pp. 73–107.

—— (1981) *The Old Testament and the Archaeologist* (Philadelphia: Fortress Press).

Landsberger, H. A. (1973) "Peasant Unrest: Themes and Variations," in: *Rural*

Protest: Peasant Movements and Society Change, H. A. Landsberger, ed. (New York, Barnes & Noble).

Lapp, P. W. (1969) *Biblical Archaeology and History* (New York: The World Publishing Co.).

—— (1970) "Palestine in the Early Bronze Age," in: J. A. Sanders (ed.) *Near Eastern Archaeology in the Twentieth Century* (Garden City, NY: Doubleday & Co.), pp. 101–31.

Laughlin, J. C. (1990) "Canaan," in: W. E. Mills (ed.) *Mercer Dictionary of the Bible* (Macon, GA: Mercer University Press), pp. 128–30.

Lemaire, A. (1994, May/June) "'House of David' Restored in Moabite Inscription," *BAR*, 20(3): 30–7.

—— (1997) "Ostracon," in: *OEANE*, vol. 4, pp. 189–91.

Lemche, N. P. (1985) *Early Israel* (Leiden: E. J. Brill).

—— (1992a) "Habiru, Hapiru," in: *ABD*, vol. 3, pp. 6–10.

—— (1992b) "Hebrew," in: *ABD*, vol. 3, p. 95.

—— (1995) *Ancient Israel: A New History of Israelite Society*, trans. by Fred Cryer (Sheffield: Sheffield Academic Press).

Leonard, A. J. (1989) "The Late Bronze Age," *BA*, 52: 4–39.

Levy, T. E. (1986) "The Chalcolithic Period – Archaeological Sources for the History of Palestine," *BA*, 49(2): 82–108.

—— (1995a) "Cult, Metallurgy and Rank Societies – Chalcolithic Period (ca. 4500–3500 BCE)," *ASHL*, pp. 224–44.

—— (1995b, July/August) "From Camels to Computers: A Short History of Archaeological Method," *BAR*, 21(4): 44–51, 64–5.

—— (1996) "Syncretistic and Mnemonic Dimensions of Chalcolithic Art: A New Human Figurine from Shiqmim," *BA*, 59(3): 150–9.

Lloyd, S. (1955) *Foundations in the Dust* (Bristol: Penguin Books).

London, G. (1989, February) "A Comparison of Two Contemporaneous Lifestyles of the Late Second Millennium BC" *BASOR*, 273: 37–55.

Longstaff, T. R. W. (1997) "Computer Recording, Analysis, and Interpretation," in: *OEANE*, vol. 2, pp. 57–9.

McCarter, P. K., Jr (1988) "The Patriarchal Age – Abraham, Isaac and Jacob," in: H. Shanks (ed.) *Ancient Israel: A Short History from Abraham to the Roman Destruction of the Temple* (Englewood Cliffs, NJ: Prentice-Hall), pp. 1–29.

—— (1992) "The Origins of Israelite Religion," in: H. Shanks (ed.) *The Rise of Ancient Israel* (Washington, DC: Biblical Archaeology Society), pp. 119–36.

—— (1996) *Ancient Inscriptions: Voices from the Biblical World* (Washington, DC: Biblical Archaeology Society).

Malamat, A. (1970) "Northern Canaan and the Mari Texts," in: J. Sanders (ed.) *Near Eastern Archaeology in the Twentieth Century: Essays in Honor of Nelson Glueck* (Garden City, NY: Doubleday & Co.), pp. 164–77.

—— (1997) "The Exodus: Egyptian Analogies," in: E. Frerichs and L. Lesko (eds) *The Exodus: The Egyptian Evidence* (Winona Lake, IN: Eisenbrauns), pp. 15–26.

—— (1998, January/February) "Let my People Go and Go and Go and Go," *BAR*, 24(1): 62–6, 85.

Massoni, S. (1985) "Elements of the Ceramic Culture of Early Syrian Ebla in Comparison with Syro-Palestinian EB IV," *BASOR*, 257: 1–18.

Mattingly, G. (1983) "The Exodus-Conquest and the Archaeology of Transjordan: New Light on an Old Problem," *Grace Theological Journal*, 42: 245–62.

Mazar, A. (1985) *Excavations at Tell Qasile, Part 2, The Philistine Sanctuary: Various Finds, the Pottery, Conclusions, Appendices Series: Qedem 20* (Jerusalem: The Hebrew University).

—— (1988) "Israeli Archaeologists," in: *BTC*, pp. 109–28.

—— (1990) *Archaeology of the Land of the Bible 10,000–586 BCE* (New York: Doubleday).

—— (1992a) "Temples of the Middle and Late Bronze Ages and the Iron Age," in: *AAIPP*, pp. 161–87.

—— (1992b) "The Iron Age I," in: *AAI*, pp. 258–301.

—— (1997) "Qasile, Tell," in: *OEANE*, vol. 4, pp. 373–6.

Mazar, A. and de Miroschedji, P. (1996) "Hartuv, an Aspect of the Early Bronze I Culture of Southern Israel," *BASOR*, 302: 1–40.

Mazar, B. (1968) "The Middle Bronze Age in Palestine," *IEJ*, 18(2): 65–97.

—— (1981, Winter) "The Early Israelite Settlement in the Hill Country," *BASOR*, 241: 75–85.

Mazar, E. (1997, January/February) "Excavate King David's Palace!" *BAR*, 23(1): 50–7, 74.

Mendenhall, G. (1970) "The Hebrew Conquest of Palestine," in: E. Campbell and D. Freedman (eds) *BA Reader* 3 (originally published in *BA*, XXV(3) (1962): 66–87) (Garden City, NY: Anchor Books, Doubleday & Co.), pp. 100–20.

Merrillees, R. S. (1986, March) "Political Conditions in the Eastern Mediterranean during the Late Bronze Age," *BA*, 49(1): 42–50.

Meshel, Z. (1978) *Kuntillet 'Ajrud: A Religious Center from the Time of the Judean Monarchy on the Border of Sinai* (Jerusalem: Israel Museum).

—— (1997) "Kuntillet 'Ajrud," in: *OEANE*, vol. 3, pp. 310–12.

Meyers, C. (1992a) "Temple, Jerusalem," in: *ABD*, vol. 6, pp. 350–69.

—— (1992b) "The Contributions of Archaeology," in: J. Suggs *et al.* (eds) *The Oxford Study Bible* (New York: Oxford University Press), pp. 48–56.

Meyers, E. M. (1984) "The Bible and Archaeology," *BA*, 47(1): 36–40.

Millard, A. R. (1992) "Abraham," in: *ABD*, vol. 1, pp. 35–41.

Miller, J. M. (1987) "Old Testament History and Archaeology," *BA*, 50(1): 55–63.

—— (1988) "Antecedents to Modern Archaeology," in: *BTC*, pp. 3–14.

—— (1991) "Is it Possible to Write a History of Israel without Relying on the Hebrew Bible?" in: D. V. Edelman (ed.) *The Fabric of History: Text, Artifact and Israel's Past* (Sheffield: Journal for the Study of the Old Testament), pp. 93–102.

Miller, J. M. and Hayes, J. H. (1986) *A History of Ancient Israel and Judah* (Philadelphia: Westminster Press).

Mommsen, H., Yellin, J. and Perlman, I. (1984) "The Provenance of the lmlk Jars," *IEJ*, 34: 89–113.

Moore, A. M. T. (1982) "A Four-stage Sequence for the Levantine Neolithic, *ca.* 8500–3700 BC," *BASOR*, 246: 1–34.

Moorey, P. R. S. (1988) "The Chalcolithic Hoard from the Nahal Mishmar, Israel, in Context," *World Archaeology*, 20(2): 171–89.

—— (1991) *A Century of Biblical Archaeology* (Louisville, KY: Westminster/ John Knox).

Moran, W. L. (1985) "Rib-Hadda: Job at Byblos?" in: A. Kort and S. Morschauser (eds) *Biblical and Related Studies Presented to Samuel Iwry* (Winona Lake, IN: Eisenbrauns), pp. 173–81.

—— (1992) *The Amarna Tablets* (Baltimore: The Johns Hopkins University Press).

Na'aman, N. (1992) "Amarna Letters," in: *ABD*, vol. 1, pp. 174–81.

—— (1994) "The 'Conquest of Canaan' in the Book of Joshua and History," in: *FNM*, pp. 218–28.

—— (1997, July/August) "Cow Town or Royal Capital? Evidence for Iron Age Jerusalem," *BAR*, 23(4): 43–7, 67.

—— (1998, July/August) "It Is There: Ancient Texts Prove It," *BAR*, 24 (4): 42–4.

Nakhai, B. A. (1997a) "Syro-Palestinian Temples," in: *OEANE*, vol. 5, pp. 169–74.

—— (1997b) "Locus," in: *OEANE*, vol. 3, pp. 383–4.

—— (1994, May/June) "What's a Bamah? How Sacred Space Functioned in Ancient Israel," *BAR*, 20(3): 18–29, 77–8.

Netzer, E. (1992) "Massive Structures: Processes in Construction and Deterioration," in: *AAIPP*, pp. 17–27.

Noth, M. (1960) *The History of Israel* 2nd edn (New York: Harper & Row).

Oren, E. D. (1992) "Palaces and Patrician Houses in the Middle and Late Bronze Ages," in: *AAIPP*, pp. 105–20.

—— (ed.) (1997) *The Hyksos: New Historical and Archaeological Perspectives* (Philadelphia: University of Pennsylvania Museum).

Oren, E. D. and Yekutieli, Y. (1992) "Taur Ikhbeineh: Earliest Evidence for Egyptian Interconnections," in: *NDT*, pp. 361–84.

Ottosson, M. (1980) *Temples and Cult Places in Palestine* (Uppsala: Almquist & Wiksell).

Palumbo, G. (1991) *The Early Bronze Age IV in the Southern Levant. Settlement Patterns, Economy, and Material Culture of a Dark Age* (Rome: University of Rome).

Palumbo, G. and Peterman, G. (1993) "Early Bronze Age IV Ceramic Regionalism in Central Jordan," *BASOR*, 289: 23–32.

Pardee, D. (1997a) "Gezer Calendar," in: *OEANE*, vol. 2, pp. 400–1.

—— (1997b) "Mesad Hashavyahu Texts," in: *OEANE*, vol. 3, p. 475.

—— (1997c) "Lachish Inscriptions," in: *OEANE*, vol. 3, pp. 323–4.

Pennells, E. (1983) "Middle Bronze Age Earthworks: A Contemporary Engineering Evaluation," *BA*, 46(1): 57–61.

Petrie, W. M. F. (1891) *Tell el Hesy, Lachish* (London: Alexander P. Watt).

Pitt-Rivers, A. L. E. (1887) *Excavations in Cranborne Chase near Rushmore, on the Borders of Dorset and Wiltshire*, vol. 1 (London).

Porat, N. (1992) "An Egyptian Colony in Southern Palestine during the Late Predynastic–Early Dynastic Period," in: *NDT*, pp. 433–40.

Pritchard, J. (ed.) (1969) *Ancient Near Eastern Texts Relating to the Old Testament with Supplement* 3rd edn (Princeton: Princeton University Press).

Raban, A. and Stieglitz, R. R. (1991, November/December) "The Sea Peoples and their Contributions to Civilization," *BAR*, 17(6): 34–41, 92–3.

Rainey, A. F. (1988) "Toward a Precise Date for the Samaria Ostraca," *BASOR*, 272: 69–74.

—— (1991, November/ December) "Rainey's Challenge," *BAR*, 17(6): 56–60, 93.

—— (1996) "Who is a Canaanite? A Review of the Textual Evidence," *BASOR*, 304: 1–15.

Rassam, Hormuzd (1897) *Asshur and the Land of Nimrod* (New York: Eaton & Mains).

Rast, W. (1992) *Through the Ages in Palestinian Archaeology* (Philadelphia: Trinity Press International).

Redford, D. (1970) "The Hyksos Invasion in History and Tradition," *Orientalia*, 39: 2–51.

—— (1997) "Observations on the Sojourn of the Bene-Israel," in E. S. Frerichs and L. H. Lesko (eds), *Exodus: The Egyptian Evidence* (Winona Lake, IN: Eisenbrauns), pp. 57–66.

Redford, D. and Weinstein, J. M. (1992) "Hyksos," in: *ABD*, vol. 3, pp. 341–8.

Redmount, C. (1995, December) "Ethnicity, Pottery, and the Hyksos at Tell el-Maskhuta in the Egyptian Delta," *BA*, 58(4): 182–90.

Reich, R. (1994) "The Ancient Burial Ground in the Mamilla Neighborhood, Jerusalem," in: *AJR*, pp. 111–18.

Richard, S. (1980) "Toward a Consensus of Opinion on the End of the Early Bronze Age in Palestine-Transjordan," *BASOR*, 237: 5–34.

—— (1987) "The Early Bronze Age – The Rise and Collapse of Urbanism," *BA*, 50(1): 22–43.

Richard, S. and Boraas, R. S. (1984) "Preliminary Report of the 1981–82 Seasons of the Expedition to Khirbet Iskander and its Vicinity," *BASOR*, 254: 63–97.

—— (1988) "The Early Bronze IV Fortified Site of Khirbet Iskander, Jordan: Third Preliminary Report, 1984 Season," *BASOR, Supplement*, 25: 107–30.

Robinson, E. (1841) *Biblical Researches in Palestine, Mount Sinai, and Arabia Petraea*, vol. 3 (Boston: reprinted in 1977, New York).

—— (1856a) *Later Biblical Researches in Palestine and in the Adjacent Regions* (Boston: reprinted in 1977, New York).

—— (1856b) *Biblical Researches in Palestine and the Adjacent Regions: A Journal of Travels in the Years 1832 and 1852*, 2nd edn, vol. 1 (London: Crocker & Brewster).

—— (1857) *Later Biblical Researches in Palestine and in the Adjacent Regions: A Journal of the Travels in the Year 1852*, vol. 3 (Boston: Crocker & Brewster).

—— (1868) *Biblical Researches in Palestine and in the Adjacent Regions: A Journal of Travels in the Year 1838*, vol. 2 (Boston: Crocker & Brewster).

Rogerson, J. and Davies, P. R. (1996, September) "Was the Siloam Tunnel Built by Hezekiah?" *BA*, 59(3): 138–49.

Rollefson, G. O. (1983) "8,000-Year-Old Human Statues Discovered at 'Ain Ghazal (Jordan)," *ASOR Newsletter*, 35(2): 1–3.

—— (1997) "'Ain Ghazal," in: *OEANE*, vol. 1, pp. 36–8.

Rosen, S. A. (1996) "The Chipped Stone Assemblage from Hartuv," *BASOR*, 302: 41–50.

—— (1997) "Tell," in: *OEANE*, vol. 5, p. 183.

Ross, J. F. (1979) "Early Bronze Age Structures at Tell el-Hesi," *BASOR*, 236: 11–21.

—— (1987) "A Bibliography of Early Bronze Age Sites in Palestine," in: *ABI*, pp. 315–53.

Sarna, N. M. (1988) "Israel in Egypt: The Egyptian Sojourn and the Exodus," in: H. Shanks (ed.) *Ancient Israel: A Short History from Abraham to the Roman Destruction of the Temple*" (Englewood Cliffs, NJ: Prentice-Hall), pp. 31–52.

Sauer, J. (1982) "Syro-Palestinian Archaeology, History and Biblical Studies," *BA*, 45(4): 201–9.

Schaub, R. (1982) "The Origins of the Early Bronze Age Walled Town Culture of Jordan," *Studies in the History and Archaeology of Jordan*, 1: 67–75.

Schaub, R. and Rast, W. E. (1984) "Preliminary Report of the 1981 Expedition to the Dead Sea Plain, Jordan," *BASOR*, 254: 35–60.

Schiffer, M. B. (1987) *Formation Processes of the Archaeological Record* (Albuquerque: University of New Mexico Press).

Schneider, T. (1994) "A Biblical Name on a City of David Bulla: Azariah Son of Hilkiah," in: *AJR*, pp. 62–3.

Schniedewind, W. M. (1996, May) "Tel Dan Stela: New Light on Aramaic and Jehu's Revolt," *BASOR*, 302: 75–90.

—— (1998, February) "The Geopolitical History of Philistine Gath," *BASOR*, 309: 69–77.

Schoville, K. N. (1978) *Biblical Archaeology in Focus* (Grand Rapids, MI: Baker Book House).

Shanks, H. (1987, July/August) "Avraham Biran: Twenty Years of Digging at Tel Dan," *BAR*, 12(4): 12–25.

—— (ed.) (1992) *The Rise of Ancient Israel* (Washington, DC: Biblical Archaeology Society).

—— (1994, March/April) "'David' Found at Dan," *BAR*, 20(2): 26–39.

—— (1996a, July/August) "Is This Man a Biblical Archaeologist?" *BAR*, 22(4): 30–9, 62–3.

—— (1996b, September/October) "Is the Bible Right After All?" *BAR*, 22(5): 30–7, 74–7.

—— (1996c) *Archaeology's Publication Problem* (Washington, DC: Biblical Archaeology Society).

—— (1996d, July/August) "Coin flip," *BAR*, 22(4): 9.

—— (1997, July/August) "Face to Face: Biblical Minimalists Meet their Challengers," *BAR*, 23(4): 26–42, 66.

Shiloh, Y. (1984) *Excavations at the City of David, I, 1978–1982. Qedem 19 Monographs of the Institute of Archaeology* (Jerusalem: The Hebrew University).

—— (1985) "The City of David: 1978–1983," in: *BAT*, pp. 451–62.

—— (1987) "The Casemate Wall, the Four Room House, and Early Planning in the Israelite City," *BASOR*, 268: 3–15.

—— (1989) "Judah and Jerusalem in the Eighth–Sixth Centuries BCE," in: *REI*, pp. 97–105.

—— (1994) "The Rediscovery of the Ancient Water System Known as 'Warren's Shaft'," in: *AJR*, pp. 46–54.

Shoham, Y. (1994) "A Group of Hebrew Bullae from Yigal Shiloh's Excavations in the City of David," in: *AJR*, pp. 55–61.

Singer, I. (1988, February) "Merneptah's Campaign to Canaan and the Egyptian Occupation of the Southern Coastal Plain of Palestine in the Ramesside Period," *BASOR*, 269: 1–10.

—— (1994) "Egyptians, Canaanites, and Philistines in the Period of the Emergence of Israel," in: *FNM*, pp. 282–338.

Soggin, J. A. (1984) *A History of Ancient Israel* (Philadelphia: Westminster).

Stager, L. (1990, February–May) "Shemer's Estate," *BASOR*, pp. 277–8, 93–107.

—— (1985, Fall/November) "The Archaeology of the Family in Ancient Israel," *BASOR*, 260: 1–35.

—— (1991) *Ashkelon Discovered: From Canaanite and Philistines to Roman and Moslems* (Washington, DC: Biblical Archaeology Society).

—— (1993) "Ashkelon," in: *NEAHL*, vol. 1, pp. 103–12.

—— (1995) "The Impact of the Sea Peoples in Canaan (1185–1050 BCE)," in: *ASHL*, pp. 332–48.

Stager, L. and Wolff, S. R. (1981, Summer) "Production and Commerce in Temple Courtyards: An Olive Press in the Sacred Precinct at Tel Dan," *BASOR*, 243: 95–102.

Stech, T., Muhly, J. and Maddin, R. (1985) "Metallurgical Studies on Artifacts from the Tomb near 'Enan, *'Atiqot*, 17: 75–82.

Steiner, M. (1998, July/August) "It Is Not There: Archaeology Proves a Negative," *BAR*, 24 (4): 26–33, 62–3.

Stone, B. J. (1995, May) "The Philistines and Acculturation: Culture Change and Ethnic Continuity in the Iron Age," *BASOR*, pp. 7–32.

Strange, J. F. (1988) "Computers and Archaeological Research," in: *BTC*, pp. 307–24.

—— (1992) "Some Implications of Archaeology for New Testament Studies," in: J. H. Charlesworth and W. P. Weaver (eds) *What Has Archaeology to Do with Faith?* (Philadelphia: Trinity Press International), pp. 23–59.

Sussman, V. (1980) "A Relief of a Bull from the Early Bronze Age," *BASOR*, 238: 75–7.

Tadmor, H. (1985) "Nineveh, Calah and Israel: On Assyriology and the Origins of Biblical Archaeology," in: *BAT*, pp. 260–8.

Taylor, J. G. (1994, May/June) "Was Yahweh Worshiped as the Sun?" *BAR*, 20(3): 52–61, 90–1.

Thompson, T. (1974) *The Historicity of the Patriarchal Narratives* (Berlin: de Gruyter).

—— (1979) *The Settlement of Palestine in the Bronze Age; Series; Beihefte Zum Tubinger Atlas Des Vorderen Orienten, Reine B, Nr 8* (Wiesbaden: Ludwig Reichert).

Toombs, L. E. (1982) "The Development of Palestinian Archaeology as a Discipline," *BA*, 45(2): 89–91.

Tubb, J. N. (1983) "The MB IIA Period in Palestine: Its Relationship with Syria and its Origin," *Levant*, XV: 49–62.

Tushingham, A. (1992, Summer) "New Evidence Bearing on the Two-winged LMLK Stamp," *BASOR*, 287: 61–5.

Ussishkin, D. (1982) "Where is Israeli Archaeology Going?" *BA*, 45(2): 93–5.

—— (1985) "Level VII and VI at Tel Lachish and the End of the Late Bronze Age in Canaan," in: *PBIA*, pp. 213–30.

—— (1987, January/February) "Lachish: Key to the Israelite Conquest of Canaan," *BAR*, 13(1): 18–39.

—— (1989) "Notes on the Fortifications of the Middle Bronze II Period at Jericho and Shechem," *BASOR*, 276: 29–53.

—— (1997a) "Lachish," in: *OEANE*, vol. 3, pp. 317–23.

—— (1997b) "Megiddo," in: *OEANE*, vol. 3, pp. 460–9.

Van Beek, G. W. (1988) "Excavation of Tells," in: *BTC*, pp. 131–67.

Van Seters, J. (1966) *The Hyksos: A New Investigation* (New Haven, CT: Yale University Press).

—— (1975) *Abraham in History and Tradition* (New Haven, CT: Yale University Press).

—— (1983) *In Search of History: Historiography in the Ancient World and the Origins of Biblical History* (New Haven, CT: Yale University Press).

Wachsmann, S. (1986, March) "Is Cyprus Ancient Alashiya? New Evidence from an Egyptian Tablet," *BA*, 49(1): 37–40.

Wapnish, P. (1997) "Middle Bronze Equid Burials at Tell Jemmeh and a Re-examination of a Purportedly 'Hyksos Practice'," in: *HNHAP*, pp. 335–67.

Ward, W. A. (1991) "Early Contacts between Egypt, Canaan, and Sinai: Remarks on the Paper by Amnon Ben-Tor," *BASOR*, 281: 11–26.

—— (1992) "The Present Status of Egyptian Chronology," *BASOR*, 288: 53–66.

—— (1997) "Summary and Conclusions," in: E. Frerichs and L. Lesko (eds) *Exodus: The Egyptian Evidence* (Winona Lake, IN: Eisenbrauns), pp. 106–12.

Ward, W. A. and Dever, W. G. (1994) *Scarab Typology and Archaeological Context: An Essay on Middle Bronze Age Chronology* (San Antonio, TX: Van Sicien Books).

Watson, P. J. (1997) "Jarmo," in: *OEANE*, vol. 3, pp. 208–9.

Weinstein, J. M. (1981, Winter) "The Egyptian Empire in Palestine: A Reassessment," *BASOR*, 241: 1–28.

—— (1984) "The Significance of Tell Areini for Egyptian–Palestinian Relations at the Beginning of the Bronze Age," *BASOR*, 256: 61–9.

—— (1991) "Egypt and the Middle Bronze IIC/Late Bronze IA Transition in Palestine," *Levant*, XXIII: 105–15.

—— (1992) "The Chronology of Palestine in the Early Second Millennium BCE," *BASOR*, 288: 27–46.

—— (1996) "A Wolf in Sheep's Clothing: How the High Chronology Became the Middle Chronology," *BASOR*, 304: 55–63.

—— (1997a) "Hyksos," in: *OEANE*, vol. 3, pp. 133–6.

—— (1997b) "Exodus and Archaeological Reality," in: E. Frerichs and L. Lesko (eds) *Exodus: The Egyptian Evidence* (Winona Lake, IN: Eisenbrauns), pp. 87–103.

Wheeler, S. M. (1956) *Archaeology from the Earth* (Baltimore: Penguin Books).

Wood, B. (1991, November/December) "The Philistines Enter Canaan – Were They Egyptian Lackeys or Invading Conquerors?" *BAR*, 17(6): 44–52, 89–90, 92.

Wright, G. E. (1937) *The Pottery of Palestine from the Earliest Times to the End of the Early Bronze Age* (New Haven, CT: ASOR).

—— (1957) *Biblical Archaeology* (Philadelphia: Westminster).

—— (1965) *Shechem: The Biography of a Biblical City* (New York: Mc Graw-Hill).

—— (1971) "The Archaeology of Palestine from the Neolithic through the Middle Bronze Age," *Journal of the American Oriental Society*, 91: 276–93.

—— (1974) "The Tell: Basic Unit for Reconstructing Complex Societies of the Near East," in: C. B. Moore (ed.) *Reconstructing Complex Societies: An Archaeological Colloquium* (Baltimore: ASOR), pp. 123–30.

—— (1983) "What Archaeology Can and Cannot Do," in: E. F. Campbell and D. N. Freedmen (eds) *BA Reader* IV; (originally published in *BA* (1971): 70–6) (Sheffield: The Almond Press), pp. 65–72.

Wright, M. (1985) "Contacts between Egypt and Syro-Palestine during the Protodynastic Period," *BA*, 48(4): 240–53.

Wright, R. B. (1997) "Photography of Fieldwork and Artifacts," in: *OEANE*, vol. 4, pp. 331–6.

Yadin, Y. (1982, March/April) "Is the Biblical Account of the Israelite Conquest of Canaan Historically Reliable?" *BAR*, VII(2).

—— (1985) "Biblical Archaeology Today: The Archaeological Aspect," in: *BAT*, pp. 21–7.

Yellin, J. and Gunneweg, J. (1989) "Instrumental Neutron Activation Analysis and the Origin of Iron Age I Collared-rim Jars and Pithoi from Tel Dan," in: *REI*, pp. 133–41.

Yoffee, N. and Congill, G. L. (eds) (1988) *The Collapse of Ancient States and Civilizations* (Tucson: University of Arizona Press).

Yurco, F. J. (1990, September/October) "3,200-year-old Picture of Israelites Found in Egypt," *BAR*, 16(5): 20–38.

—— (1997) "Merenptah's [*sic*] Canaanite Campaign and Israel's Origins," in E. S. Frerichs and L. H. Lesko (eds), *Exodus: The Egyptian Evidence* (Winona Lake, IN: Eisenbrauns), pp. 27–55.

Zeder, M. A. (1996) "The Role of Pigs in Near Eastern Subsistence: A View from the Southern Levant," in: J. D. Seger (ed.) *Retrieving the Past: Essays on Archaeological Research and Methodology. In Honor of Gus W. Van Beek* (Winona Lake, IN: Eisenbrauns), pp. 297–312.

Zertal, A. (1991, September/October) "Israel Enters Canaan – Following the Pottery Trail," *BAR*, 17(5): 28–47.

Zevit, Z. (1984, Summer) "The Khirbet el-Qom Inscription Mentioning a Goddess," *BASOR*, 255: 39–47.

Ziffer, I. (1990) *At That Time the Canaanites Were in the Land: Daily Life in Canaan in the Middle Bronze Age 2,2000–1550 BCE* (Tel Aviv: Eretz Israel Museum).

Zohar, M. (1993) "Dolmens," in: *NEAEHL*, vol 1, pp. 352–6.

Zorn, J. R. (1994) "Estimating the Population Size of Ancient Settlements: Methods, Problems, Solutions, and a Case Study," *BASOR*, 295: 31–48.

Index